I0199878

MODERN JEWISH HISTORY

BRYAN EDWARD STONE AND JONATHAN L. FRIEDMANN, SERIES EDITORS

Also in the series:

Commodore Levy: A Novel of Early America in the Age of Sail, by Irving Litvag

Contesting Histories: German and Jewish Americans and the Legacy of the Holocaust, by Michael Schuldiner

The Jewish Women Prisoners of Ravensbrück: Who Were They?, by Judith Buber Agassi

Karski: How One Man Tried to Stop the Holocaust, by E. Thomas Wood and Stanisław M. Jankowski

Love, Norm: Inspiration of a Jewish American Fighter Pilot, by Norman M. Shulman

"Non-Germans" under the Third Reich: The Nazi Judicial and Administrative System in Germany and Occupied Eastern Europe, with Special Regard to Occupied Poland, 1939–1945, by Diemut Majer

Pillar of Fire: A Biography of Stephen S. Wise, by A. James Rudin

Songs of Sonderling: Commissioning Jewish Émigré Composers in Los Angeles, 1938–1945, by Jonathan L. Friedmann and John F. Guest

The Tailors of Tomaszow: A Memoir of Polish Jews, by Rena Margulies Chernoff and Allan Chernoff

Transcending Darkness: A Girl's Journey out of the Holocaust, by Estelle Glaser Laughlin

Unwanted Legacies: Sharing the Burden of Post-Genocide Generations, by Gottfried Wagner and Abraham J. Peck

Jewish Historical Societies

Navigating the Professional-Amateur Divide

EDITED BY JOEL GEREBOFF AND
JONATHAN L. FRIEDMANN

TEXAS TECH UNIVERSITY PRESS

This book is typeset in EB Garamond. The paper used in this book meets the minimum requirements of ANSI/NISO Z39.48-1992 (R1997). ♾

Designed by Hannah Gaskamp
Cover image: Concordia Club picnic, Los Angeles, early 1900s. Photo courtesy of the Western States Jewish History Association.
Cover designed by Hannah Gaskamp

Library of Congress Cataloging-in-Publication Data

Names: Gereboff, Joel D., editor. | Friedmann, Jonathan L., 1980– editor. Title: Jewish Historical Societies: Navigating the Professional-Amateur Divide / edited by Joel Gereboff and Jonathan L. Friedmann. Description: Lubbock, Texas: Texas Tech University Press, [2023] | Series: Modern Jewish History | Includes bibliographical references and index. | Summary: "A scholarly examination of local and regional Jewish historical societies in the United States that considers their contribution to historical memory and suggests what they might offer to the future."—Provided by publisher.
Identifiers: LCCN 2022055296 | ISBN 978-1-68283-181-6 (cloth)
Subjects: LCSH: American Jewish Historical Society. | Jews—United States—History
Classification: LCC E184.J5 J5566 2023 | DDC 973/.04924—dc23/eng/20221116
LC record available at https://lccn.loc.gov/2022055296

Printed in the United States of America
23 24 25 26 27 28 29 30 31 / 9 8 7 6 5 4 3 2 1

Texas Tech University Press
Box 41037
Lubbock, Texas 79409-1037 USA
800.832.4042
ttup@ttu.edu
www.ttupress.org

To Jody Myers (1954–2022), whose extraordinary scholarship on local Jewish history drew out the larger significance thereof.

Contents

Preface

Anyone researching or teaching history must consider and defend the choice of topic, the intended audience, and why the knowledge produced and disseminated matters. In many ways, deciding on the second of these elements—the intended audience—greatly impacts the position on the first and third. While analysis of any historical question ought to be rigorous, utilizing critical methodologies and attending to the range of relevant variables, historians foreground their work in what they determine to be valuable for their target audience. Although in principle the conclusions of historical investigations should hold true irrespective of who is doing the research, envisioning who will receive that information invariably shapes which historical subjects or findings are deemed significant. For example, while an investigation into some aspect of American history should be taught the same way whether one is in an American or an Australian setting, it is obvious from school curricula that this information is given greater importance for American students. All knowledge may ideally contribute to broader understandings of social, cultural, and political processes. But, for a variety of reasons, certain groups or individuals place greater emphasis on particular bits of knowledge.

Most who teach the history of Jews and Judaism speak to a variety of audiences. They interact with students and scholars of diverse backgrounds at colleges, universities, and conferences, while at the same time engaging members and leaders of Jewish communities. In both cases, they presume the details and interpretations they share are of inherent and objective value. Beginning in the nineteenth century, historians of Jews have been seen as vital contributors to Jewish identity, helping Jews to understand and reflect on what it means to be Jewish and how they want to live as Jews. These questions are uniquely important to Jews, but of limited interest to non-Jews—even as the information marshalled to address these queries may, for other reasons, have import for broader audiences. Through studying larger developments and more localized topics, academically trained historians of Jews (the majority of whom are themselves Jewish) stake out positions on the above matters. By contrast, amateur history buffs typically explore minutiae related to a local Jewish community or personality without reflecting analytically.

The genesis of this book was the editors' mutual interest in examining how local and regional Jewish historical societies have approached these issues and what contributions they make to a range of audiences, including Jews of the area, broader Jewish and non-Jewish communities, and scholars of various disciplines.

Joel Gereboff has taught the history of Jews, including American Jews and Judaism, both at public, secular universities and at a range of Jewish institutions. He has also published on a number of topics related to researching and teaching the history of Jews and Judaism. Among these is an article, now a quarter century old, on the roles of local and regional Jewish historical societies. His interest in such organizations stems in part from his own background. Growing up in Rhode Island, he knew of the Rhode Island Jewish Historical Association, the earliest of the now more than forty local and regional Jewish historical societies in the US. His mother was a member of the society, and he spoke with her often about their activities, especially the scholarly presentations delivered at their annual meetings. He came to discover that, over the years, she had accumulated more than half of the annual journals published by the association. Several years ago, at the request of the journal's editor, Joel wrote a reflection on his returning home for graduate education and studying under his mentor, Dr. Jacob Neusner. In composing the essay, he took into consideration the audience who would read the piece and his deep appreciation for Jack, as he was known. The opportunity to collaborate on this book with Jonathan Friedmann, a colleague and co-editor of several other volumes, inspired Joel to investigate in depth the largely unexplored history, activities, and roles of local and regional Jewish historical societies.

In 2018, Jonathan Friedmann was brought on as president of the Western States Jewish History Association (WSJHA) and director of the association's online museum, the Jewish Museum of the American West. At that time and for decades prior, WSJHA was synonymous with its quarterly journal, *Western States Jewish History*, which began in 1968 and ceased publication in 2018. Wishing to retain the association's popular—even "folksy"—appeal while simultaneously introducing academic standards, Jonathan reconceived WSJHA as having "two faces" or "serving two masters": the lay, mostly Jewish, audience, who visit the online museum, give donations, and invite speakers to present at programs, and the academic audience, who are the primary readers of the recently revived, biannual, peer-reviewed journal and a growing slate of scholarly books (including this one).

Several people have graciously assisted the editors with materials, insights, and information. Our gratitude goes to Gary P. Zola, executive director of the Jacob Rader Marcus Center of the American Jewish Archives (AJA) and the staff of AJA; Bernard Wax, late former director of the American Jewish Historical Society (AJHS); Jeffrey Gurock, former associate editor of *American Jewish History*, and the staff of AJHS; David Epstein and Gladys Sturman, retired co-publishers of *Western States Jewish History*; Fred Rosenbaum, founding director of Lehrhaus Judaica; Mark Bauman, editor of the journal sponsored by the Southern Jewish Historical Society; Lisa Kranseler, executive director of the Washington State Jewish Historical Society; Joanna Church, director of collections and exhibits at the Jewish Museum of Maryland; Wendy Turman, deputy director of the Capitol Museum in Washington, DC; Larry Bell, executive director of the Arizona Jewish Historical Society; Zachary Baker, retired curator of Stanford University's Judaica and Hebraica collections; Rachel Leket-Mor, Jewish studies librarian at Arizona State University (ASU), and Francoise Mirguet, associate professor of Hebrew at ASU; and Sivan Siman-Tov, archivist for the Jewish Historical Society of Southern California (JHSSC). Special thanks to Ava F. Kahn, former research associate at the Western Jewish History Center of the Judah L. Magnes Museum, and Stephen Sass, president of JHSSC, for generously reading and offerings comments on an earlier draft.

Jewish Historical Societies

Introduction

JONATHAN L. FRIEDMANN AND JOEL GEREBOFF

Since the early 1950s, local and regional historical societies have served as an integral part of the American Jewish landscape, providing community outreach, housing archives, fostering research, and publishing historical studies. The mission statement of the Rhode Island Jewish Historical Association, founded in 1951 and the first such society, set the template for groups that would form in other locales:

> To procure, collect, and preserve books, records, pamphlets, letters, manuscripts, prints, photographs, paintings, and any other historical material relating to the history of the Jews of Rhode Island; to encourage and promote the study of such history by lectures and otherwise; and to publish and diffuse information as to such history.

These efforts are motivated by the vested interests of hobbyists, enthusiasts, history buffs, local boosters, and Jewish leaders, who support, maintain, and fill the rosters of the organizations. Their aims include localizing Jewish identity; creating continuity with the area's past; instilling pride among Jewish residents; and promoting a positive Jewish image in the larger community. Often connected to these is a desire to "set the record straight" through advocating for Jewish representation in general histories.

These aspirations can be beneficial on a communal level, as they seek to ground Jews in the places they live and encourage healthy relationships with their neighbors. However, the accompanying activities often fall short of academic history standards. By mostly focusing on Jewish success stories, constructing uncomplicated narratives, isolating local stories from patterns of Jewish history, bypassing critical analysis, and largely ignoring broader ethnic, racial, religious, and socioeconomic developments, the programs and publications of Jewish historical societies tend to be more celebratory than scholarly and more apologetic than accurate—much to the chagrin of trained historians of American Judaism.

These tendencies are not limited to Jewish groups. Amateur history of all sorts favors description over analysis, clean narratives over unsavory details, notable figures over average people, and certain ethnicities over others. In an attempt to improve the quality of historical research and presentation, the American Association for State and Local History (AASLH) published a guidebook for its more than 5,500 institutional and individual members and other interested readers, including history teachers, volunteers and employees of history organizations, history museum workers and docents, "spare time" researchers and archivists, and the like. The book's epilogue, written by John R. Dichtl, executive director of the National Council on Public History, is subtitled "Moving History from Nice to Essential."[1] Dichtl presents six priorities of the AASLH Council and Aspirations Task Force to better "provide leadership and resources for [those] who preserve and interpret state and local history to make the past more meaningful to all people."[2]

1. Serve as a "town square" for historical organizations and history practitioners (amateur and professional) to develop relationships and share resources with diverse communities.
2. Expand online courses, webinars, and workshops for volunteers and employees of member organizations.
3. Build relationships with scholars in traditional history programs, who can both inform what is taught in public history and take advantage of materials and information gathered by historical societies.
4. Organize national outreach to "avocational historians": genealogists, reenactors, lifelong learners, museum docents, lay historians, etc.

5. Make connections with international groups to better situate state and local history in relation to global movements of populations, resources, and ideas.
6. Encourage historians and history practitioners to expand the types of stories they tell, invite more people and views into the interpretive process, and reevaluate how decisions are made regarding what is worth preserving.

The list includes a crucial reminder: "All history is local, but it doesn't occur in a vacuum."

AASLH's priorities are applicable to Jewish local and regional historical societies, which would profit from formalized relationships between similar groups, historical training for lay members, partnerships with professional historians, a national network for "avocational historians," collaborations with international organizations, and expanding what constitutes "history" and "history makers." These would go a long way in facilitating the maturation of Jewish historical societies, in terms of both what they preserve and how they present it. While many of their pursuits are useful and well-constructed—with a few demonstrating high-caliber programs and publications—the prevalence of outdated notions, simplistic storytelling, unacknowledged biases, and overall unevenness suggests a need for guidance and guidelines.

Unfortunately, despite the early intentions of the American Jewish Historical Society and American Jewish Archives to provide centralized support for groups across the country, there is no national association for the forty-plus Jewish local and regional historical societies. Such organizations do exist for Jewish libraries (Association of Jewish Libraries), museums (Council of American Jewish Museums), and genealogical societies (International Association of Jewish Genealogical Societies), which offer programs, conferences, and resources for their members. In the absence of a national body, many historical societies continue to perpetuate boosteristic interests of their founders, produce work of limited academic merit, and generally operate insularly (save for those that engage with non-Jewish local historical societies and/or universities).

Yet Jewish history, even in a popular vein, need not be self-censoring, whitewashed, or unsophisticated. Hyman "Hy" Berman, the late University of Minnesota professor and public historian, modeled how to navigate the popular-scholarly divide. Turning down an invitation to be president of the American Jewish Historical Society in the mid-1960s—citing unease at being labeled a "professional Jew"—Berman nevertheless remained active in Jewish groups and causes. He was also a regular guest on the public television program *Almanac*, becoming the face of public history in Minnesota. University colleagues would scoff, "Look at him, he's on *Almanac* again talking to people instead of writing another book that only three people will read." In truth, Berman's peer-reviewed writings were narrowly focused and saturated with "academese," but his lectures, television talks, and newspaper columns were crisp and congenial—all without being roseate or triumphalist. This balance reflected Berman's view that history—even difficult or critical history—was vital for everyone. In a speech written for Minnesota governor Rudy Perpich in 1977, Berman stressed the importance of cultivating a historical awareness, especially in communities:

> A community without a knowledge of its past is like a person with amnesia. It can exist and function from day to day, but its lack of memory leaves it without a feeling of purpose, direction, or identity. A sense of history is recognizing the influence of the past in the very web of our daily lives—in our habits of thought and speech, in the streets we walk through, in the ways we earn a living. It is in the touch of humility that comes with knowing that wherever we are in life, we stand upon the shoulders of those who have gone before.[3]

This book charts the development, undertakings, successes, shortcomings, and possible future of local and regional Jewish historical societies in the United States. The lead chapter, by Joel Gereboff, explores the challenges of constructing and presenting Jewish history, and disparities between amateur historians and professionals in regard to standards, tools, methods, analysis, and contextualization. Following an overview of key players, major themes, representative organizations, and recurring critiques, the chapter proposes ways to address the key question: Can Jewish history on the local and regional levels be more inclusive, better integrated with broader trends of Jewish and general history, and improved according to scholarly norms and expectations of history?

Following this prelude are six chapters by leaders of local and regional Jewish historical societies, all with doctoral degrees in studying historical and cultural developments: George M. Goodwin of the Rhode Island Jewish Historical Association; Jonathan L. Friedmann of the Western States Jewish History Association; Mark K. Bauman of the Southern Jewish Historical Society; Catherine Cangany of the Jewish Historical Society of Michigan; Jeanne E. Abrams of the Rocky Mountain Jewish Historical Society; and Lawrence Bell of the Arizona Jewish Historical Society. Appearing in the order in which they were founded, with Rhode Island (est. 1951) launching the first such group and Arizona (est. 1981) yielding the newest of the groups included here, the selected societies cover major regions of the country—New England, Midwest, South, Southwest, and West—and, as such, are representative of the broader phenomena of American Jewish historical societies.

Although colored by distinct geographical features and developments, these groups share a number of pertinent traits, varying rather in degree than in kind. For example, most were formed by a small group of Jewish residents who aimed to retrieve, preserve, and present the area's Jewish history. Believing that Jewish contributions were ignored, downplayed, inaccurately reported, or, worse, intentionally swept aside in the historical record, these nostalgic founders—usually men (and a few women) of financial means and social prominence—initiated their advocacy projects independent of institutional support from synagogues or Jewish agencies. In most cases, these founders were history buffs, although some had studied history at the university level. Often, they were joined by academics with some knowledge of Judaism or Jewish history, and/or Jewish community professionals on a voluntary basis (not as representatives of their institution). In many cases, their initial efforts to correct the record were successful, with the historical societies becoming fixtures of the Jewish landscape and community at large through public exhibits, educational offerings, sponsoring local initiatives, and collaborating with both Jewish and non-Jewish organizations. Moreover, many have become "go to" places for anyone seeking historical information about the area's (and sometimes the broader) Jewish past.

Typically, the groups' early efforts centered on collecting and organizing archives of local Jewish history, including printed and handwritten documents, photographs, oral histories, memorabilia, objects, and ephemera. Such archives served as "evidence" of a place's Jewish roots and were—and still are—used by history buffs to make this point. The archives have proven useful for students and scholars conducting historical research, journalists and documentarians telling stories, and professional and amateur genealogists constructing family trees. The associations themselves use the materials to create onsite and virtual exhibits. Some, like Arizona, retain their own archive; some, like Rocky Mountain, partner with universities; and others, like Western States, have donated their archives to established institutions. In all cases, accessibility of archival materials has become central, with digitization and online cataloging playing increasing roles.

Publishing historical research is a priority for some societies, including Rhode Island, Southern, and Western States. To varying levels of intention and success, the societies' journals try to balance the interests and approaches of amateur and professional history writing—the former generally comprising descriptive accounts and the latter involving critical analysis and broader contextualization. A key question for publishing societies is how to acknowledge the "warts" while still fostering Jewish pride. Most groups rely heavily on lay members and backers, who invest in a positive Jewish self-image; but the groups also want to attract readers and solicit articles from academia.

Balancing a popular versus professional focus similarly factors into conferences and speaker series, with some societies, like Michigan and Arizona, carefully selecting scholarly presenters capable of connecting with lay enthusiasts. Bringing hobbyists and trained historians together, both in publications and in conferences, tends to enhance the work of all involved: amateurs become acquainted with academic norms and the "big questions" in the field, while professionals learn to communicate their work more accessibly.

As time goes on, the enthusiasm of historical society founders tends to wane, especially in places like Arizona and Southern California, where transplants from other regions far outnumber longtime Jewish residents with ties to the "land." In such instances, finding new ways to reach out, especially to younger generations, becomes paramount. Diversifying programs to include contemporary and more general topics (notably around the Holocaust and intercultural dialogue), hosting prominent speakers, film screenings, and outside organizations, connecting with college and university Jewish and religious studies programs, participating with local museums and associations, and developing an online presence are all common outreach strategies.

Funding needs differ from group to group, with some, like Arizona, carrying a paid staff and undertaking building projects; others, like Rocky Mountain, having a university faculty position; others, like Southern, Michigan, and Rhode Island, with one or two salaried professionals; and still others, like Western States, functioning as an all-volunteer organization. Operating expenses are covered by a combination of endowments, grants, membership dues, individual donations, ticket sales, and, in the case of Rocky Mountain, university budgets. Financial and membership challenges also vary, with some, like Rhode Island, having ample funds but limited membership, and others, like Michigan, facing both membership and funding concerns. Costs likewise depend on whether the group owns or rents a location or, as with Western States, has no brick-and-mortar site.

Justifying a localized Jewish identity is another shared concern. Location-specific Jewishness was an implicit and motivating factor for the founders of Jewish historical societies, who celebrated and linked themselves to their local Jewish forebears. While this is still largely true for society leaders and members, the extent to which a local or regional Jewish identity matters to Jews as a whole—as opposed to a more general Jewish identity supported by synagogues, Jewish Community Centers, Zionist organizations, and other Jewish affiliations and activities—remains an open question. A major challenge moving forward will be articulating and advocating the relevance of local and regional Jewish history, particularly as the societies' members are predominantly retirees.

Despite their significant and, in many cases, longstanding presence in American Jewish life, local and regional historical societies are an underexamined phenomenon. Combining macro and micro studies of the subject, this volume hopes to modestly fill the gap and offer insights into what these organizations have been, are now, and might yet be.

Historical grounding is imperative for an understanding of community and self. Equally essential is the type of information that makes up that history, as well as how that information is recounted and interpreted. No individual or community exists in isolation; human history is complex, multilayered, and interwoven. "All history is local, but it doesn't occur in a vacuum."

1. John R. Dichtl, "Epilogue: Moving History from Nice to Essential," in *An American Association for State and Local History Guide to Making Public History*, ed. Bob Beatty (Lanham, MD: Rowman and Littlefield, 2017), 230–31.
2. "About Us," American Association for State and Local History, https://aaslh.org/about/.
3. Hy Berman and Jay Weiner, *Professor Berman: The Last Lecture of Minnesota's Greatest Public Historian* (Minneapolis: University of Minnesota Press, 2019), 151.

1

Local and Regional Jewish Historical Societies

Goals and Roles

JOEL GEREBOFF

Over the course of the 1940s and 1950s, three developments signaled the growing importance of the study and presentation of the history of American Jews. These were: (1) efforts to improve the quality of research and publications regarding American Jews, focused particularly on the American Jewish Historical Society and resulting in other national organizations dedicated to scholarship on American Jews and to the training of a coterie of scholars to pursue such research; (2) the numerous, nationally sponsored local activities celebrating the tercentenary of the first Jewish community in America, many of which exhibited constructions of the history of Jews in the United States; and (3) the founding of the first of what are today more than forty local and regional Jewish historical (or heritage) societies. While the first two developments have been analyzed extensively—with attention to what they indicate about growing efforts to use history as a way to represent the Jews of America to themselves and to the broader American society—little has been written on the history of local or regional Jewish historical societies, let alone analyzing them in terms of what they reveal about the significance, both for American Jews and non-Jews, of researching and conveying the history of Jews in a variety of media.

We open with a discussion of the first two developments and then offer an extensive analysis of the histories, missions, activities, and publications of local Jewish historical societies. This chapter focuses on the ways in which each party promoting the three developments understands the project of historical research and representations of the past. Central to this are questions of how they negotiate tensions between objective, dispassionate scholarship, which seeks to better understand the history of Jews in the United States, the history of the Jews on a global level, and the history of America more broadly—especially as these are manifest in particular locales—and, by contrast, the use of history to ground or bolster Jewish identity. In essence, what are the roles of local and regional Jewish historical societies? Are they strictly institutions that serve as *sources* for learning about the history of Jews, or are they also *resources*: arenas for Jews to explore and enact ways to be Jewish and for non-Jews to think about how they, as individuals or members of diverse subgroups, form part of and contribute to American society and culture? Can Jews engage in research related to Jewish history without compromising the standards that typically define academic scholarship? Does the claim or assumption that Jewish historical investigations reveal the reasons for and contents of being Jewish align with the neutrality that generally underlies academic research? From the beginning of the nineteenth century onwards, much of the inward-looking historical research on the Jews has viewed such endeavors as a key to defining the core meaning and purpose of being Jewish, often framed in essentialist terms. This proposition has been challenged over the decades by historians who take what they define as a more academic approach, seeking to make sense of Jewish history as part of a more general study of history, the humanities, and the social sciences.

Others have documented efforts to raise the quality of research into the history of American Jews and Judaism and to professionalize the field. Accordingly, our discussion is limited to only several aspects of those developments. These include delineating the recurrent tension between advancing a discipline using methods and theories shared by other academic disciplines and the desire to produce knowledge and information that speak to uniquely Jewish goals, such as forming Jewish identity and promoting the acceptance and status of American Jews. This review will also address geographic concerns regarding the significance of focusing on local, regional, or only national aspects of American Jewish history. In sum, the overarching query is why anyone should devote time and energy to studying and producing programs and publications regarding the history of American Jews.

Professionalizing and Improving Research and Publications on American Jewish History

Beginning in the early 1940s, three Jewish academics—Salo Baron, Oscar Handlin, and Jacob Rader Marcus—came to recognize the significance of American Jewish history.[1] Each saw the present state of research and writing on the history of American Jews as woefully deficient. Their motivations to improve the field were several. On the one hand, they strove to encourage the serious study of American Jews in a way resembling how American history and the broader history of the Jews were being pursued in institutions of higher education. They hoped to train scholars who would, in time, occupy academic appointments in such institutions. Additionally, both Baron, the holder of the Miller Chair in Jewish History at Columbia, and Marcus, professor of Jewish history at Hebrew Union College (HUC), were historians of European and, in many ways, global Jewry. They were cognizant that, with the already evident decimation of European Jewry, America would soon be home to the largest Jewish population in the world. As such, they felt that American Jews—and Americans in general—needed a more accurate and more complex understanding of the history of American Jewry.

In their view and that of Handlin, a professor of American history at Harvard whose scholarship focused on what was then the novel topic of immigration, the study of American Jewish history was a domain comprised nearly entirely of amateurs. The list of pejorative terms applied to the "scholarship" of these nonprofessional "historians" took account of the range of topics, agendas, and deficient methods. Their work was deemed "amateurish," "antiquarian," "tombstone history," "ancestor worship," "filiopietistic," "nonobjective," "parochial," and driven by celebratory and apologetic goals. These untrained writers consistently failed to situate their topics within the context of either American history or the broader world history of the Jews. Moreover, the publications were largely descriptive, did not critically evaluate evidence, were often far too limited to support the conclusions drawn, and did not include the range of factors often determinative of historical developments, such as social, political, or economic forces.

While American Jews sought to construct, display, communicate, and celebrate their history through a range of media, the primary focus of Baron and Marcus was the American Jewish Historical Society (AJHS).[2] Since its founding in 1892, AJHS had not given rise to much in the way of excellent scholarship. Before briefly discussing the organization's history, it is also important to situate the efforts of Baron, Marcus, and Handlin within broader trends in the professionalization of historical scholarship in America as directed by academics with positions at research universities.

The development of the discipline of American history has been documented in several studies.[3] The 1880s was a time of growing importance for the field of history in the American university, as well as the formation of the first academic national society for historians, the American Historical Association (AHA). Although dominated by historians from universities in the East, AHA for many years strove to be inclusive. Individuals who worked in historical societies, high school history teachers, and archivists were all welcome during its early years. A parallel organization, the Mississippi Valley Historical Association (MVHA), was launched in 1907, partly as a result of the efforts of professionals at a number of state historical societies in the Midwest (between the Allegheny and Rocky Mountains). Over time, AHA narrowed the definition of "historian" to those employed at research universities. A short while later, MVHA, which in 1965 became the Organization of American Historians, followed suit. During its initial phase, MVHA focused on what was called "applied history," which aimed at supplying governments and other agencies with historical knowledge to address policy issues. Treating this as a legitimate goal of historical inquiry was due in part to the influence of Robert Shambaugh, superintendent of the State Historical Society of Iowa and a professor at the University of

Iowa, where the historical society was centered. Another defining feature of the MVHA was its agreement with Frederick Turner's thesis of the frontier: regions beyond the East Coast as locations for the flourishing of American democracy. Jacob Marcus's vision of American Jewish history would later come to espouse a similar emphasis on the Midwest and a rejection of the centrality of the East Coast.[4]

Despite these wider understandings of what Robert Townsend terms the "historical enterprise," the broad conglomerate of individuals interested in the discipline of history, AHA upheld a narrow view of the "history profession" and failed to attend to the concerns of archivists, employees of historical societies, and those teaching history at institutions below the university level.[5] Members of these other groups had been "professionalized" within the structure of the AHA, but in time withdrew to form independent societies: the Society of American Archivists (1937) and the American Association for State and Local History (1940). An overarching concern among university-based historians was research that had a national focus, employed objective scientific methods, and was framed conceptually. It is worth noting, however, the narrowness of what was seen as "real" American history. From the 1940s through much of the twentieth century, historians largely concerned themselves with the experiences of the Anglo-Saxon Protestant founders of the United States and their wealthy and more socially and politically established descendants.[6] Examining the history of the United States or analyzing the lives of "minorities," immigrants, women, or what would be called "ethnic groups" did not begin until the late 1960s.[7]

Efforts to raise the standards of American Jewish historical studies during the 1940s overlapped with similar efforts at research universities during that period. As noted, one of the aims of these historians was to gain acceptance for the study of American Jewish history, both in universities and within the broader field of Jewish history. To achieve this goal—as well as internally Jewish-focused aims—required working with AJHS and, in Baron's words, "turning it around."

Established in 1892, AJHS is the oldest American ethnic society devoted to historical research and publication. The call to form the society was issued by Cyrus Adler, who had a PhD from Johns Hopkins University and was supported by East Coast laypeople, with Oscar Strauss having a leading role. A variety of factors contributed to the formation of the group, including the celebration that year of the 400th anniversary of Columbus's "discovery" of America and the growing nativism and anti-Semitism present in American society. Adler had an academic vision in mind. He aimed to form an organization that would "attempt at collecting, preserving and publishing data having reference to the settlement and history of Jews on the American continent."[8] Among the invitees were several of the small number of Jews with university appointments at the time, as well as American Jewish lay leaders and rabbis. Concurrently, as is clear from AJHS's statement of "objects" on the opening page of its journal, *Publications of the American Jewish Historical Society*, the group also had defensive and apologetic goals, along with the filiopietistic interests of some founders to tell their family histories. The statement begins: "The object of this Society is to collect and publish material bearing upon the history of our country." It goes on to note that some Spanish and Portuguese Jews were present on the voyage that led to the founding of America, and that Jews had participated in the Revolutionary War. These observations are summarized thus: "The genealogy of these men and the record of their achievements will, when gathered together, be of value and interest to the historian and perchance contribute materially to the history of our country." Anticipating objections from non-Jews (and probably many Jews), it continues: "The objects for which this Society was organized are not sectarian but American. The co-operation of students of history and of all persons who have an interest in the work of this Society is cordially invited."

Jeffrey Gurock, Hasia Diner, Elisabeth Kaplan, and others note that the founders of AJHS sought to promote and defend Jewish honor and status, and to use historical research for the formation of a model of Jewish identity—goals similar to those of other ethnic historical societies of the period, which also used historical claims for the purpose of legitimizing their place in America.[9] From her reading of the minutes from the meeting convened by Adler, Kaplan observes that, in calling for locating and collecting (archiving) documents scattered and potentially soon to be lost regarding the history of American Jews, they saw these activities as "the means by which to achieve a larger mission: to mold a cohesive and positive image of American Jewry, one which would combine their understandings of themselves as American Jews and of Judaism with their perceptions of Americans and America."[10] Although the terms "ethnic" and "identity" are anachronistic, as neither was in use at that time, the group essentially sought to formulate an "ethnic identity" for American Jews. This approach was reflected in their avoidance of discussions about what it meant to be a Jew, other than to be a loyal American. Participants agreed that being Jewish in America required some degree of accommodating "American values," and that Jews who were highly separationist did not align with their conception of American Jewish identity.

Until the early 1940s, AJHS managed to survive and continue to hold annual meetings, acquire some archival material, and maintain, for the most part, an annually published journal. But as Gurock details in his history of the society, it was an orphaned child of the Jewish and academic worlds: housed in two rooms at the Jewish Theological Seminary in New York, it had no serious or readily accessible archive, was under the lay leadership of an insular and controlling president, and employed just one professional librarian. The quality of the articles published in the society's journal, *Publications*, typically suffered from the aforementioned string of adjectives applied by Baron, Handlin, and Marcus.

These efforts illustrate tensions between the desire to transform the study of American Jewish history into an academic endeavor and ethnic-focused goals of disseminating historical knowledge to address challenges of being Jewish in America and promote thriving Jewish communities.[11] Pursuing these goals need not compromise the quality of historical scholarship nor degenerate into apologetics; both should be "objective," rigorous, and conceptually sound in answering specific questions. However, the choice and handling of topics may well be skewed if practical applications are guiding the way. The professionalized field of American historical research had already largely rejected "applied history," and that remained the case until the emergence of "public history" in the late 1970s. Similarly, the emergence of "social history," which at times found expression in ethnic and/or women's or feminist historical research, also sought to draw on such investigations for advancing changes in society. These novel approaches also experienced pushback or outright rejection from university-based historians, who saw them as violating professional standards. To better understand these tensions, we will discuss Baron, Handlin, and Marcus separately, and then compare their similar and conflicting objectives.

Salo Baron took the lead in seeking to transform the study of American Jews into a serious scholarly field. He trained a number of doctoral students who were the first to complete dissertations on topics related to American Jewish history and sought academic appointments for them. He worked to raise the caliber of AJHS and its publication. He invited non-Jewish university professors of American history to speak at AJHS annual meetings. In 1954, he organized a joint session of AHA and AJHS at the AHA conference, intending both Marcus and Handlin to be key presenters. Most significant in this regard, Baron convened the Peekskill conference in conjunction with the celebration of the American Jewish Tercentenary in 1954. The meeting attempted to assess the state of scholarship in American Jewish history and establish plans for aligning it with the broader academic community. Both Jewish and non-Jewish professionals attended the meeting. Although it would take until the 1970s for AJHS to achieve consistently high standards in its publication and a greater role for the growing number of formally trained scholars of American Jewish history, Baron's efforts were central to the reformulation of AJHS and the advancement of American Jewish studies at the university level.

In addition to these academic goals, Baron had specifically Jewish objectives. He subscribed to the view that accurate and sophisticated historical knowledge was essential for the well-being and survival of American Jews.[12] In his lengthy AJHS presidential address in 1950, Baron detailed the numerous scholarly desiderata for the group, concluding, "The time seems indeed to have come for our society to assume its rightful place as a major constructive force in the cultural life of the American Jewish community."[13] He made a similar comment in his opening statement at the Tercentenary Conference on American Jewish Sociology, convened by the Conference of Jewish Relations, of which he served as president: "On the basis of this experience, I feel confident that the present Conference will likewise leave a permanent imprint on Jewish cultural life."[14] In his opening remarks at the Peekskill conference, Baron observed that only in the last fifteen or twenty years had a number of important works dealing with major phases of Jewish history in the United States been published: "They have laid the foundations for thorough investigations of the historic experience of American Jewry and the Jewish contribution to American civilization to be conducted on a level comparable with that of writings in other phases of American and Jewish history."[15] While this remark underscored the need to contextualize the American Jewish experience within American and broader Jewish global history, Baron nevertheless stressed the "contributions" of Jews—an emphasis characteristic of apologetic and defensive writings.

Baron's encouragement of scholarly analyses of various Jewish communities, while flowing from his own work on the topic (and primarily aligned with the urban history focus of American historical research), also had a practical goal.[16] The AJHS-sponsored studies of Jewish communities were published by Columbia University Press as part of the Jewish Communal History Series. A parallel initiative was a series of community studies undertaken by the Center for American Jewish History, headed by Professor Moshe Davis at the Jewish Theological Seminary of America. These studies were produced by joint initiatives of local rabbis and amateur researchers working with professional historians.[17] The topics and contextual analyses were consistent with academic inquiries of the time. Yet they were also of value to local Jewish leadership. With attention to the range of social, economic, demographic, political, and social factors that shaped and formed Jewish life in America, professional and lay Jewish leaders could better assess and formulate programs to speak to the needs of Jews. These projects reaffirmed Baron's hope, articulated at a 1942 meeting of Jewish social and communal workers, that research guided by modern social and historical sciences "may be destined to render a historic service lesser to none performed by their predecessors in other ages of great transformation."[18] As Diner and Gurock point out, Baron was essentially an elitist who envisioned professional academics and intellectually sophisticated Jewish leaders as the primary audience for the type of scholarship he sought to foster.

Oscar Handlin, the child of immigrants and the first Jew to be tenured in the history department at Harvard, also played a crucial role in professionalizing and raising the quality of the study of American Jewish history. Hasia Diner has offered a detailed analysis of Handlin's bifurcated scholarly career.[19] Handlin is best known for his Pulitzer Prize–winning study *The Uprooted*, which describes the quintessential immigrant to America as a peasant removed from his land and deposited in urban America among others from different cultural backgrounds. As Diner observes, this immigrant experience was not, in fact, that of most Jews who landed in America. Indeed, Handlin's scholarly writings and presentations at academic conferences seldom treated Jews as the subject matter. Yet, Handlin was an activist within the Jewish community, especially in terms of upgrading the quality of scholarship on American Jews. He spoke frequently to Jewish audiences and published articles in Jewish newspapers, magazines, and nonprofessional journals. In several pieces for *Commentary*, he deplored the dismal state of publications on American Jews: "What passes now for history is an accumulation of details of little consequence, only slightly related either to the problems of the present or to the real people of the past."[20]

Handlin took a prominent role during the 1954 American Jewish Tercentenary, participating in the Peekskill conference and authoring two works related to the history of American Jews. His doctoral student, Moses Rischin, composed a review and analysis of existing scholarship on American Jewish history for which Handlin wrote a foreword.[21] Although Handlin disapproved of writings that were "overlaid with an apologetic tone, filiopietism and excess zeal to demonstrate the contributions of particular groups of ancestors to American history," he hoped that competently produced studies of American Jewish history would result in fellow citizens—and fellow historians—recognizing "the important part played by Jews in the making of American civilization."[22]

Perhaps the most revealing of Handlin's views appeared in his 1954 book, *Adventure in Freedom: Three Hundred Years of Jewish Life in America*.[23] Reviews for the book were mixed, in part because of Handlin's overly positive interpretation of the benefits America offered to Jews. Like the peasant immigrants described in *The Uprooted*, for the Jews, "The American crossing was liberating. In every area of life the confining regulations fell away and man was left free." Critics of the book saw in it an assimilationist agenda. Handlin did not advocate this, but in some ways foresaw it.[24] A similar statement on the advantages of studying American Jewish history appears in *Commentary*, which he wrote following a 1948 conference on the state of American Jewry:

> Such historical perspective has a critical function in our society where many Jews now call themselves Jews not for purposes of traditional religious observance, but for some other reason. . . . People whose ties to the group are ethnic, the recollection of a common ancestry, find particularly important to know their own history, to seek in the past the sources of their present consciousness as Jews. . . . Unless they have a clear conception of the past of the group, they fall victims to disastrous myths and remain torn by cultural and personal conflicts. . . . [Such accounts may speak to Jews] troubled only by the answers they must give children who demand an explanation of the vague line that divides them from their neighbors.[25]

Whatever distinctly Jewish outcomes Handlin envisioned, he actively engaged in efforts to advance the study of Jews in America.

The third scholar central to the transformation of this scholarship, Jacob Rader Marcus, served as professor of history at Hebrew Union College in Cincinnati. In 1942, even earlier than Baron and Handlin, Marcus offered the first course in American Jewish history at an institution of higher learning. To be sure, Marcus's base of operation was a Jewish institution where he helped train American rabbis, and this Jewish communal agenda informed his multiple activities directed at enhancing the field. Yet, his endeavors—including his voluminous books on American

Jewish history,[26] founding of the American Jewish Archives (AJA) in 1947, training of doctoral students in American Jewish history, promoting the writing of local Jewish history (professional and amateur), and participating in AJHS, which he served as president from 1957 to 1959—testify to his singular contribution to the historical study of American Jews. Marcus stressed the importance of the "scientific method" in studying history, by which he meant assembling numerous primary texts and subjecting them to analysis. In the spirit of Leopold von Ranke, he valued "the facts." These facts did require interpretation, although Marcus's approach was limited compared to that of Baron, who more fully embraced a social-economic methodology and complex contextualization within Jewish and broader societal trends.[27]

Crucial to understanding Marcus's oeuvre was his emphasis on studying American Jews who lived beyond the East Coast. He founded AJA in part to address deficiencies he saw in the AJHS archives, but also out of a desire to document the lives of Jews across the country, especially in the Midwest and through to the Pacific. Marcus was also keenly interested in the lives of "ordinary Jews," not just the elite, although in the end AJA—as a result of his contacts with HUC graduates—came to feature large holdings on Reform synagogues and Reform rabbis. While there is no evidence that Marcus was influenced by MVHA, which likewise sought to expand the study of American history beyond the East Coast patrician class, Marcus's vision of America in many ways harmonized with that of MVHA.

Although Marcus did train a number of significant PhD students in American Jewish history at HUC, he also saw a legitimate role for "amateurs" and those he called "semi-pros," including rabbinic students who wrote theses on topics in American Jewish history. In his 1957 presidential address to AJHS, Marcus spoke of professional historians taking an interest in the field. Yet, he also recognized that "it would not be unrealistic to assume that the study of American Jewish history will ever produce a school of professional historians of any size." He posited that "Paid and professionally trained college men, are not the only ones who can write history. Some of the great historians in this country had no formal training and never taught history in a collegiate institution." He affirmed that gifted lovers of American Jewish history could also write *good* history:

> They can if they but prepare themselves. To write history it is important to have an appreciation and knowledge of historic method. Once the amateur has learned to identify documents and papers of historical value and to evaluate them critically, he is on the way to being in the same category as the professional historian whom he admires.[28]

To help facilitate the study of local Jewish history in particular, Marcus issued a 1953 booklet entitled, *How to Write the History of an American Jewish Community*.[29] Directed at would-be historians, the booklet begins: "Our sense of identification with our American homeland and our age old Jewish history and tradition encourages us to look with pride upon our dual past." Marcus assured the reader: "Actually it is not too difficult to write the history of the Jews of your town, and we can promise you that you will find the task not only enjoyable but even a fascinating one."[30] For Marcus, even basic descriptive studies of local Jewish communities had value, so long as they were grounded in a range of potentially relevant primary sources. As such, his vision of who may (and perhaps ought to) participate in American Jewish history aligned with that of laypeople who fostered the creation of local and regional Jewish historical societies. While Marcus did not elucidate his theoretical assumptions, Gary Zola, executive director of AJA's Jacob Rader Marcus Center, has identified five themes underlying Marcus's approach to the study of American Jewish history. These speak to the scholarly and more Jewishly focused aims of Marcus's research.[31]

1. American Jewish history is consistently influenced by historical experiences of the Jewish people.
2. American Jewish history has a practical benefit: it illustrates our understanding of contemporary issues in American Jewish life.
3. American Jewish history possesses inspirational value; it instills Jewish pride and strengthens Jewish identity.

4. American Jewish history is, at its core, the study of the lives of individual Jews interrelated with their ethnic-religious community in America.
5. American Jewish history lends support to the historically based assertion that the Jewish experience is immortal.

These themes combine insights emerging from historical analyses and a set of religiously grounded convictions. Which of these assertions are conclusions Marcus derived from historical study, and which were the very presuppositions motivating that research? One hears in these five themes the integration of Marcus the scholar and Marcus the Reform rabbi. For example, in explicating the fifth of these themes, Zola observes:

> Marcus believed that civilizations and nations may rise and fall, but as long as Jews cling to their ethical legacy they can never be obliterated. . . . He regularly concluded his public lectures by pointing out that the core essence of American Jewry, indeed that of the Jewish people, had been distilled in the prophet Micah's (6:8) famous maxim: "It is told of thee, O man, what is good and what the Lord requires of thee; only to do justice, love mercy and walk humbly with thy God."[32]

Marcus also tended to fill his books with copious details and anecdotes about the lives of all types of Jews. In many ways, this is similar to biographical sketches that appear in publications of local and regional Jewish historical societies. A key difference is that Marcus often draws on more primary sources and weaves the lives of individual Jews into a larger narrative involving broader aspects of American Jewish life.

Jeffrey Gurock has compared the views of Marcus and Baron regarding the importance of the public knowing of the subject. "Marcus was more a public historian [than was Baron]," writes Gurock. "He was very concerned with personally educating the American Jewish public, both through writing guides to how amateurs could write their own communal history with objectivity and sophistication and through his journal *American Jewish Archives*, which he called his 'magazine' and which was designed from its inception to speak to more than just scholars."[33] Gurock concludes: "All told, while we revere Baron as the paradigmatic academic Jewish historian, who typified the successful rarefied professional, a status to which so many of us aspired, we adore Marcus for his scholarship, his commitment to teaching our subject and his determination to have the American Jewish historian walk within the community and actively contribute to the perpetuation of Jewish life in this country."[34]

The 1954 tercentenary celebration provided an early display of certain views about the lessons of American Jewish history for both Jews and the general public. Initiated by AJHS, the Tercentenary Committee—comprising 300 members and headed by Ralph Samuel, who had held leadership positions at the Federation of Philanthropies in New York and the American Jewish Committee, and Simon H. Rifkind, a former federal judge—programmed numerous major national events. They also provided guidance, programming information, and travelling exhibits for the more than 400 celebrations held in Jewish communities across the United States.[35] Official reports boasted that there were so many local observances that it "would be impossible to record them all."[36] Despite their being proposed by AJHS, trained historians did not play a central role in formulating or executing the various celebrations.[37] The Peekskill conference, organized by Baron, undertook a formal part in the tercentenary observances, which, on the whole, occasioned broader interest in American Jewish history—although mediated through narratives advanced by the various events.

The tercentenary commemorated the 1654 arrival of America's first Jewish community, consisting of twenty-three Jews of Spanish-Portuguese descent who left Brazil for New Amsterdam (New York) and formed Congregation Shearith Israel. In the official summary of the anniversary celebration, David Bernstein stressed: "Even at the middle of the twentieth century, American Jews felt impelled to supplement the authentic American impulse to publicize the antiquity of their roots in the country with the desire to remind themselves and their Christian neighbors that these roots made each of them as early American as the mostly stately daughters of the American revolution."[38] This declaration of the overlap of American and Jewish values was directed at Jews and non-Jews alike. Describing the intention of the showcase production, committee chair Ralph Samuel highlighted the imprint of Jews "in every circle and corner of Jewish life" and "how a so-called minority group can thrive in a climate of freedom and democracy."[39] Robert Rifkind, chairman of the 350th celebration in 2004, recognized the centrality of "Jewish contributions" in how American Jews represented their history. Conscious of previous celebrations, especially the tercentenary, Rifkind stated: "American Jewry no longer felt obliged to proclaim its patriotism or its fidelity to America's highest values. Nor did American Jewry feel the need to declaim on contributions that Jews had made to America. They were too conspicuous to require comment."[40]

Several Jewish thinkers and organizations objected to the shoehorning of Jewish self-understanding and self-representation into the tercentenary. Jewish labor groups, for instance, staged their own counter-celebrations focusing on Yiddish culture and the role of workers in American Jewish life. Horace Kallen, the coiner of the concept of "cultural pluralism," stressed that American Jews should create a more democratic communal polity in order "to play its part in the orchestra of the pluralistic American people." In this way, they would enjoy the same status as all distinct groups in America and would not need to seek recognition of their legitimacy. Zionist and traditionalist thinkers saw the theme and programming as far too assimilationist. And, in the view of many critics, the committee's goal of inclusiveness actually led to a limited formulation of the content of Jewish identity.[41]

The popular appeal of American Jewish history is evidenced in the themes of the tercentenary, the mindset of its formulators, and the large number of American Jews who participated nationwide. The fact that the 300th anniversary of a Jewish community in America spoke to so many Jews indicates the resonance of the celebration's core message: American Jews felt at home in America, while also relishing in having non-Jews recognize them. Unsurprisingly, contributions of Jews to America took center stage. As David Bernstein explained, "It was important to recognize the vitality and value of the past in the United States. It was gratifying to hear the expressions of respect from fellow-citizens of other faiths. And it was helpful to consider the prospects for the future."[42]

As already mentioned, a key question is what these activities present as the contents and lessons of American Jewish history. While the programs of Jewish historical societies are often intended for Jews and non-Jews, the lectures they sponsor, like those sponsored by other Jewish groups and institutions, are predominantly attended by Jews. What do the attendees hope to hear? In several publications, Diner reflects on her experiences in the Jewish community as an academically trained, university-employed professor of American Jewish history. One paper, delivered in 2007 at a joint session of the Polish American Historical Association and the Immigration and Ethnic History Society at a meeting of AHA, speaks of the pressures of "serving two masters." Diner primarily defines herself as a member of the academic community. However, she is also beholden to the financial support of American Jewish donors and communal institutions, especially when she is involved in Jewish community programs. From the 1970s onwards, American Jews have invested in Jewish studies with the aim of shoring up the identity of Jewish college students and, at times, serving as Jewish representatives on university campuses. Most professors object to these roles. Yet, as Diner notes, it would be ungracious not to recognize the many local Jews (often seniors) who attend lectures and conferences on campus and help fund Jewish studies programs. She feels obligated to make herself available to Jewish organizations and institutions by speaking in such settings, or by writing articles in popular Jewish newspapers. She understands that people who attend her public lectures come "with deep passions about the American Jewish past and with their already fixed ideas about those developments, why they took place and what they meant. . . . They tend to see history as a matter of praising heroes and blaming villains. To them American Jewish history serves to confirm identity and shore up communal solidarity."[43]

Gurock also notes ongoing tensions between the academic and the popular within AJHS as it sought to address the interest of its many non-academic members and donors who received its journal, *American Jewish History*. Since 1970, academics in the society have gained greater editorial control over the journal and who publishes in it. He observes that, on occasion, a more popular article has still appeared in the journal, with the typical traits of historic anecdotes or facts about a famous or obscure American Jew. At one point, a proposal appeared to either reframe the journal or to publish a separate, more popular magazine on American Jewish history.[44]

In a recent piece, Diner recounts giving numerous talks during the observance of the 350th anniversary of Jews in America (2004–2005) and indicates her discomfort with the sort of rhetoric common to those programs: "I had and continue to have problems with the idea of historians operating under the banner of 'celebration,' as much of our professional project involves critical distance from our subjects. 'Analysis' or 'criticism' rather than 'celebration' seems to me to be the focus of our [academics'] activity."[45] These comments capture tensions between engaging in scholarly pursuits and what seems to be valued when the same historians speak to the Jewish public.

Diner has also written on American historians' general neglect of the nation's Jewish history, including in an article co-authored by Tony Michels for the *Organization of American Historians' Newsletter*.[46] David Hollinger, one of the foremost historians of American ethnicity, responded to the complaint, contending that, for the most part, the communal perspective of American Jewish history—with an eye toward engaging and fostering the Jewish community—makes it undesirable for general historians.[47] In her reply to Hollinger, Diner argued that this perceived emphasis is overstated, and that many scholars of American Jewish history now focus on "Jews at the margin." At the same time, she agreed with Hollinger that "the old 'contributions' approach" remains an "albatross that hangs around the neck" of American Jewish history: "Many of us cringe when we peruse older works in American Jewish history, the type of books and articles that dominated the field from the 1880s through the 1970s, which celebrated the clustering of Jews in one field or another and their important contributions to this or that aspect of American history."[48]

Diner captures the challenges of being a professional historian of American Jewry. While she claims that, after the 1970s, the field of

American Jewish history has moved beyond devotion to "contributors" and "contributions," her other comments indicate that general Jewish audiences continue to desire celebratory presentations. Her remarks serve as a bridge to our description and analysis of local and regional American Jewish historical societies. At the foreground are questions concerning what sorts of activities and programming these societies engage in, the nature of their publications, whether they can serve more than just parochial interests, and if they can be sources for credible Jewish historical studies.

Evaluating the Organizations

Little scholarship has been produced on local or regional American Jewish historical societies. Outside of passing comments in scattered sources and one brief article listing the societies, only two critical papers—one by Jonathan Sarna and one by me—have assessed the impact of these institutions and proposed models for their improvement.[49] Thus, despite the existence of more than forty such organizations, making them a common presence in American Jewish life, they have not attracted much attention. This is similar to the general scholarly neglect of historical societies, save for publications sponsored by the American Association for State and Local History, which have reviewed and offered suggestions for such groups.[50]

Comments referring to local and regional historical societies, their archives, or their publications most often appear in larger discussions of research concerning Jewish communities. One of the sessions at the tercentenary conference examined issues related to local and regional studies. Four papers were presented, followed by a discussion involving both academics and amateur historians. As Jeffrey Gurock observes:

> The Peekskill Conference also revealed that these professors were willing to share their newfound interest in American Jewish history with the amateur historians, including persons with long-affiliation with the society. It was, for them, self-evident that dedicated and literate laymen and rabbis, with proper professional guidance and encouragement could rise above filiopietism and apologetics, to compose useful historical

> statement that might also affect the future course of American Jewish life. Professionals saw real possibilities for improvement particularly in the area of local and regional history, a subdiscipline that had always attracted resident buffs ready to uncritically glorify their community's or synagogue's achievement.[51]

The professional historians stressed that good scholarship should relate local developments to the interpretation of national movements. Morris Schappes, who taught at several universities and edited *Jewish Currents*, reported that an important list of naturalized Jews had been published in the first issue of *Rhode Island Jewish Historical Notes*.[52] That journal was launched the same year as the Peekskill conference, indicating that at least some academically oriented historians took note of what was, in fact, the first journal published by a local Jewish historical society.

Local and regional Jewish historical societies appear as topics in other articles published after the 1954 conference. In several instances, these essays note the ongoing challenge of how to write good local and regional history, due to the general neglect of this area by professionally trained historians. When Abraham Duker presented a survey of publications on local Jewish history at the 1960 annual meeting of AJHS, he noted that the tercentenary "celebration brought to the attention of American Jews the uses of history for the purpose of raising their status as Americans. . . . The excitement engendered by the historical event was channeled in a number of communities into local history projects which have been instrumental in sponsoring historical research."[53] A footnote in the published version cites four local Jewish historical societies—Rhode Island, Maryland, Michigan, and Southern—along with the journals they published (Michigan and Southern California were without journals at the time).[54]

Duker gave mixed reviews of the publications he surveyed: "[I]t is too early to write a substantial synthetic history on the basis of these studies; many large and small communities have not yet been studied; from that which has been written, a pattern of a model local history seems to be evolving," noting Marcus's guide for writing the history of an American Jewish community. "Many publications are not of very high quality and some can be described as inferior." According to Duker, the status and training of the writers were largely to blame: "Persons well trained in research, possessed of insight in the process of history and endowed with a gift of writing, are increasingly making their mark in the field. Of course, the untrained and amateur part time historians will always be with us, certainly as authors of histories of small communities. . . . The semi-professional needs guidance beyond references to sources and help in the formation of the outline."[55]

Diner commented on the successes and limitations of local and regional Jewish history efforts in the early 1990s. She underscored the importance of archives, some of which have assisted articles published by the societies:

> Local and regional Jewish historical societies have played an important role in the collection and publication of many of these sources. Their archives are rich in primary materials. Moreover, the Jewish Historical Societies of Rhode Island, Michigan, Washington, DC, and New Haven have also published large amounts of material. While such articles and books may not quite match a standard of professional scholarship, they are an important and immensely rich basis for research and interpretation.[56]

Of the Jewish society publications, *Southern Jewish History* is most consistent in producing high-caliber academic articles, followed by *Rhode Island Jewish Historical Notes,* which occasionally includes such articles. The other journals are more mixed in this regard.

Gurock's study of AJHS notes the plenitude of inquiries regarding American Jewish history that were sent to and answered by the society during the 1950s and 1960s: "Many of these inquiries came from amateur buffs interested in their local community's history." Specifically, many letters came from members of local and regional Jewish historical societies that supported, and were encouraged by, the national society. Gurock states positively: "A number of these groups established local journals. In these organs diligent investigators informed their friends and associates about little known facts or aspects of their community's history even as they studiously avoided the bluster, hyperbole and defensiveness that once characterized the form of amateur writing."[57]

Gurock identifies "the society's most troubling policy dilemma" as "navigating the interests of readers and board members of AJHS."[58] This predicament continued during the editorship of Henry Feingold and Marc Lee Raphael from the 1970s to the 1990s. AJHS never quite resolved the matter, as financial support for the society mainly came from non-professional members and a few generous board members who preferred the inclusion articles aimed at attracting broader readership. Some suggested publishing two journals: *American Jewish History* for academics and a second journal, *American Jewish Heritage*, for an interested popular audience. According to Gurock, "Executive council members who were closely aligned with the burgeoning local societies were particularly exercised that their type of community history—readable, accessible, popular accounts—did not appear in the *Quarterly*,[59] while 'esoteric, not interesting, not contemporary' academic investigations seemingly dominated the journal."[60] During the 1970s, the council resolved to work on a single journal that would more consistently balance the interests and needs of both academic and general readers. The journal, however, continued to disproportionately include the former to maintain its scholarly quality and standing. Many of these articles dealt with developments in limited locales or were studies of specific individuals in such locales. But they were scholarly in terms of their methodologies and contextualization. In this crucial way, they differed from the type of articles amateur history buffs tended to write.

The same challenges of how to discuss local and regional history persisted during Gurock's time as associate editor of the journal (1982–2002). One difference in the type of local history he favored was the inclusion of quantitative data, which "raised the eyebrows" of amateur history buffs. Despite his generally negative view of local Jewish historiography, he and Raphael did include "local studies with national relevance." But, as Gurock states, "the national journal has not published during our tenure, much local history. One reason is that local buffs are more often than not content to write for their own local journals." The omission of such studies from the journal had an impact on the society: "The national organization certainly needs the moral and financial support of these local groups. And to the extent that they [those who publish in local Jewish history journals and readers of those works] feel separate from Waltham, Massachusetts, it surely impacts on their commitment to the *AJH*'s survival."[61]

It is crucial to note here the distinction between local and regional studies. Most of the comments cited above refer to writing pertaining to local or at most statewide history. In terms of "regional" studies, while the Tercentenary Conference's session was on "local and regional Jewish history," only a handful of articles have discussed with care the notion of regionalism in American Jewish historiography.[62] The concept has been addressed particularly regarding claims of uniquely Southern and Western Jewish histories.[63] Among the regional Jewish historical studies are the Rocky Mountain Jewish Historical Society, Jewish Society of the Upper Midwest, Western Jewish History Center (originally part of the Magnes Museum and now part of the University of California, Berkeley), and Western States Jewish History Association.

In 1994, John Higham, a leading historian of immigration and ethnicity, published what is to date the only significant comparative analysis of ethnic historical societies.[64] Tracing the history and character of several such groups from their inception in the 1890s until a century later, Higham presented a three-period typology. The most recent phase of these organizations, dating from the 1970s, is the era of "academic particularism," in which "the agenda of leading ethnic historical societies is predominantly academic." According to Higham, AJHS's move to Brandeis raised the status of the society in parts of the academic world. (The headquarters of AJHS later returned to New York to the Center for Jewish History.) While lay interests were not completely ignored, support for AJHS "in the Jewish community at large has eroded." Meanwhile, "local Jewish historical and genealogical societies have spread like wildfire in the last fifteen years attracting more and more the interest and contributions the national group needs. These local societies reflect the growing desire of American Jews to preserve their families through a history centered in particular communities, now that identity as American no longer needs to be proven."[65]

Higham's observations were supported by a conversation he had with Bernard Wax, then executive director of AJHS. Wax made these points explicit in his printed reply to Higham's piece. Although aware of the impact that local Jewish historical societies had on the nationally oriented AJHS, Wax nevertheless assisted local groups and published the only detailed listing of them, containing brief descriptions of each. Information reported in that list came from a questionnaire distributed to all known Jewish historical societies in the United States and Canada. "The resulting listing demonstrates the wide-ranging diversity and activity of the local state and regional institutions of this nature," Wax wrote. "It also shows the boom in interest in the field of American Jewish history, one of which we anticipate will continue to rise over the years."[66] AJHS's interest in local and regional Jewish historical societies, while not formally structured, is also evident from comments a decade earlier by AJA director Jacob Marcus. Reflecting on the completion of twenty-five years of publishing the *American Jewish Archives Journal*, Marcus provided a positive review of developments in American Jewish historical studies since 1948. According to Marcus, the interest aroused by the tercentennial celebrations "eventuated in an American Jewish historiography which is now a scientific discipline and has begun to produce works of quality. . . . In addition to the national depositories of AJA and AJHS, numerous smaller American Jewish associations have developed for the study of city, state and regional Jewish communities and are now publishing their own magazines."[67] In light of Marcus's efforts to collect documents from local Jewish communities (often with the aid of HUC graduates), and his guidance on how amateurs should write such histories, it seems that he approved of this development.

The above comments summarize the limited remarks about local Jewish historical societies in academic publications. While not entirely ignored, their history, activities, and publications have not received much discussion. At most, a few scholars have noted their existence, with the majority of comments being dubious about their academic value. Scholars have shown little interest in discussing the roles these groups play in the Jewish community, or what an analysis of them might contribute to the study of Jews in America. As noted, only Sarna and I have explored these issues.

Sarna initially presented his remarks to the Rhode Island Jewish Historical Association.[68] He framed the significance of studying history in terms of "we"—the value it has to "us." "We" here refers in part to historians, irrespective of their identities. However, by the end of his presentation, "we" comes to mean that Jews who study their past also help to shape future Jewish goals and self-perceptions. Noting the habitual failure of organizations to articulate why American Jewish history is important, why local Jewish history is worth pursuing, and how history should be preserved, Sarna offered the following points:[69]

1. We study local Jewish history because it teaches us we have a history. We have learned to respect the power of tradition, and we know that we have been shaped by those who came before us. One of the tasks of every Jewish historian, and every Jewish historical society, is to demonstrate that we actually have a continuous history dating back some 3,500 years, and dating back in America—and in Rhode Island—to the mid-seventeenth century. But it is important not to rewrite that history to conform to present wishes, for present personal and political reasons.
2. The purpose of engaging in historical studies is to remind us that we have a usable history, a history that can teach us something about the present. Without history, the present lacks both context and perspective. The ability to place a contemporary problem into a broader and sometimes different perspective is one of the most important functions of history.
3. Jewish history, especially local Jewish history, teaches us we have a variegated history, a history that is rich and diverse. History properly studied counters ethnocentrisms. One of the great tasks facing local and regional Jewish community historical societies is to broaden our perspective on American Jewish history: to make it frankly less New York centered. We need to highlight what made

American Jewish history in its myriad locations throughout the United States both different and unique.

4. Local Jewish history shows us that we have an organic history; that differences and distances notwithstanding, we are nevertheless related to one another; we form one world. Local Jewish history can teach us about the ties that bind; those that bind us as human beings to one another; those that bind us as Jews to one another; and those that bind Rhode Island Jews to other Jewish communities in the United States and beyond.
5. Local Jewish history reminds us we have a history that binds us across time. We are, in other words, not only bound to one another, we are also part of the ongoing process of history. History fights dangerous present-mindedness.

Sarna further stressed the centrality of preserving records in combatting distortions of history—including those by demagogues—and, to that end, recommended placing the Rhode Island Jewish Historical Association's records in proper archives. To move forward, we must learn from our past. The study of history is a creative act and a means of inspiring individuals and communities to forge ahead. The efforts of historical societies to study and understand the diverse lives of the Jews of the past might very well stimulate new ideas, new approaches, and new directions for American Jewry in the decades ahead. For Sarna, preservation and engagement with the past give us tools to shape our future confidently and creatively.

Sarna views local and regional historical societies as contributing, first and foremost, to the lives and self-definition of contemporary Jews in particular locales. Understanding events and situations of the past, recognizing the factors that led to those developments, and drawing connections between multiple time periods can inspire Jews to reflect on why they ought to be Jewish and what being Jewish means to them. Some aspects of Sarna's claims are debatable, such as whether the history of Jews is "organic." The study of Jewish history also should consider those Jews who ceased to identify as such, as well as those who objected to the way some other Jews thought or behaved. Indeed, there were (and still are) Jews who found nothing usable in the past, however accurately or inaccurately they perceived it.

The other specific function of historical societies is to preserve records and archive resources. Collecting such information can benefit anyone—Jewish and non-Jewish—who seeks to learn about an area's Jews, Jewish groups, and/or Jewish communities. Missing from Sarna's analysis is discussion of the importance of publishing archived materials or historical accounts drawing on such documents. Still, one might surmise from Sarna's having published this article in the Rhode Island society's journal—as well as his assessment that "the Rhode Island Jewish Historical Association is among the most active and successful of these local historical societies"—that he saw merit in such publications.[70]

Sarna concludes that local and regional Jewish historical societies can help us decipher why Jews in the past did what they did, including: "[H]ow they struggled to overcome problems and challenges posed by American society, and how they emerged to become part of one of the greatest Jewish communities in all of Jewish history, might very well stimulate new ideas, new approaches and new directions for American Jewish life in the decades to come."[71] The potential for historical society members to make connections between their own lives and accurate reconstructions of past Jewish lives points to a forward-looking, open-ended objective. The past does not necessarily determine how Jews or Jewish communities must function or behave in the future. In this regard, although he does not use these words, Sarna sees local Jewish historical societies as arenas for discussions about the past that inform ideas for the future.

We will later return to this model for how local and regional Jewish historical groups can address concerns of Jews for their own future and, depending on their inclusiveness, for their broader communities. In what follows, we describe and analyze the history, missions, activities, and publications of numerous American Jewish historical societies. These observations will lead to a proposal for how well-functioning groups might use academic-level tools and methods to benefit an area's Jewish and non-Jewish residents.

Of course, beyond this utilitarian focus, which is our subject here, there is also the possibility of gaining knowledge for its own sake. Having a greater understanding of history can be interesting and valuable in and of itself. Moreover, it can be assumed that when non-Jewish academics write on Jewish history—even in the journals of these societies—they are not doing so primarily for the benefit the Jewish community.

Local and Regional Jewish Historical Societies

Since 1951, at least forty-five local and regional Jewish historical societies have been formed. A list of these organizations, organized by their date of formation, appears in the appendix to this volume. Of these groups, roughly forty are still active in one form or another. Information about these societies was gleaned from previously cited articles, websites of the various groups, and essays appearing in their own publications.[72] We have also read representative selections from their publications, reviewed their indices (when available), and communicated with professionals employed by several of the groups.[73] Additionally, we contacted past and present employees of AJHS and AJA.[74] Certainly, descriptions and analyses of these groups would be enriched by examining internal correspondence and minutes of meetings. Learning more about their programming, such as the number of attendees at their various events, specific details of lectures and exhibits, and other types of programs, would also add depth to this discussion. Regardless of these limitations, the evidence examined suggests a number of commonalities among these groups, as well as some differences.

Jewish historical societies are not the only organizations or institutions that engage the Jewish past on the local or regional level. Geographically focused Jewish museums, archives, and genealogical groups also seek to preserve and present historical information. While in some communities a single institution performs all these functions, in many others distinct entities serve these roles. In several cases, such as the Jewish historical societies of Maryland, Washington, Milwaukee, and Oregon, the study of history has been subsumed within a Jewish museum and is now guided by the museum's leadership. In cities such as Atlanta and New Orleans, where no historical society exists, the Jewish museum acts as the leading historical institution.[75] In Savannah, Pittsburgh, Philadelphia, Nashville,

Cleveland, Kansas City, and elsewhere, there are Jewish institutions housing community archives of various types but no formal historical society.

It is worth noting that Jewish museums have a national professional organization, the Council of American Jewish Museums, that sponsors annual conferences and other activities; genealogical groups have the International Association of Jewish Genealogical Societies, through which groups can share information and ideas; and Jewish archivists can network with their peers through the Association of Jewish Libraries. However, there is no coordinating body for the staff or members of local or regional Jewish historical societies. The closest approximation is the webpage of AJHS, which contains a list and links to some of these groups, along with other types of organizations.

The formation, development, and trajectories of the various historical societies are fairly similar. Most grew out of the interests and desires of a small number of local individuals. Founding members were often already engaged in local or regional history and were themselves amateur history buffs. They were typically joined by local rabbis and Jewish community professionals. In some cases, an academic also played a role in the group's formation or maturation. Typically, it took some time for these institutions to gain stability, but most continued as shoestring operations run by laypeople, lacking sufficient (or any) office space, and without official support from centralized Jewish communal bodies, such as a community council or federation. In other cases, the historical society emerged from an existing community institution, such as a Jewish community center or a non-Jewish organization.[76] Although some organizations are listed as "affiliates of the AJHS," there is no formal relationship between the local or regional societies and the national group. Even so, groups often reference the national society with the intention of heightening the commitment of group leaders and raising the group's status in the local community.[77] Jacob Rader Marcus, founder of AJA, also encouraged the formation and activities of several of the groups, publishing brief greetings in the societies' journals and/or speaking at their meetings.[78] But, again, there is no sustained connection between AJA and the various Jewish historical societies.

A number of groups were also stimulated into existence by national, state, and local historical celebrations.[79] In several instances, non-Jewish organizations contributed to the formation of the societies or supported these efforts.[80] The launching of two groups, Memphis and Upper Midwest, was assisted through contact with other Jewish historical societies, Southern and El Paso respectively. Finally, concerns about historic preservation or the disappearance of earlier records of Jewish settlement also played a formative role in these organizations.[81]

Historical societies vary in terms of the size of their dues-paying membership and fundraising initiatives. In several cases and in more recent years, paid employees—often with advanced training in history or archival studies—serve as the ongoing leadership of the societies and are supported by volunteers. The work of these professionals can be viewed as "public history." In sum, many of the organizations have become stable, have offices, have space for an archive, and sponsor a range of activities.

Mission statements or charters provide a partial sense of a society's goals and, in some cases, the motivations of its founders (see appendix). We begin with an analysis of those statements, followed by additional information pertaining to the founding purposes of select societies. The discussion highlights tensions between a commitment to academic work and the desire to speak to Jewish individual and community needs. The central goal of many of these organizations is to procure, collect, and preserve materials related to the lives of Jews of the locale. These records include documents, photos, material objects, and memorabilia from individuals, businesses, organizations, and synagogues. These primary sources are sometimes supplemented by oral histories collected or conducted by the societies. This data is made available to scholars, history enthusiasts, and the broader community via a range of programs, including lectures, exhibits, conferences, and publications. The intended audience consists of both Jews and non-Jews, although membership consists mostly of the former.

The activities have diverse objectives. Having access to the history of the Jews of a region fosters serious research, which itself may have multiple foci. Some groups seek to correct the historical record with accurate information about the Jews—an aim occasionally cited in mission statements and accounts of a group's founding. A common purpose is to ensure that the history of local Jews appears in general histories of the area. Many societies explicitly speak of Jewish "contributions, accomplishments, achievements." These terms appear in the mission statements of Indiana, Hartford, North Shore (Massachusetts), Staten Island, Columbus, New Mexico, Memphis, Orange County, South Florida, and Southern Nevada. While the history presented, either through lectures or exhibits, may be factually correct, it is often shaded by an agenda of fostering pride and respect. This outcome-orientation finds additional expression in the claim that by understanding their past, Jews can shape their future (Michigan, Maryland, Columbus, Memphis) or gain a sense of continuity, legacy, or heritage (Hartford, Dallas, Rocky Mountain, Staten Island, Fairfield, Upper Midwest). Although not explicit in their mission statements, the activities of some groups are also strongly flavored with elements of nostalgia, such as tours of previous Jewish areas of settlement or of existing buildings that no longer house Jews or Jewish institutions.

Several challenges arise from presenting historical evidence for the purpose of fostering Jewish identity. First, the accuracy—and, more importantly, the selectivity—of data about earlier Jews can radically skew engagement with the Jewish past. Are all aspects of earlier phases of Jewish life in a location preserved and presented, or are potentially undesirable elements omitted? Are oral histories taken primarily of Jews who were leaders in the Jewish community or had achieved prominence in the general community? Is the past celebrated or is it analyzed? What type of analysis is utilized? What factors are considered in accounting for past events and their possible connections to current features of Jewish life in the area? Are connections drawn to developments in the broader community and/or national or international factors, both Jewish and non-Jewish? Finally, what is the manner of presenting the information: is it highly didactic, providing "the correct account of the Jewish past," or do the lectures, exhibitions, writings, and other projects encourage discussion and competing points of view that, in turn, occasion open-ended conversations about the type of Jews and Jewish community they seek to foster in the present and future?[82]

As the preceding attests, historical societies are involved in a range of activities including archival endeavors; recording and transcribing oral histories; hosting lectures; holding conferences; staging local or traveling exhibits; conducting tours of historic Jewish locations (by foot, bike, or bus); erecting historical markers; cleaning up unkempt Jewish cemeteries; producing educational materials for schools and institutions; and publishing materials, especially books, journals, and newsletters. Analyzing all these activities would require an enormous amount of time and pages and would not necessarily be more helpful than a summary. In what follows, we focus on archival work and publications, with brief remarks on the lectures and conferences.

The range of materials collected in a society's archive can be diverse in form. As noted, an archive might include written records pertaining to individuals, businesses, Jewish communal organizations, and synagogues; photographs and memorabilia of various sorts; artifacts, such as sacred objects, furniture, and clothing; and items pertaining to domestic and commercial activities, such as food production and consumption. Precisely what each society collects is not evident from their websites or publications. Individual archivists must ultimately decide what to solicit, what to discard, and what to keep. To borrow the title of Elisabeth Kaplan's essay, "we are what we collect."[83] Choices generally reflect the type of history the organization wishes to present, as well as its views about the present and future. Access to these collections—and periodic displays drawn from them—also serves to restrict the types of histories that can be researched and who is able to conduct such research. A related consideration is how much of a given archive is now digitized and searchable and thus accessible to inquirers from around the world.

Many historical societies maintain their own archives (Rhode Island, Southern California, Washington, DC, Maryland, Hartford, Dallas, Oregon, North Shore, Central New Jersey, New Jersey, Columbus, Arizona, Nebraska, Fairfield, Memphis, New Jersey–Metro West, Iowa, Milwaukee, Orange County, Western Massachusetts, Southwest Florida). Most of these are not available online. Several societies (Indiana, Delaware, New Mexico) house their archives in a state or public institution. The archives of several other societies are kept in university libraries (Chicago, Michigan, New Haven, Rocky Mountain, Texas, San Diego, Washington State, Upper Midwest, South Carolina, Southern Nevada, Western States). Lists of the holdings, sometimes only partial, are accessible online. The Institute of Southern Jewish Life (ISJL) represents a hybrid model. It conducts numerous activities, including visiting rabbis and education programs for Jewish schools, but has also employed a historian for a couple of decades, acts as an archive with an oral history program, and publishes the online *Encyclopedia of Southern Jewish Life* (isjl.org). The Museum of Southern Jewish Life, located in New Orleans, Louisiana, is an offshoot of ISJL. The holdings of Jewish archives can serve as sources for various types of scholarly projects.

The multiplication of archives underscores the longstanding barriers to centralizing archives relevant to American Jewish history. During the 1950s, national organizations including AJHS, AJA, YIVO, and Yeshiva University tried and failed to create a single national Jewish archive.[84] More recently, the Center for Jewish History in Manhattan (est. 2000) has successfully integrated the holdings of five Jewish institutions and made them available through one search engine. Such consolidation of archives was an aspiration shared by Baron and Marcus and, in Marcus's case, partially achieved with AJA. Marcus established branches of AJA at the Los Angeles and New York campuses of Hebrew Union College. He commended the archives of the Jewish Historical Society of Michigan and encouraged other groups to establish archives as well. His recommendation was that such archives include not only original copies but also photocopies of documents held in other repositories. Baron similarly called for regional branches of AJHS, complete with archival holdings.

Local Jewish societies also disseminate knowledge (and sometimes encourage discussions) about the history of Jews via lectures, conferences, and publications. The lectures are generally intended for mixed Jewish and non-Jewish audiences, as are the publications. Conferences primarily serve the interests of society members. Southern, Texas, and New Mexico hold annual weekend conclaves in different parts of their state or region, which may include visits to Jewish sites, Shabbat programming, and lectures.

Southern has long been committed to scholarly presentations, despite the desire of some members for more popular historical lectures. New Mexico has a mixture of scholarly and popular presentations at its conferences, but academics are always included on the program. Texas shades more in the nonacademic direction. The Rhode Island society's annual meeting has featured academic papers over the years. Academics also appear regularly at the semiannual meetings of the South Carolina society.[85]

In addition to popular books on selected aspects of an area's Jewish history, many societies have published journals, magazines, or newsletters (see appendix). Rhode Island, Southern, Western States, Michigan, Maryland, Indiana, Washington, DC, Hartford, Rocky Mountain, and Nebraska have produced journals or magazines, mostly containing articles of sizeable length. Societies including Rhode Island, Southern, Hartford, Delaware, Oregon, Chicago, Texas, Nebraska, New Mexico, Washington, Memphis, South Carolina, and Iowa have also published annual or quarterly newsletters. Most of these periodicals are still being produced, with only Washington (*Nizkor*) and Iowa (*CHAIowan*) having ceased publication. The newsletters usually share a similar format: greetings from the organization's president and/or lead professional staff; announcements of upcoming programs; lists of donors to the group; solicitations of donations; necrologies; and brief articles on some aspects of the area's history, often with accompanying photographs. These writings typically pertain to a notable Jewish individual, organization, synagogue, or historic occurrence. Most lack documentation and are narrowly focused, and a good number are reminiscences. As such, their value to scholarly research is limited. They fulfill the aim of fleshing out the Jewish history of a locale through information pertaining to an individual, family, group, organization, synagogue, or nostalgic concern. They generally lack contextualization within the broader Jewish or American history, even related to developments on the local level.

The oldest Jewish historical societies published journals regularly for many years, with several still being issued. These include Rhode Island, Southern, Michigan, and Indiana. No longer appearing are long-running journals of Maryland, Washington, DC, Rocky Mountain, and Nebraska, and journals of much shorter duration, Connecticut and El Paso. *Western States Jewish History*, a quarterly that began under the Southern California society and continued with the Western States Jewish History Association, ceased publication in 2018 after fifty years. The journal has since been relaunched as a biannual, peer-reviewed academic journal.

The types of writings published by the Washington, DC, society provide a helpful view. The editorial policy and manuscript guidelines specify the following:

1. Analytical works that argue a thesis about Washington Jewish history and document the original and secondary sources on which they draw.
2. Other researched manuscripts, typically descriptive, offering insights into an historical issue or providing a Jewish or Washington context to a subject not generally addressed from the perspective.
3. Works of family history, personal reminiscences, firsthand accounts of historic events or interviews with participants in these events. Oral history interviews must be accompanied by analysis placing the material in context.
4. Pictorial essays or documents.
5. Other material judged by the publication committee as being relevant to the purposes of the society.

The editors of the Washington, DC, journal clearly recognize the necessary qualities of what constitutes a scholarly paper. Essays of that sort are analytical, advance a thesis, and document the claims with primary and secondary sources. If one added to these criteria the need to situate the historic topic within broader American or Jewish factors and developments, then the articles would be of a scholarly nature. However, these aims are rarely achieved.

The five types of articles cited above appear in many of the local and regional Jewish historical journals, with varying frequency and depth of analysis and contextualization. Articles belonging to some of the above categories are, at best, potentially relevant primary source material for well-written scholarly pieces. In particular, competent oral histories, even without detailed analyses, can be useful to scholarly writers, as can be presentations of photographs and documents. But such works are primarily of interest to nonprofessional readers. Many of the articles in the journals align more with items 2 and 3—that is, a high percentage are descriptive essays and personal reminiscences or firsthand accounts. In many cases, primary evidence does not appear in footnotes, and despite guidelines calling for articles of type 2 to be set in broader contexts, this generally does not occur. There is also little analysis of the person, institution, or event described. If references to primary data are included, such as contemporaneous newspaper accounts, then at least the material can be double-checked—even if the descriptive account is selective. Overall, the studies do not answer conceptually formulated questions, other than who did what and when they did it.

Of the journals published by local and regional historical societies, the journal of the Southern Historical Society has most consistently published scholarly caliber papers. Rhode Island has many such articles, often including detailed primary information, such as transcriptions or reproductions of public and private documents. Essays in these journals tend to be lengthy, spanning fifteen pages or more. Throughout its history, *Southern Jewish History* has been edited by an academic, Mark Bauman, and articles must pass peer review. Academics or trained professionals, such as archivists, have written many of those essays. *Rhode Island Jewish Historical Notes* has published articles by professors and students writing under the supervision of academics. Papers by individuals holding doctorates or advanced degrees in history, although not employed by institutes of higher learning, also appear regularly in that journal. But there are also numerous reminiscences and descriptive accounts of institutions and individuals, with most containing footnotes referencing primary sources. In recent years, the Rhode Island journal has had an editor with a doctorate. *Rocky Mountain Jewish Historical Notes* also published academic-level essays, although generally shorter in length. One can attribute this orientation to the editorship of scholars holding academic appointments, including John Livingston and Jeanne Abrams. Articles in *Michigan Jewish History* have varied over time. Until the later 1990s, the papers were mostly written by amateur history buffs and were less scholarly, although some were of considerable length. With the appointment of a full-time, professionally trained staff, volumes from the last two decades have included a fair number of well-framed and finely documented pieces, often in the fifteen-page range. A similar trajectory characterized articles in *Generations*, the journal of the Maryland Jewish Historical Society, under the editorship of Avi Decter, director of the Jewish Museum of Maryland, and assisted by a trained staff including a historian and others in the community. In the journal's latter years, issues were often centered on a theme and contained well-documented essays speaking to broader trends in American and American Jewish history. Many of the articles also included glossy photos. Images printed in Rhode Island, Southern, Rocky Mountain, and Michigan appeared less frequently and in lower resolution than those found in *Generations*. Finally, the preponderance of articles in *Indiana Jewish History* and Washington, DC's *The Record* are reminiscences and descriptions without consistent documentation or contextualization.

The above review demonstrates ways in which various historic societies have defined their goals and audiences. Each is committed to the preservation of sources, including via oral histories. To varying degrees, each sees its activities as contributing to scholarly work, be it simply in collecting and preserving primary data, or, in a few cases, producing articles of a conceptual-analytical nature. The organizations envision Jewish and non-Jewish groups and individuals as their audiences. They regularly emphasize Jewish contributions and accomplishments and in many cases occasion nostalgia for what once was. They also seek to enrich the present and future lives of their Jewish members, readers, and program attendees.

It is important to explore how this last goal might be achieved without compromising the quality of historic evidence or the analysis thereof. Local and regional Jewish historical societies are vital in selecting and disseminating information that fosters ongoing explorations and conversations about the future, particularly that of American Jews. This does not mean that all Jewish historical societies share the same attitude or approach. Although most are engaged in history to serve Jewish individuals and communities, others view themselves as historical societies first and Jewish institutions second. Mark Bauman, editor of the journal of the Southern Jewish Historical Society, speaks for the latter:

> We've had two non-Jewish presidents both of whom have published work on southern Jewish history. . . . We've also had numerous speakers and conference attendees who do not "identify as Jews" because they are non-Jews. I and the historians in the field that I know pick topics that interest us or where we've come across primary sources/information that strikes our fancy, not because of some sort of communal goal or identity issue.[86]

Nevertheless, the goals of the group's leadership and academic contributors are not always aligned with how the audience perceives the group or uses its materials. Laypeople especially want to learn about themselves and very often use local and regional Jewish historical research as a source of pride. The next section proposes how these resources can best serve Jews in drawing on the past to construct Jewish identities in the present and future.

Jewish Historical Societies as Resources for Jews (and Others)

Over twenty-five years ago, I published an essay entitled "Integrating Local Jewish Historical Societies and Public History."[87] The concerns and conclusions offered in that paper remain relevant today. The 1995 article presented a vision for how well-functioning, critically disposed local and regional historical societies could serve as both *sources* and *resources* for the study and creation of American Jewish history. Two understandings of "sources" were given: historical societies can be repositories of information relevant to the academic writing of American Jewish history and can themselves be viewed as part of American Jewish history and thus subject to analysis. By contrast, as "resources," historical societies can play a role in shaping the future of their communities. If these organizations include the range of those who identify as Jews and involve scholars of American Jewish history in their discussions and programming, they can move beyond propounding nostalgic, self-aggrandizing, or parochial accounts. Considering the full range of past and present Jews—successful, unsuccessful, famous, anonymous, and everyone in between—they can serve as forums, active agents, and resources for composing new visions of what being Jewish means today and in the future.

My arguments relied on claims made in postmodernist and poststructuralist thought and studies of local historical societies—especially those connected to public history, museum studies, and collective memory. My intention was to break down the hard dichotomy between academic and amateur historians and to call for greater cooperation between them. Even academic research, while open-ended, critical, and focused on explanation, is not entirely apolitical. At a minimum, all historians subscribe to the idea that what they are researching and writing about is compelling and worth knowing. The very choice of a topic to investigate inherently turns the historian into an advocate. All historians have underlying commitments; what is required is making those commitments explicit.

Like that earlier paper, this section considers public history, museum studies, and local archives of ethnic groups. Proposals for programs in public history first emerged in the late 1970s. Part of the impetus was to generate employment opportunities for doctoral candidates and recent PhDs at a time when academic positions were limited. Although there are differing understandings of what exactly public history (or applied history) is, a common view is that, rather than primarily engaging with other scholars, public historians interact with a range of publics in any number of institutional settings, including museums, historical societies, national parks, governmental agencies, and private corporations. Lately, employment in public history has shrunk for graduates of doctoral programs, due to a reduction of funding for institutions and the present saturation of those organizations with earlier doctoral graduates. Still, scholars continue to teach and reflect on the nature of public history, now often on an international level.[88]

In his introductory textbook for the practice of public history, Thomas Cauvin delineates a vision for what public historians do and how they can do it well: "Public historians put great emphasis on the ways in which the public uses the past. The concept of usability is at the core of public history." To Cauvin, public history is based on collaboration, requires an entrepreneurial spirit, and encourages shared authority: "Shared authority relates to the demonstration of the knowledge-building process. In other words, audiences are not passively consuming knowledge produced by expert historians. Many public historians would today accept that public history is not doing history for the general public but with them."[89] In Cauvin's model, academically trained historians working in public institutions, including historical societies, must learn to collaborate and share authority with members of the public who attend the institution's programs.

Scholarship in museum studies, including writings focused on Jewish museums, likewise advocates a participatory approach.[90] Avi Decter has examined the interpretation of American Jewish history in a range of museums, most of them non-Jewish. His book on the subject concludes with a chapter titled, "Toward Next Practice." He chose this wording, rather than "best practices," partly because of rapid cultural, demographic, communal, and technological changes: "[W]e cannot stay with what is safe and agreed upon or even best practices but need to work on the next iteration of practice that looks to the future."[91] Taking note of younger museum visitors, who have been raised in the digital age and who expect interactive experiences, Decter recommends that public historians in museum settings recalibrate themselves as "enablers" instead of "providers." At the core of history is the telling and creating of compelling stories and narratives. As such, museums must practice "audacious hospitality," meaning that visitors have opportunities to tell their own stories in relation to the museum exhibits. "Audacious hospitality requires effort," Decter writes, "but the engagement, intimacy, and immediacy of the experience can produce a host of new narratives and ideas, deep connections and corps of community ambassadors. Equally important, audacious hospitality gives us a chance to get feedback on the stories we tell ourselves, as well as those we relate to our communities."[92] These observations and recommendations emphasize the importance of polyphonic narratives. As Decter writes:

> Story will continue to trump all other modes of interpretation as it always has in the past. Our challenge in telling stories of American Jews, or of any other religious, ethnic, cultural, or racial group will be twofold: First, we ourselves are going to need to deepen our understanding of what makes a compelling story and what is the best and most engaging way of telling the story. Our second challenge will be, in an age of visitor-centered experiences, how to leave enough room in our storytelling so that our users and constituents can share their narratives as well. Facilitating a multiplicity of next narratives while negotiating the boundaries of our authority will be very challenging. But if we elect to adapt to novelty, the history of our plural communities will continue to engage, inform and inspire.[93]

These points are relevant to the endeavors of local and regional historical societies, especially as many of them operate in part as museums. How the staffs of these institutions interact with their visitors (participants) will determine their success in gathering narratives, as well as the meaning attendees derive from their experiences.

A final pertinent topic concerns the intersection of archival practices and notions of ethnicity and ethnic communities. Recent scholarship argues for a more inclusive approach to archival work, recognizing the culturally constructed nature of ethnicity, internal debates among those who identify as members of an ethnic group, and the inherently group-defining impact of archival practices.[94] Jewish historical societies must reflect on these issues because much of their energy and perceived value center on collecting and preserving a range of sources related to the history of Jews. A consistent assertion is that archivists must work with communities and not simply be passive recipients of documents. Archivists are active researchers, interpreters, and powerful agents of documenting the past and thereby shaping the future. To the extent that they strive to include documents and evidence about more typical members of an ethnic group, not just the elite, they help to construct—and perhaps expand—the boundaries of the community. Archivists are pivotal to the construction of community, consolidating its identity and shaping its memory.[95]

Joel Wurl, former deputy director of the Division of Preservation & Access at the National Endowment for the Humanities, has also written on the role archives and archivists play in proposing and negotiating ethnic identity on both individual and group levels. He calls for archivists to "cultivate an openness of thought of how ethnic community life is actually transacted through communication structures that might not be familiar to the shelves of our repositories. It is only through an appreciation of ethnic communities as environments of originating context that we can liberate ourselves from constricted thinking about the evidence of ethnicity."[96] In other words, archivists should not see their work as merely preserving history but as facilitating memory. Instead of viewing themselves as custodians of a group's historical documents, they should operate through a model of distributed responsibility.[97]

To better understand how local and regional historical societies can be effective participants in their communities, let us return to the activities of the country's first state historical society, the Rhode Island Historical Society, founded in 1822. Albert T. Klyberg, former director of the association, wrote one of the few essays detailing the importance of publishing on local Jewish history.[98] In his 1999 essay, he characterized *Notes*, the Rhode Island Jewish Historical Association's journal, as "a rich index to the Rhode Island Jewish experience, a series of doorways into fascinating stories, a very important document of life here stretching back more than three centuries, and a model of local history and ethnic history scholarship for us all. We wish we had equivalents for all the major groups in our community. There is much of value here for Jew and non-Jew alike."[99] Klyberg added, "Here are the linkages and intersections for many groups, to work together to understand our common origins and the differences as well that makes life in the state so special."[100] He then turned to what was, at the time, an effort to build a museum, Heritage Harbor, in downtown Providence. The museum project was conceived to include many ethnic and other types of groups that comprised—and still comprise—the Rhode Island experiment. The inclusive nature of the intended museum, which would have examined differences and commonalities among the groups, was grounded in careful historical studies of the past and inspired by President Washington's words to the Jewish congregation in Newport: "Happily the government of the United States gives to bigotry no sanction, to persecution no assistance." Although the museum was never built, Heritage Harbor persists as a foundation offering grants for historical projects that carry forward the original vision.

Klyberg's concluding remarks are a fitting way to end this chapter: "I think that as our close association flourishes, as understanding and true affection grows, our Heritage Harbor partnership will develop such a permanent bond that no one group in our community will ever have to face evil alone again."[101] If local and regional Jewish historical societies are invested in conversations between diverse reconstructions of the past from multiple voices, they can serve as active resources for sharing and shaping visions of the future rooted in detailed accounts of the past.

1. Jeffrey Gurock, "From *Publications* to *American Jewish History*: The Journal of the American Jewish Historical Society and the Writing of American Jewish History," *American Jewish History* 81, no. 2 (1993–94): 155–270; Jeffrey Gurock, "Cyrus Adler's Vision of American Jewish Historical Writing," *American Jewish History* 101, no. 4 (2017): 489–99; Elisabeth Kaplan, "We Are What We Collect, We Collect What We Are: Archives and the Construction of Identity," *The American Archivist* 63 (2000): 126–51; Hasia Diner, "American Jewish History," in *Oxford Handbook of Jewish Studies*, ed. Martin Goodman (New York: Oxford University Press, 2002), 470–90; and Jason Lustig, "Building a Home for the Past: Archives and the Geography of American Jewish History," *American Jewish History* 102, no. 3 (2018): 375–399.
2. See Beth S. Wenger, *History Lessons: The Creation of American Jewish Heritage* (Princeton: Princeton University Press, 2010).
3. For helpful delineations of the history of historical research in the United States, see Peter Novick, *That Noble Dream: The "Objectivity Question" and the American Historical Profession* (Cambridge: Cambridge University Press, 1988); Ian Tyrrell, *Historians in Public: The Practice of American History 1890–1970* (Chicago: University of Chicago Press, 2005); Robert Townsend, *History's Babel: Scholarship, Professionalization and the Historical Enterprise in the United States, 1889–1940* (Chicago: University of Chicago Press, 2013; Michael Kammen, "The Mississippi

Valley Historical Association, 1907–52," in *The Organization of American Historians and the Writing and Teaching of American History*, ed. Richard S. Kerkendall (New York: Oxford University Press, 2011), 17–32; William H. Chafe, "One Hundred Years of History: Extraordinary Change, Persistent Challenges," in *The Organization of American Historians and the Writing and Teaching of American History*, ed. Richard S. Kerkendall (New York: Oxford University Press, 2011), 59–62.

4. On the history of state historical societies, including differences between private "gentlemen"-type East Coast groups and the more inclusive Midwestern groups, see David Russo, *Keepers of Our Past: Local Historical Writing in the United States 1820s–1930s* (New York: Greenwood, 1988); Leslie H. Fischer Jr., "Historical Societies As History: A Review Essay," *The Wisconsin Magazine of History* 81, no. 1 (1997): 55–58; and Alea Henle, "Preserving the Past, Making Histories: Historical Societies in the Early U.S." (PhD diss., University of Connecticut, 2012).
5. The terminology of enterprise, discipline, and profession is used by Townsend in his charting of the history of the AHA. Robert Townsend, *History's Babel: Scholarship, Professionalization and the Historical Enterprise in the United States, 1889–1940* (Chicago: University of Chicago Press, 2013), 3.
6. Hasia Diner captures this contradiction of American historians who, despite framing their work as nationally and universally focused, were in fact highly parochial. Diner, "American Jewish History," 474.
7. The history of the recognition and varying degree of integration of "ethnic, minority, and women's studies" within American universities is well told. Regarding the discipline of history, see, for example, Alan M. Kraut and David A. Gerber, eds., *Ethnic Historians and the Mainstream: Shaping America's Immigration Story* (New York: Routledge, 2013).
8. Cited in Gurock, "Cyrus Adler's Vision of American Jewish Historical Writing," 491.
9. Gurock, "From *Publications* to *American Jewish History*," 160. Little has been written about the history of ethnic historical societies other than John J. Appel, *Immigrant Historical Societies in the United States, 1880–1950* (New York: Arno, 1980), and John Higham, "The Ethnic Historical Society in Changing Times," *Journal of American Ethnic History* 13, no. 2 (1994): 30–44.
10. Kaplan, "We Are What We Collect," 130. The title of her work underscores the

inherent connection between archival activity and determining the boundaries of identity of the group whose materials comprise the archive.

11. While these scholars played a central role in altering the nature of AJHS, their efforts would not have been successful if Lee Friedman, the newly elected president of the society and a layperson, did not agree with and actively work to achieve this outcome.
12. Gurock, "From *Publications* to *American Jewish History*, 212; Diner, "American Jewish History," 473.
13. Salo W. Baron, "American Jewish History: Problems and Methods," *Publications of the American Jewish Historical Society* 39, no. 3 (1950): 266.
14. Salo W. Baron, "Opening Statement," *Jewish Social Studies* 17, no. 3 (1955): 176. Baron closed his comments at an AJHS session honoring him in 1982 by referring back to his "Presidential Report," where he spoke of his hope that AJHS would be a positive communal force in shaping the cultural destinies of American Jewry. Salo W. Baron, "Reply to Professor Abraham Karp's Address," *American Jewish History* 71, no. 4 (1982): 500.
15. Salo W. Baron, "Conference Theme," *Publications of the American Jewish Historical Society* 46, no. 3 (1957): 137.
16. Two reviews of scholarship in urban history covering the 1940s and 1950s are Blake McKelvey, "American Urban History Today," *American Historical Review* 57, no. 4 (1952): 919–29, and Eric E. Lampard, "American Historians and the Study of Urbanism," *American Historical Review* 67, no. 1 (1961): 49–61.
17. Moshe Davis, "Preface: 'And Seek the Peace of the City,' The Program of the American Jewish History Center," in *The History of the Jews of Milwaukee*, ed. Louis J. Swichkow and Lloyd P. Gartner (Philadelphia: Jewish Publication Society of American, 1963): vi–xii.
18. Salo W. Baron, *Steeled by Adversity: Essays and Addresses in American Jewish Life*, ed. Jeanette M. Baron (Philadelphia: Jewish Publication Society, 1971), 471–72.
19. Hasia Diner, "Oscar Handlin: A Jewish American Historian," *Journal of American Ethnic History* 32, no. 3 (2013): 53–61.
20. Oscar Handlin, "New Paths in American Jewish History," *Commentary* 8 (January 1949): 389. Handlin's earlier essay in that journal was, "Our Unknown American Jewish Ancestors: Fact and Myth in History," *Commentary* 6 (January 1948): 104–10.

21. Moses Rischin, *Inventory of American Jewry* (Cambridge, MA: Harvard University Press, 1954).
22. Oscar Handlin, "Foreword," in Moses Rischin, *Inventory of American Jewry* (Cambridge, MA: Harvard University Press, 1954), vii.
23. Oscar Handlin, *Adventure in Freedom: Three Hundred Years of Jewish Life in America* (New York: McGraw-Hill, 1954).
24. For largely negative comments on this book—as well as on a competing book published that year by Rufus Learsi (pseudonym of Israel Goldberg), *The Jews in America: A History* (New York: World Publishing Company, 1954)—see Joshua Bloch, "American Jewish Historiography: A Survey of Some of the Literature on the History of the Jews in America," *Jewish Quarterly Review* 45, no. 4 (1955): 441, and the reviews cited there.
25. Handlin, "New Paths in American Jewish History," 393.
26. For a critical review of Marcus's scholarship, citing a lack of discretion in including numerous examples of individuals without sufficiently formulating larger interpretive theses, see Moses Rischin, "Review of *The Colonial Jew, 1492–1776*, Jacob R. Marcus," *William and Mary Quarterly* 30, no. 2 (1973): 353–55, and Moses Rischin, "Review Essay: Jacob Rader Marcus: Historian-Archivist of Jewish Middle America," *American Jewish History* 85, no. 2 (1997): 175–81.
27. Critical discussions of Marcus's approach and contributions include Lance Sussman, "'Historian of the Jewish People': A Historiographical Reevaluation of the Writings of Jacob R. Marcus," *American Jewish Archives Journal* 50 (1998): 10–21; Jon Butler, "Jacob Rader Marcus and the Revival of Early American History, 1930–60," *American Jewish Archives Journal* 50 (1998): 28–39; Gary P. Zola, "Jacob Rader Marcus and the Dynamics of American Jewish History," in *The Dynamics of American Jewish History: Jacob Rader Marcus's Essays on American Jewry*, ed. Gary P. Zola (Hanover, MA: Brandeis University Press, 2004), xiii–xxxi; Jonathan Sarna, "Jacob Rader Marcus (1896–1995)," in *The Dynamics of American Jewish History: Jacob Rader Marcus's Essay on American Jewry*, ed. Gary P. Zola (Hanover, MA: Brandeis University Press, 2004), 3–12; and Kevin Proffitt, "Jacob Rader Marcus and the Archive He Built," in *New Essays in American Jewish History Commemorating the Sixtieth Anniversary of the Founding of the American Jewish Archives*, eds. Pamela Nadell, Lance Sussman, and Jonathan Sarna (Cincinnati: American Jewish Archives, 2010), 5–18. Diner mentions very little about Marcus

in her survey article, "American Jewish History." For a rich discussion of Marcus's reasons for founding AJA and his sense of its relationship to AJHS, see Jason Lustig, "Building a Home for the Past: Archives and the Geography of American Jewish History," *American Jewish History* 102, no. 3 (2018): 375–400.

28. Jacob R. Marcus, "Address of the President," *Publications of American Jewish Historical Society* 46, no. 4 (June 1957): 465–66.
29. Jacob R. Marcus, *How to Write the History of an American Jewish Community* (Cincinnati: American Jewish Archives, 1953).
30. Ibid., 1.
31. Zola, "Jacob Rader Marcus," xiii–xxxi.
32. Ibid., xxx.
33. Jeffrey Gurock, "Jacob Rader Marcus, Salo W. Baron, and the Public's Need to Know American Jewish History," *American Jewish Archives Journal* 56 (1998): 23–27.
34. Ibid., 26.
35. The official report on the events appears in David Bernstein, "The American Jewish Tercentenary," *American Jewish Yearbook* 57 (1956): 101–18. Detailed analyses of this anniversary observance, often compared with either the 250th anniversary in 1905 or the 350th anniversary in 2004–2005, include Judith Friedman Rosen, "In Search of . . . Early American Jewish Anniversary Celebrations: 1905–54," *American Jewish History* 92 (2004): 481–97; Arthur A. Goren, "A 'Golden Decade' for American Jews 1944–55," in *A New Jewry? America Since the Second World War*, ed. Peter Medding (New York: Oxford University Press, 1992), 3–20; and Wenger, *History Lessons*, 210–19.
36. Bernstein, "The American Jewish Tercentenary," 108–12.
37. For the tercentenary, AJHS conducted an essay contest for college students on American Jewish history. With the national committee, it sponsored an Office of Historical Information, providing factual material regarding the observance: Bernstein, "The American Jewish Tercentenary," 115. Baron chaired the Committee on Research and Publications, which promoted Jewish scholarship and biographies and convened the Peekskill conference. At the direction of the national committee, Baron's subcommittee was supposed to produce a lasting scholarly memorial of the tercentenary as a contribution for future generations. The publications committee proposed a ten-volume documentary history of

American Jews, but only the first three volumes were completed.

38. Bernstein, "The American Jewish Tercentenary," 101–2.
39. Wenger, *History Lessons*, 218.
40. Cited in ibid., 224–25. Judith Friedman Rosen summarized the Tercentenary Committee's mission: "[It] was to effectively promote the contributions of American Jews to American society": Friedman Rosen, "In Search of," 484.
41. These critical comments on the tercentenary celebrations are noted in Friedman Rosen, "In Search of," 487–94; Arthur A. Goren, "A 'Golden Decade,'" 15–18; and Wenger, *History Lessons*, 220–21. For a critical evaluation of such celebrations in one location, see David Weinfeld, "Two Commemorations: Richmond Jews and the Lost Cause During the Civil Rights Era," *Southern Jewish History* 23 (2020).
42. Bernstein, "The American Jewish Tercentenary," 118.
43. Hasia Diner, "The Study of American Jewish History: In the Academy, in the Community," *Polish American Studies* 65, no. 1 (Spring 2008): 54.
44. Gurock, "From *Publications* to *American Jewish History*," 254.
45. Hasia Diner, "Looking Back on American Jewish History," in *American Jewry: Transcending the European Experience?*, eds. Christian Wiese and Cornelia Wilhelm (London: Bloomsbury, 2017), 355. A summary of the 350th celebration appears in Alice Herman and Steven Bayme, "Celebrating the 350th," *American Jewish Yearbook* 106 (2006): 115–32.
46. Hasia Diner and Tony Michels, "Considering American Jewish History," *OAH Newsletter* 35, no. 4 (2007): 9, 18.
47. David Hollinger, "Communalist and Dispersionist Approaches to American Jewish History in an Increasingly Post-Jewish Era," *American Jewish History* 95, no. 1 (March 2009): 1–32.
48. Hasia Diner, "Why American Historians Really Ignore American Jewish History," *American Jewish History* 95, no. 1 (March 2009): 38. In a study examining the trope of the "Jewish contribution to civilization," David Biale traces the notion of two twentieth-century American Jewish thinkers and concludes, "No longer do Jewish scholars feel compelled to defend the Jewish contributions to the civilization in which they now feel themselves entirely at home." David Biale, "Louis Finkelstein, Mordecai Kaplan, and American 'Jewish Contributions to Civilizations,'" in *The Jewish Contribution to Civilization: Reassessing an Idea*, eds. Jeremy Cohen and Richard Cohen (Oxford: Littman Library of Jewish Civilization, 2008), 185–97.

49. Jonathan Sarna, "What's the Use of Local Jewish History?" *Rhode Island Jewish Historical Notes* 12, no. 1B (1995): 77–83, and Joel Gereboff, "Integrating Local Jewish Historical Societies and Public History," *Shofar: An Interdisciplinary Journal of Jewish Studies* 13, no. 3 (1995): 53–72.
50. See, for example, Carol Kammen, *On Doing Local History*, 3rd. ed. (Lanham, MD: Rowman and Littlefield, 2014); Carol Kammen, "On Doing Local History: The Future Survival of Historical Societies," *History News* 59, no. 1 (2004): 3–4; and David Kyvig, Myron A. Marty, and Larry Cebula, *Nearby History: Exploring the Past Around You*, 4th ed. (Lanham, MD: Rowman and Littlefield, 2019).
51. Gurock, "From *Publications* to *American Jewish History*," 222. Comments on the work of the American Jewish History Center at the Jewish Theological Seminary note collaborations among local individuals and professionally trained historians.
52. Moshe Davis and Isidore S. Meyer, "First Seminar: Local and Regional History; Proceedings of the Conference of Historians Convened by the American Jewish Historical Society on the Occasion of the 300th Anniversary of the Settlement of the Jews in the United States, Held at Peekskill, New York, Sept. 12th and 14th, 1954," *Publications of the American Jewish Historical Society* 46, no. 3 (1957): 184–85. In reference to this paper and others, Zachary Baker observes: "Local historical societies can be among the most useful repositories of genealogical information." He goes on to write that the Rhode Island journal "is a highly professional journal and contains many articles of direct relevance to the genealogist. . . . Its publication activities provide an example for newer societies to follow and the amount of material which its members and scholars have been able to uncover regarding the Jewish communities of this small state provide only a faint hint of the massive quantities of information that surely can be gathered and published concerning Jews in other states." Zachary M. Baker, "Local Jewish History and Genealogy: The Rhode Island Experience," *Toledot: The Journal of Jewish Genealogy* 2, no. 2 (Fall 1978): 14–15.
53. Abraham Duker, "An Evaluation of Achievement in American Jewish Local Historical Writing," *Publications of the American Jewish Historical Society* 49 (June 1960): 215–53.
54. Ibid., 215–16 and n8. A Southern Jewish Historical Society had been established during the 1950s and published single volumes in 1958, 1959, and 1963 before the organization disbanded. This organization and journal served as precursors

of the society established in 1976 and current journal but should not be confused with them. Bernard Wax, the director of AJHS beginning in the mid-1960s, also draws this connection between the tercentenary and the formation of local historical societies and credits those celebrations with the reinvigoration of AJHS. Bernard Wax, "Comment: Solutions to Contemporary Problems of National Ethnic Historical Societies," *Journal of American Ethnic History* 13, no. 2 (Winter 1994): 59–62. On two occasions, the AJHS journal has published lists of local and regional Jewish historical societies besides publishing three brief reports on the initial meetings of the Southern California Jewish Historical Society, which was identified as an affiliate: "Local Jewish Historical Societies in the United States and Canada," *American Jewish Historical Quarterly* 59 (1969): 118–20; "Local Jewish Historical Societies in the United States and Canada," *American Jewish Historical Quarterly* 66, no. 4 (1977): 538–40; Julius Bisno, "Southern California Jewish Historical Society," *Publications of the American Jewish Historical Society* 42, no. 4 (1953): 420–23; Julius Bisno, "The Third Annual Meeting of Southern California Jewish Historical Society," *Publications of the American Jewish Historical Society* 46, no. 2 (1956): 120–21; and Benjamin Dworkin, "Southern California Jewish Historical Society Meeting of Officers and Governing Board," *Publications of the American Jewish Historical Society* 46, no. 2 (1956): 122–23.

55. Duker, "An Evaluation of Achievement," 244–45.
56. Hasia Diner, *A Time for Gathering: The Second Migration, 1820–1880* (Baltimore: Johns Hopkins University Press, 1992), 292.
57. Gurock, "From *Publications* to *American Jewish History*," 246. Henry Feingold offered a mixed assessment of local history publications in his review of two books on Philadelphia and one on Washington, DC. Most of the articles in the latter book first appeared in the publication *The Record*, the journal of the Jewish Historical Society of Washington, DC. While noting the quality and contribution of one of the essays, Feingold lists the typical deficiencies of the others, including their brevity and the overstating of their importance and relevance to broader issues beyond the local. He concludes: "Local history, we now know, doesn't have to be written that way. When done well it can serve as a building block for the larger historical story." Henry Feingold, "Review of *Jewish Life in Philadelphia*, by Murray Friedman, *Philadelphia Jewish Life, 1940–85*, by Murray Friedman, *The Jews of Washington, D.C.: A Communal History Anthology*, by David Altshuler,"

in *American Jewish History* 76, no. 4 (1987): 522–28.

58. Gurock, "From *Publications* to *American Jewish History*," 263.
59. The AJHS journal has had three names over the course of its history: *Publications of the American Jewish History Society* (1892–1962), *American Jewish Historical Quarterly* (1962–1978), and *American Jewish History* (1978–present).
60. Gurock, "From *Publications* to *American Jewish History*," 254–56.
61. Gurock, "From *Publications* to *American Jewish History*," 268–69.
62. See, for instance, a roundtable discussion on "Regionalism: The Significance of Place in American Jewish Life," *American Jewish History* 93, no. 2 (2007): 113–27.
63. Mark Bauman has also addressed this issue in various publications. In an extended conversation with him (September 16, 2020), and in several emails, he has most graciously shared a good deal on the history and goals of the Southern Jewish Historical Society and its journal, *Southern Jewish History*. He is now writing an article that suggests limitations on the claim that regionalism can serve as an analytic approach to the study of American Jewish history. In addition, there have been several special issues of *American Jewish History* on the Jews of the South and one on Western Jews. Additional studies of Western Jews have been edited by Moses Rischin, John Livingston, Ava Kahn, Ellen Eisenberg, and others.
64. John Higham, "The Ethnic Historical Society in Changing Times," *Journal of American Ethnic History* 13, no. 2 (1994): 30–44. The only other comparative discussion of ethnic historical societies took place at a meeting of the AHA. Introductory comments from that session by its conveners, Anna Jaroszynska-Kirchman and Suzanne M. Sinke, appear in their article, "Ethnic Historical Associations at the Crossroads: An Introduction," *Polish American Studies* 65, no. 1 (2008): 7–10.
65. Higham, "The Ethnic Historical Society in Changing Times," 39.
66. Wax, "Local Jewish Historical Societies in the United States and Canada," 228–46. Wax had an extended conversation with Joel Gereboff on September 24, 2020, during which he shared many details of his own activities with AJHS, particularly regarding his interactions with local Jewish historical societies. Wax helped found the modern Southern Jewish Historical Society and served as its long-time treasurer.
67. Jacob Rader Marcus, "After Twenty-Five Volumes," *American Jewish Archives Journal* 26, no. 1 (1974): 3–4.

68. Sarna, "What's the Use of Local Jewish History?" 77–83.
69. The following points are largely excerpted from Sarna, with some transitional language occasionally added.
70. Sarna, "What's the Use of Local Jewish History?" 77.
71. Ibid., 83.
72. Seebert J. Goldowsky, "Local Jewish History—The Rhode Island Experience," *Rhode Island Jewish Historical Notes* 6, no. 4 (1974): 622–28; Seebert J. Goldowsky, "The Genesis of an Amateur Historian, or Ruminations on How I Got That Way," *Rhode Island Jewish Historical Notes* 11, no. 1 (1991): 63–66; Seebert J. Goldowsky, "History of the Rhode Island Jewish Historical Association," *Rhode Island Jewish Historical Notes* 12, no. 3 (1997): 376–80; Bisno, "Southern California Jewish Historical Society," 420–23; Bisno, "The Third Annual Meeting of Southern California Jewish Historical Society," 120–21; Dworkin, "Southern California Jewish Historical Society Meeting," 122–23; Bernard Wax, "Ruminations about the SJHS," *Southern Jewish History* 10 (2007): 1–4; Saul J. Rubin, "The Pioneer Period of the SJHS (1976–1983)," *Southern Jewish History* 10 (2007): 5–11; Janice Rothschild Blumberg, "The Distance Traveled: Reminiscences of Twenty-Five Years in SJHS," *Southern Jewish History* 10 (2007): 13–26; Eric L. Goldstein, "Making History: An Interview with Saul Viener," *Southern Jewish History* 10 (2007): 39–88; Eli N. Evans, "Reflections on the Past and Future of the Southern Jewish Historical Society," *Southern Jewish History* 10 (2007): 89–101; Allen A. Warsen, "Founding Our Society," *Michigan Jewish History* 1, no. 1 (1960): 1–2; Judith Levin Cantor, "Documenting the Past for Future Generations: Celebrating the 40th Anniversary of the Jewish Historical Society of Michigan," *Michigan Jewish History* 39 (1999): 27–33; Edie Resnick, "The Jewish Historical Society of Michigan is Celebrating," *Michigan Jewish History* 49 (2009): 4–15; Sylvan M. Dubow, "The Jewish Historical Society of Greater Washington: Its Archival Program," *American Archivist* 30, no. 4 (1967): 575–80; *Celebrating 50 Years, 1960–2010: 50th Annual Meeting, Program and Commemorative Booklet* (Jewish Historical Society of Greater Washington and Lillian and Albert Small Jewish Museum, November 14, 2010); Louis F. Cahn, "The Early Days of the Jewish Historical Society of Maryland," *Generations* 1, no. 1 (1978): 2–13; Anita Kassof, "Maryland's Treasure House: The Jewish Museum and Its Collections," *Generations* (2000): 35–42; Barry Kessler, "Chronology:

Jewish Museum of Maryland," *Generations* (2000): 46–51; Max Einstandig, "The Beginning of the Indiana Jewish Historical Society," *Indiana Jewish History* 29 (1993): 5–12; and Charles B. Bernstein, "The History of the Chicago Jewish Historical Society: Its First Year, January 1977–January 1978," *Chicago Jewish Historical Society* (1978).

73. Thank you to Lisa Kranseler of the Washington State Jewish Historical Society, Joanna Church of the Jewish Museum of Maryland, Wendy Turman of the Capitol Museum in Washington, DC, and, especially, Mark Bauman of the Southern Jewish historical Society.

74. Thank you to Gary P. Zola and the staff of AJA, the staff of AJHS, its retired executive director Bernard Wax, and Jeffrey Gurock and Zachary Baker for answering questions and sharing information.

75. The collection of the Western Jewish History Center of the Judah L. Magnes Museum in Berkeley, California, is now part of the University of California. It began as an archive and also sponsored research, exhibitions, lectures, and publications. It did not define itself as a historical society; hence, it is not included in our index. On the founding of the organization, see Celeste L. McLeod, "Historical News and Comments: Western Jewish History Center," *American Jewish Historical Quarterly* 58, no. 2 (1968): 271–77, as well as its current website: https://magnes.berkeley.edu/.

76. Hartford grew from travelling exhibitions initiated by the cultural committee of the Jewish Community Center. Northern New Jersey originated from an oral history project sponsored by the local YMHA. Iowa has roots in the local Jewish Federation. Milwaukee was initiated by the Women's Division of the local Jewish Federation. Washington State grew from an archive project of the Women's Division of the local Jewish Federation. Southern Nevada originated as an initiative of the University of Nevada library.

77. Southern California, Washington, DC, and North Jersey claim formal affiliation with AJHS, while Southern, Indiana, Hartford, Chicago, and North Shore note assistance or outreach to AJHS. Abraham Duker suggested a role that AJHS could play in local and regional Jewish history: "While there has been a significant growth in publications, collections and in the organization of local historical societies, even the most optimistic will not contend that our community is sufficiently conscious of the needs of the field of American Jewish History. . . . The

American Jewish Historical Society should devote some of its resources in terms of counseling and public education, to the encouragement of research on the local scene, particularly in smaller communities. National organizations should educate their local affiliates to maintain records, appoint historians and commission the writing of their own histories. This will accrue not only to the benefit of local history but it will also help the writing of histories of national organizations, of which there are too few. . . . The establishment of local or state-wide Jewish historical archives in the larger communities will help to popularize the needs of American Jewish history." Duker, "An Evaluation of Achievement," 252–53. No such sustained efforts were ever made.

78. Marcus spoke at an opening meeting of the Washington, DC, group. The Indiana society contacted him to see if AJA would be interested in their archival materials. With reference to the first southern organization, Marcus's greetings appear in "Foreword," *The Journal of the Southern Jewish Historical Society* 1, no. 1 (1958): 3; "Greetings, Jewish Historical Society and Similar Societies," *Michigan Jewish History* 1, no. 1 (1960): 3.
79. Tercentenary celebrations helped inspire the formation of the Rhode Island, Southern California, first Southern, and Michigan societies. Additional factors, such as an anniversary of the founding of a synagogue or a broader celebration in the community, also contributed to the launching of the societies. The bicentennial of the United States led to the forming of societies in Chicago and the North Shore of Massachusetts.
80. The Rhode Island group was supported by the Rhode Island Historical Society, the Maryland group by the Pearce Museum, and the Chicago group by the Museum of Science and Industry, which had a relevant exhibit.
81. The decay of a Lloyd Street Synagogue was one of two contributing factors to forming the Maryland society. Concern for preserving an early synagogue was also a key motivation for the societies in Washington and Arizona. In Dallas, the destruction of an older synagogue stimulated creation of the Jewish historical society. The disappearance of earlier Jewish institutions provoked the interest of the founders of the Michigan, Texas, and South Carolina groups.
82. It is interesting to compare the above mission statements with those of AJHS and AJA. The current website of AJHS (ajhs.org) specifies its mission as fostering "awareness and appreciation of American Jewish heritage and to serve as a national

scholarly resource for research through the collection, preservation and dissemination of materials relating to American Jewish history." Other than "appreciation of the American Jewish heritage," most of the mission is academic. Appreciating what Jews have done or contributed still smacks of the apologetic goal of instilling pride within Jews. AJA defines its mission in exclusively scholarly terms: "The AJA's educational mission is to give access and expose learners to primary source documents relating to the entirety of the American Jewish experience from its earliest manifestations to the present day. Primarily, these include records of enduring value created by organizations and individuals consisting of correspondence, photographs, memoirs, minutes and reports, genealogical records and audio-visual materials. We aspire to assist educators by encouraging and providing access, understanding and interpretation of source materials relating to American Jewish history, by the creation of educational resources, including but not limited to, lesson plans, curricula, and exhibits. The mission of AJA is to serve not only as a repository of source material, but also as a research center and an agency for the dissemination of scientific data on the history of the American Jewish experience. This goal is primarily achieved through our semi-annual periodical, *The American Jewish Archives Journal*, which has been in continuous publication since 1948 and is now available for free on our website." There is no explicit mention in this self-description, nor in that of AJA, of a distinctly Jewish-oriented mission. On the surface, AJA and AJHS are entirely neutral and scholarly, even as AJA is part of a Jewish institution (Hebrew Union College–Jewish Institute of Religion).

83. Kaplan, "We Are What We Collect," 126.
84. See Jason Lustig, "Building a Home for the Past: Archives and the Geography of American Jewish History," *American Jewish History* 102, no. 3 (2018): 375–400.
85. Information about these conferences appears in the publications of each society. With regard to the decision of the Southern group to maintain high quality academic presentations, see Rubin, "The Pioneer Period of the SJHS (1976–1983)," 5–11.
86. Mark Bauman, email to author, August 16, 2022.
87. Gereboff, "Integrating Local Jewish Historical Societies and Public History," 53–72.
88. Barbara J. Howe, "Reflection on an Idea: NCPH's First Decade," *The Public Historian* 11, no. 3 (1989): 69–85; Spencer R. Crew, "Public History: Past and

Present," in *The Organization of American Historical Writing and Teaching of American History*, ed. Richard S. Kerkendall (New York: Oxford University Press, 2011), 301–5; Otis L. Graham Jr., "Discovering Public History in an Unlikely Place, UC Santa Barbara, 1976 and After," in *The Organization of American Historical Writing and Teaching of American History*, ed. Richard S. Kerkendall (New York: Oxford University Press, 2011), 317–22; Philip Scarpino and Daniel Vivian, "What Do Public History Employers Want?" *Report of the Joint AASLH-AHA-NCPH-OAH Task Force on Public History Education and Employment*, https://ncph.org/wp-content/uploads/2019/02/What-do-Public-History-Employers-Want-A-Report-of-the-Joint-Task-Force-on-Public-History-Education-and-Employment.pdf; James B. Gardner and Paula Hamilton, "The Past and Future of Public History: Developments and Challenges," in *Oxford Handbook of Public History*, eds. Paula Hamilton and James B. Gardner (New York: Oxford University Press, 2017), 1–25; Thomas Cauvin, "The Role of Public History: An International Perspective," *Historia Critica* 68 (2018): 3–26; Thomas Cauvin, *Public History: A Textbook of Practice* (New York: Routledge, 2016).

89. Cauvin, *Public History*, 13–14.

90. Recent publications on Jewish museums include Natalia Berger, *The Jewish Museum, History and Memory, Identity and Art from Vienna to Bezalel National Museum, Jerusalem* (Leiden: Brill, 2017); Avi Decter, *Interpreting American Jewish History at Museums and Historic Sites* (Lanham, MD: Rowman and Littlefield, 2017); Avi Decter, "New Vistas on Jewish History and Culture," *Sh'ma* 31, no. 5 (2001): 1–2; Deborah Waxman, "Review of the National Museum of American Jewish History, Philadelphia," *Pennsylvania History* 79, no. 1 (2012): 65–75; Jenna Weismann Joselit, "Best-in-Show: American Jewish Museums Exhibitions, and the Search for Community," in *Imagining the American Jewish Community*, ed. Jack Wertheimer (Hanover: Brandeis University Press, 2007), 141–53; Barbara Kirshenblatt-Gimblett, "From Ethnology to Heritage: The Role of the Museum," in *Museum Studies: An Anthology of Contexts*, ed. Bettina Messias Carbonell (Malden, MA: Blackwell, 2012), 199–205; Grace Cohen Grossman, "Project Americana: Collecting Memories and Exploring the American Jewish Experience," in *New Beginnings: The Skirball Museum Collection and Inaugural Exhibit*, ed. Grace Cohen Grossman (Los Angeles: Skirball Cultural Center, 1996), 89–109;

Grace Cohen Grossman, "Jewish Museums in America," *Encyclopedia Judaica*, 2nd ed. (New York: Macmillan Reference, 2007), 631–34; Yaara Shteinhart Moghadam, "Practitioners and Practices in Museum Jewish Education" (PhD diss., Jewish Theological Seminary, 2011); David Clark, "Jewish Museums: From Jewish Icons to Jewish Narratives," *European Judaism* 36, no. 2 (2003): 4–17; and David Clark, "Jewish Museums: Performing the Present through Narrating the Past," *Jewish Cultural Studies* 4 (2008): 271–92.

91. Decter, *Interpreting American Jewish History*, 205.
92. Ibid., 214.
93. Ibid., 218.
94. Works on ethnicity and archives include Richard Cox, "Foreword," in *Identity Palimpsests: Archiving Ethnicity in the U.S. and Canada*, eds. Dominique Daniel and Amalia Levi (Sacramento: Litwin, 2014), ix–xiv; Dominque Daniel and Amalia S. Levi, "Introduction: From Containing to Shaping to Performing Ethnicity in Archives," in *Identity Palimpsests: Archiving Ethnicity in the U.S. and Canada*, eds. Dominique Daniel and Amalia Levi (Sacramento: Litwin, 2014), 1–11; Jeannette A. Bastian and Ben Alexander, "Introduction, Communities and Archives—A Symbolic Relationship," in *Community Archives: The Shaping of Memory*, eds. Ben Alexander and Jeannette Allison Bastian (London: Facet Publishing, 2009), xxi–xxiv; Joel Wurl, "Ethnicity As Provenance: In Search of Values and Principles for Documenting the Immigrant Experience," *Archival Issues* 29, no. 1 (2005): 65–76; and Fiona Casson, "The Small Politics of Everyday Life: Local History Society Archives and the Production of Public Histories," *Archives and Records* 38, no. 1 (2017): 45–60.
95. Bastian and Alexander, "Introduction," xxi.
96. Wurl, "Ethnicity As Provenance," 69.
97. Carol Kammen advances similar ideas. She explores the role and position local historical institutions need to adopt in relation to their communities if they seek to be effective. If such institutions intend to continue to function as community educators, this requires "seeing and responding to community needs, being part of the local landscape rather than sitting apart from it, and cooperation with other cultural institutions and with public officials." They must "understand the modern, living community it serv[es], not just the descendants of those buried in the local cemetery." Kammen, *On Doing Local History*, 160.

98. Albert T. Klyberg, "A Rhode Island Historian Looks at the *Rhode Island Jewish Historical Notes*," *Rhode Island Jewish Historical Notes* 13, no. 1 (1999): 9–16.
99. Ibid., 10.
100. Ibid., 15.
101. Ibid., 16. For information on the foundation and its vision, visit https://heritage-harborfoundation.org.

2

Rhode Island Jewish Historical Association

Latecomer and Pioneer

GEORGE M. GOODWIN

For three quite obvious reasons, Rhode Island merits a place of honor within studies of American and perhaps international Jewish history. Indeed, for Jewish visitors from near and far, the Ocean State has become a hallowed destination as both a religious and a patriotic shrine.

Consecrated in 1666, Newport has the oldest intact Jewish cemetery in North America. According to a map drawn for the British admiralty in 1777, it was located on Jew Street. Newport's synagogue, identified on the same map as "Jews' Synagogue," was located near the cemetery on Griffin Street. In 1823, this byway was renamed Touro in honor of two brothers who helped preserve and sustain both holy places.

Congregation Jeshuat Israel's home had been dedicated in 1763, thirty-three years after the construction of North America's first synagogue, the home of Congregation Shearith Israel in New York City. But its first synagogue on Mill Street was demolished in 1818 in order to build a larger one on the same site, and its second lasted only until 1833, when another was built on Crosby Street.

The third reason for Rhode Island's prominence within American Jewish history also relates to its colonial synagogue but through a two-dimensional object. George Washington had made his first visit to Jeshuat Israel in 1780, when it housed Rhode Island's General Assembly and sessions of the Supreme Court. In advance of his second visit, as president, in August 1790, Washington received a letter from a congregational leader, Moses Seixas, who wrote on behalf of "the children of the stock of Abraham." Seixas characterized the new government "which to bigotry gives no sanction, to persecution no assistance." In his reply to "the Hebrew Congregation in Newport," Washington not only echoed the *hazzan*'s words but further extolled the blessings of liberty and freedom.[1]

The president's reply, regaled for generations as "the Washington Letter," was enshrined within the Newport synagogue until about 1950, when it was sold mysteriously to a private collector. The Morris Morgenstern Foundation later lent it to B'nai B'rith's Klutznick Museum in Washington, DC, but then sequestered it in a vault in Maryland. Between 2012 and 2015, this providential letter was lent to the new National Museum of American Jewish History in Philadelphia, where it should be perpetually enshrined.

Fortunately, additional structures in Newport still mark the presence of its early Jewish colonists—loyalists and patriots alike. Many documents found in the city's archives and others also shed significant light on the Jewish community's early inhabitants. And there are holy objects, such as Torahs and *rimonim*, as well as other works of art, scattered among various museums. All these rarities exemplify and evoke Newport's rich Jewish past.[2]

Thus, it would seem almost inevitable that a Rhode Island Jewish historical organization would eventually be established to protect, study, and celebrate the state's quite remarkable legacy. Indeed, one was, but not until 1951.

Yet, this was our country's first state or local Jewish historical organization. So, it may also be appropriate to say that the Rhode Island Jewish Historical Association was created "as early as" 1951. And the organization is itself a fourth reason why the study of Rhode Island Jewish history is possible, enlightening, and rewarding.

Beyond Newport

It also seems notable, at least in retrospect, that the Rhode Island Jewish Historical Association (RIJHA) was founded by Jews in Providence and that its basic purpose was to augment and, in some sense, counterbalance the study of Jews in colonial and federal Newport. The state's more recent Jewish history began a few decades after 1822, when the last Jew had departed Newport and others began to settle at least temporarily in Providence.[3]

By the late nineteenth century, Jews lived not only in Rhode Island's largest cities but also in many small towns and more distant crossroads. And during the post–World War II era, decades after Providence was eclipsed as America's twentieth largest city, Jews accelerated their exodus from cities to suburbs and then to former vacation spots.

Consequently, Rhode Island failed in establishing a central authority, a statewide Jewish Federation, until 1970, seventy-five years after Boston organized its own, which became a prototype for many of North America's Jewish communities. Despite herculean efforts, Rhode Island Jewry remains scattered and perhaps divided, unable or unwilling to perceive itself as part of a larger community, which could easily relate, at the very least, to its closest New England neighbors.

National Jewish Historical Societies

What were some of the milestones that led to the state's charter of RIJHA on September 11, 1951? The most obvious had been the creation of the American Jewish Historical Society in New York City in 1892. Indeed, the society was not only the first but would become the country's oldest continuously functioning ethnic historical organization.[4] Originally located within the Jewish Theological Seminary of America, this eminent historical organization moved to the campus of Brandeis University, in Waltham, Massachusetts, in 1967 and remained there until 1999, when it returned to Manhattan to become a founding member of the Center for Jewish History.[5]

In the spring of 1988, when the American Jewish Historical Society's annual conference was held in Providence, RIJHA served as its host. This was one of the society's best-attended conferences in many years—and perhaps one of the more stimulating.

Thanks to the Straus family of New York City, there was a little-known connection between Providence's Jewish community and Brown University. Oscar Straus, the society's founding president, was better known as America's first ambassador to Turkey and later as the first Jewish cabinet member (Theodore Roosevelt's secretary of commerce and labor from 1906 through 1909). He was also a lawyer and a self-taught historian, who became deeply interested in Roger Williams, Rhode Island's founder.

David Blaustein, the third rabbi of Providence's Temple Beth-El, from 1892 to 1898, had studied Semitics at Harvard College from 1889 to 1893, without earning a bachelor's degree.[6] There he became a close friend of Oscar's nephew, Jesse Isidor Straus, who did graduate with the class of 1893. Subsequently, Jesse entered the family's business, Macy's department stores, ultimately becoming its president and then serving as FDR's ambassador to France from 1933 until his death in 1936.

In 1898, Rabbi Blaustein earned a master's degree in Brown's department of biblical literature and history of religions, and he became the university's first Jewish instructor when he taught Semitic languages on a part-time basis from 1897 to 1899. Thus, Blaustein probably became instrumental in Brown's courtship of the Straus family, which resulted in Oscar receiving an honorary doctor of literature degree in 1896. In 1912, after delivering the annual Washington birthday address at Brown, Oscar also spoke at Beth-El's new synagogue and was accompanied by Brown's president, William Faunce, a Baptist minister. Eventually, the university received a Straus bequest of $10,000.

In 1894, only two years after becoming president of the American Jewish Historical Society, Oscar Straus published *Roger Williams: The Pioneer of Religious Liberty*,[7] which contributed to the scholarly and popular restoration of Williams's stature. Oscar also named his son Roger Williams Straus, and his grandson became Roger Williams Straus Jr.

Jesse Straus's younger son, Kenneth, graduated from St. George's, the elite Protestant boarding school near Newport, in Middletown, Rhode Island, before matriculating at Harvard with the class of 1927 and earning a master's at Harvard Business School in 1931. The Straus family's bequest to Brown proved to be relatively modest, however, for in 1924 Oscar and his brothers donated $300,000 to Harvard. Perhaps it should also be mentioned that Rabbi David Blaustein left Temple Beth-El through Isidor Straus's encouragement to become superintendent of New York City's Educational Alliance, a Jewish organization that Isidor had helped found.

Information about Rabbi Blaustein, the Straus family, and Brown might suggest that almost all research about American Jewish history can be conducted—or at least initiated—on a local basis. Such details enrich and strengthen broader and deeper historical discussions and investigations. The danger, of course, is losing sight of a far larger, more complex picture.

No doubt the creation of the American Jewish Archives (AJA) on the Cincinnati campus of Hebrew Union College (HUC), in 1947, also inspired the founding of RIJHA. Rabbi William G. Braude, a 1931 alumnus of the Cincinnati campus, was surely acquainted with the archives' founder, Rabbi Dr. Jacob Rader Marcus, who would become known as "the founding father and dean" of American Jewish historical studies. Soon after his ordination in 1920—even before earning his doctorate in Berlin in 1925—Marcus joined the HUC faculty and remained a beloved professor there until his death in 1995. So, presumably, Marcus was one of William Braude's professors.

A few dozen letters in Temple Beth-El's archives, written between 1945 and 1980, are addressed to "Jake" or "Bill." In his first letter to Prof. Marcus, Rabbi Braude asked him to verify the year that the Temple had been founded (1844 or later?). In his 1947 letter to Rabbi Braude, Prof. Marcus thanked him for his introduction to a layperson, David Adelman, while visiting Providence. In 1951, Adelman would become RIJHA's founding president. In a 1957 letter, the pulpit rabbi asked the professor if he planned to speak at Touro. If so, could he also speak at Beth-El? A year later, Prof. Marcus asked Rabbi Braude if some of his father's papers could be donated to AJA, and they were. In 1984, "Jake" thanked "Bill" for sending both parts of his autobiographical reflections, which had been published in RIJHA's journal in 1981 and 1982.[8] In 1984, however, the professor explained that AJA could not accept twenty-five boxes of the pulpit rabbi's sermons; rather, twenty-five or thirty "representative samples" would suffice. Ultimately, eight boxes were accepted, and many more boxes and filing cabinets remain at Beth-El.

Prof. Marcus also sent Rabbi Braude annual requests for financial donations to AJA. The Cincinnatian called these "*schnorr*" letters, and he dutifully sent thank-you notes for gifts received. Temple Beth-El's library also subscribed to AJA's journal since its inception in 1948. The library eventually bound the first thirty-three volumes for continual, if not perpetual, use. It also purchased many of Marcus's books.

Rhode Island Historical Society

The earliest precedent within Rhode Island for the creation of RIJHA was likely the Rhode Island Historical Society, a privately funded and governed institution. When established in 1822, it was the fourth oldest state historical society in the country.[9] But to what extent was the historical society a prototypical organization for Jews?

The Rhode Island Historical Society's first home, known as "The Cabinet," was built on Waterman Street, on the northern periphery of the Brown University campus, in 1844. Fashioned in the Greek Revival style, it was a structure only thirty feet wide, fifty feet deep, and twenty-nine feet high.[10] The organization acquired its second home nearly a century later, in 1941, when John Nicholas Brown, a scion of the university's founding family, purchased the former John Brown House, one of the state's grandest, built in 1788 at 52 Power Street, on the southern edge of the Brown campus. A few days after the attack on Pearl Harbor, he sold it to the society for a dollar. Mr. Brown and his family continued to live in their own magnificent mansion, the Nightingale-Brown House, built in 1791 at 357 Benefit Street, before donating it in 1995 to the university as the John Nicholas Brown Center for Public Humanities and Cultural Heritage.

Beyond its location, prominence, and hospitality, however, the Rhode Island Historical Society's influence on the creation of RIJHA was probably tangential. Unquestionably the fiefdom of blue bloods, the historical society had only gradually begun to study history or collect in a more objective manner. William Greene Roelker Jr., who served briefly as its librarian and then as its director from 1940 to 1953, personified the organization's antiquarian and sentimental approach. He descended from Rhode Island nobility, Roger Williams and two colonial-era governors, the William Greenes (Sr. and Jr.), and belonged to such organizations as the Society of Colonial Wars in Rhode Island, the Rhode Island Society of the Cincinnati, and the Society of Mayflower Descendants. Educated at Groton and Harvard, he did not earn a master's degree in history (at Harvard) until 1939, shortly before joining the historical society's staff. He had worked previously in advertising and banking. But Roelker prevailed upon his board of trustees to acquire the John Brown House, significantly expand the society's membership, and in 1942 launch a new quarterly journal, *Rhode Island History* (to replace two discontinued series). Typically thirty-two pages in length, it focused on the state's Yankee hegemony and artistry.

No doubt Roelker also deserves some credit for hiring Clifford P. Monahan as the historical society's next librarian. This Maine native, a graduate of Bowdoin College, happened to be a member of the Sons of the American Revolutionary Society. His ancestor, Joseph Hubbard Jr., a native of Berwick, Maine, had served as a corporal in the Massachusetts militia. Quite likely, he was impressed by the Jewish history buffs' curiosity and commitment as well as their pursuit of accuracy. Perhaps Monahan also encouraged these Jewish adventurers to establish a journal.

Leaders of the Rhode Island Jewish Historical Association must have felt welcome at John Brown House, for they held annual meetings there for two decades. But in 1951, for example, thirty-three other organizations also held meetings there. There was no auditorium, so meetings were probably held in the Washington Room, a kitchen annex decorated with handmade wallpaper showing scenes from the president's inauguration in New York City. Nevertheless, RIJHA's creation was never mentioned among the occasional brief announcements published in *Rhode Island History.*

During William Roelker's leadership, the historical society's membership increased significantly, from about 500 to 1,400 individuals or couples. A decade after the founding of RIJHA, however, Jewish names were still extremely scarce on the historical society's published rosters. Likewise, there were no Jews among the thirty-eight members of the historical society's eight standing committees. And the same was true in 1970.

The first Jewish officer of the historical society's board was Frank Licht (1916–1987), who was elected vice president in 1980 and served two years. He was not exactly a risky choice, however. After having served as a Democratic state senator from 1949 to 1956, Licht was appointed a Superior Court judge and served as president of Providence's General Jewish Committee. In 1968, elected by a slight majority, Licht became Rhode Island's first Jewish governor (of two), and two years later he was reelected but chose not to run for a third term. Most likely, Licht felt no need to serve as the historical society's president, but it was probably easier being elected governor.[11]

Historic Preservation Movement

Given that Rhode Island's nickname is "the Ocean State," some of its residents and visitors may quip, "Yes, it's drowning in history." Such a feeling becomes abundantly clear when surveying the state's scores of local historical organizations and almost countless architectural landmarks. The designation of such landmarks did not begin until the late nineteenth century, when, for example, the Rhode Island Society of the Sons of the American Revolution placed a bronze plaque on Brown University's original building, the College Edifice, built in 1770, noting its occupation by "patriot forces and their French allies" during the Revolutionary War.

Providence did not establish its Preservation Society until 1956, when numerous edifices, both grand and relatively humble, were threatened by decay or demolition. Not surprisingly, moreover, John Nicholas Brown led the battle against architectural apathy and served as the Preservation Society's first president. It should also be mentioned, however, that in 1936 this scholarly and soft-spoken activist had commissioned Richard Neutra, a Viennese-born Jewish architect who had settled in Los Angeles, to design "Windshield," a major, modern vacation home on Fishers Island, New York.[12]

A prominent Jew also played a major role in the city and state's evolving and never-ending preservation movement (or battle). His effort involved far more than rescuing one historic building, however. Indeed, for Baptists and civil libertarians alike, this was a sacred space. In 1931, the same year that he became the first Jewish justice of Rhode Island's Supreme Court, J. Jerome Hahn donated the property known as "the Roger Williams Spring" to the city that Williams had founded. This property, cleared of dilapidated industrial and commercial buildings to form a park, was located across Main Street from where Williams and his followers purchased land from the Narragansetts and built their first settlement in 1636. As explained by two bronze plaques marking the entrance to the park, Justice Hahn's gift was made in memory of his father, Isaac, an émigré textile manufacturer who in 1884 had been the first Jew elected to public office (as a state representative) in Providence. In 1965, through legislation approved by President Lyndon B. Johnson, the Department of the Interior purchased the park and has preserved and operated it as the Roger Williams National Memorial to honor the concept of "Liberty of Conscience."[13]

Preservation and Recognition of Touro Synagogue

The creation of RIJHA in 1951 followed a far more convoluted commemorative project that had occurred, understandably, in Newport. Like Touro Street, Jeshuat Israel Synagogue acquired its nickname in 1823, following a bequest by Abraham Touro, a son of the congregation's first *hazzan*, Isaac, to care for both the Jewish cemetery and the house of worship. In 1854, a bequest by Isaac's younger son, Judah, provided similar funds, and both brothers, who had lived beyond Rhode Island, were buried in Newport's Jewish cemetery. The Touro legacies were not intended to preserve the synagogue as a museum but instead to provide a home for a new or revived Jewish congregation. Meanwhile, North America's first Jewish congregation, Shearith Israel in New York City, became the trustee for such an endeavor, and it oversaw summer services held at Touro during the 1850s, for example.[14]

At the turn of the twentieth century, two groups of Eastern European Jewish immigrants, who had settled in Newport, vied for Touro's use. In 1902, Rhode Island's Supreme Court gave its approval to one, and it eventually prospered. No later than 1932, on the occasion of the bicentenary of George's Washington's birth, the ritual of a ceremonial reading of Moses Seixas's letter to the president—and his reply—was established. In 1936, Morris Gutstein, Touro's rabbi from 1932 to 1943, published *The Story of the Jews of Newport*, which was the first comprehensive study of this subject.[15] It led to many detailed and critical studies, including, for example, important biographies of Judah Touro and Aaron Lopez.[16]

But Touro Synagogue was not designated a National Historic Site by the Department of the Interior until 1946, and this designation had nothing to do with efforts by Rhode Islanders—Jewish or Gentile.[17] The idea originated in 1944, when Arthur Hays Sulzberger, the publisher of the *New York Times* and a descendant of an original Jeshuat Israel family, sought the federal government's designation of three significant houses of worship—Protestant and Catholic churches and a synagogue—to symbolize and commemorate Americans' unity during World War II. Such architectural expression would be impressively achieved in 1956, under Jewish auspices, through the creation of the Three Chapels on the campus of Brandeis University.[18]

In 1946, despite much opposition by an advisory group of architectural historians, Oscar Chapman, the acting secretary of the Department of the Interior during the early days of the Truman administration, gave his approval for the designation of Touro. The synagogue was selected for two principal reasons: its elegant yet understated design by Peter Harrison, a major colonial architect (and loyalist) from Newport, and the structure's use as Rhode Island's General Assembly during the close of the Revolutionary War.[19]

Thus, the federal government's designation had nothing to do with the celebration of religious liberty, a theme embraced in 1947 through the creation of the Society of Friends of Touro Synagogue National Historic Shrine. Nevertheless, the reading of the Seixas and Washington letters, often by a leading state or federal elected official, became an annual ritual. Indeed, a reader in 1958 was none other than President Eisenhower, a frequent vacationer in Newport.

In 1963, as a result of the Friends' national fundraising campaign to honor Touro's bicentenary, the synagogue was fully restored. In 1982, following nearly two decades of efforts, Touro was portrayed on an American postage stamp to commemorate the 250th anniversary of Washington's birth.[20]

In 1998, the National Trust for Historic Preservation, a private organization chartered by Congress in 1949, joined the Department of the Interior and the National Endowments for the Arts and Humanities to form a consortium, Save America's Treasures, which could receive and administer federal grants. Consequently, in 2003, Interior's regulations were further modified, allowing historic structures still used for religious purposes to receive federal funding. As a result, Touro Synagogue received a $375,000 preservation grant and designation by the National Trust as one of its twenty-seven "historic sites." The land and structure are still owned by New York City's Shearith Israel, however.

Recent additions to and alterations of the Touro property have included the creation of Patriots Park, the placement of some small Holocaust memorial plaques within the park, and in 2009 the construction of the Ambassador John L. Loeb Jr. Visitors Center. These efforts further demonstrate that the reinterpretation of Touro's importance is never-ending.

American Jewish Tercentenary

No doubt, the seven incorporators of RIJHA were uplifted and propelled by a patriotic spirit as well as Jewish pride. Indeed, each reservoir of emotion fed the other. The incorporators happily foresaw local celebrations of the American Jewish Tercentenary in 1954. Indeed, many celebrations were documented within the first issue of the association's journal, *Rhode Island Jewish Historical Notes*, which began publication in June of that year.[21] The documentation of celebrations extended to the third issue (June 1955), which was dubbed "The American Jewish Tercentenary Issue" and ran to 226 pages.

The numerous celebrations included a program held at the Roger Williams Spring, another in Providence's Veterans Memorial Auditorium (which featured an address by James P. Adams, the director of the Rhode Island Historical Society), and a service sponsored by the State Council of Churches held in the First Baptist Meetinghouse in America, the oldest

Baptist congregation in the US. Still another tercentenary service was held within the sanctuary of the new home of Temple Beth-El, the congregation's third, where the featured speaker was President Abram Sachar of Brandeis University. The Providence Public Library organized a "Jewish Tercentenary Exhibit," and the Museum of Art at Rhode Island School of Design presented "The House of God," an exhibition of Jewish ceremonial art from Rhode Island synagogues and homes throughout the state. The relatively new medium of television was also put to good use. A half-hour show, "The Jewish Heritage," was broadcast on WJAR on February 13,1955.

The most enduring result of the tercentenary celebrations was probably a scholarly article by David C. Adelman that was published in the July 1954 issue of the Rhode Island Historical Society's journal, *Rhode Island History*. This impressive study, titled "Strangers: Civil Rights of Jews in the Colony of Rhode Island," ran twelve pages.[22] In his first sentence, Adelman, who was identified as a Providence lawyer and president of RIJHA, noted the dual celebrations of the American Jewish Tercentenary and the centenary of Providence's Temple Beth-El. In his second paragraph, he proclaimed, "Jews owe no greater debt of gratitude to any man in the history of the United States than Roger Williams."[23] Adelman not only examined a multitude of seventeenth- and eighteenth-century legal documents but was also able to publish photos of four belonging to Newport's Superior Court as well as the State Archives.

Of course, the American Jewish Tercentenary occurred within a far larger political and social context, which included, for example, the cessation of the Korean War. Although there were no obvious ramifications in Rhode Island, a great many Jews were also no doubt frightened, if not stigmatized, by the victimization of the Hollywood Ten, for example, and other brethren during the McCarthy era. Indeed, Julius and Ethel Rosenberg had been executed at Sing Sing Prison on June 19, 1953.

RIJHA's Founders

The driving force behind the creation of RIJHA—and its president for no fewer than fifteen years—was in fact David C. Adelman (1892–1967), a son of Eastern European immigrants and a Providence native. Dr. Seebert J. Goldowsky, the association's seventh president and a longtime editor of its journal (1962–1978; 1983), referred to his friend and colleague as the organization's "founding father." In his 1974 article about RIJHA's history, which was reprinted in 1991 on the occasion of the association's fortieth anniversary, Goldowsky also characterized the organization as "the first in the country devoted to the scientific study of local Jewish history."[24]

Adelman graduated from Providence's Classical High School in 1910 and Brown University four years later. Like most of Brown's Jewish students, he commuted from home to campus and did not belong to a fraternity. Adelman earned his law degree, probably again as a commuter, at Boston's Northeastern University and was admitted to the Rhode Island Bar in 1919, shortly after his military service during World War I. For nearly two decades, while building his own practice, the association's founder, who became active in Republican politics, served on the staff of several of the state's legislative committees. He belonged to numerous Jewish fraternal organizations and, as a member of Temple Beth-El, served as its volunteer archivist.

Rabbi William G. Braude asked him to write a congregational history, and Adelman wanted to do so, but he could not proceed after determining that too many early records had been lost or destroyed in a fire. Seebert Goldowsky built on many of Adelman's published articles when he too was eventually asked to write a congregational history, which was published in 1989.[25]

As Goldowsky explained in his 1974 article about the association's history, Adelman's interest in Rhode Island "Americana" began in childhood and evolved through book collecting. According to Adelman, "at first subconsciously but later deliberately" he began to search for Jewish "historical items."[26] Eventually, this self-taught but driven historian sought to correct errors that had been published in the journal of the American Jewish Historical Society, for example. In 1936, he published *The Life and Times of Judah Touro*.[27] This was the same year that he spoke on this topic to the Touro (Jewish) Fraternal Association in Providence, when it celebrated the state's tercentenary. Having eagerly continued to collect vast amounts of Jewish historical materials, Adelman would eventually need a home beyond his own residence to store them.

Born between 1881 and 1907, the six additional RIJHA incorporators were the children of immigrants or immigrants themselves. Only one of the incorporators had been born in Rhode Island. Two had earned doctor of philosophy degrees, although neither in history. But given how much the incorporators had overcome and achieved in their lives, their lack of formal historical training seemed unimportant.

The eldest incorporator and only woman, Matilda J. Pincus (1881–1954), had been born in nearby Fall River, Massachusetts. Her deep sense of patriotism was surely felt through the military service of her father, Newman, during the Civil War. He settled in Providence in 1866 and soon joined Rhode Island's second congregation, Sons of Israel, which had been chartered in 1854.[28] Matilda, having been confirmed at Temple Beth-El in 1895, eventually became a president of its alumni association as well as a teacher in its religious school and the congregation's first librarian and archivist. Nearly a lifelong resident of South Providence, the site of Beth-El's second home, she did not live long enough to enjoy its third home, which opened on the city's East Side a few months after her passing.

Only a year younger than "Mattie" was Alter Boyman (1882–1966), a Romanian immigrant who settled in Providence in 1908. Having been required to support himself, he was unable to earn the equivalent of a high school education. Nevertheless, in 1927, he began to chair the publication of *Providence Passover Journal*, a Yiddish-English newspaper devoted to labor Zionism. Although nominally successful in the clothing business, Boyman found his true calling as a leader of numerous Jewish communal organizations. For example, following World War I, he represented the American Jewish Relief Committee. In 1935, he was a delegate to the World Jewish Congress. Boyman also helped lead the Hebrew Free Loan Association, Jewish Orphanage, Miriam Hospital, Jewish Home, and Jewish Family Service.

By contrast, Arthur J. Levy (1897–1972) enjoyed a privileged upbringing as well as professional distinction. A native of New York City who grew up in Pawtucket, Rhode Island, he followed David Adelman to Brown and graduated in 1919.[29] Levy worked briefly as a sports editor at the *Providence Tribune* before earning his law degree in 1923 at Boston University. Five years later, he helped establish his own firm, which lasted two decades. In 1950, a year before RIJHA was chartered, he was elected president of the Rhode Island Bar Association—the first Jew to hold that office. Levy also became the founding editor of the Bar Association's journal from 1952 through 1954, but he was particularly devoted to Jewish Family Service, serving as its founding president for a decade. As president of Temple Beth-El's Brotherhood, he no doubt knew David Adelman on a social as well as a professional basis.

Levy was in more than one way a visionary. Beginning in 1944, he chaired Beth-El's building committee, which led to a thoroughly modern structure designed by Percival Goodman, a New Yorker. In 1935, Levy had considered another modernist, William Lescaze from Philadelphia, for the design of his own home, steps from Narragansett Bay in Cranston.

Bernard "Beryl" Segal (1900–1980) had been born in Romania and immigrated to Providence as a child. Like Alter Boyman, he was a Yiddish speaker and writer. In fact, Segal's wife, Chaya, was a Boyman cousin. Segal graduated from Brown in 1927 and earned a master's degree in science from the University of Rochester. Having graduated from Rhode Island College of Pharmacy in 1940, he practiced pharmacy, including thirty years on the staff of Miriam Hospital. Also a devoted teacher of Hebrew, he taught at several synagogues, including Beth-El, where he was both a member and a close friend of Rabbi Braude. Segal became widely known in the Jewish community for his numerous articles in the *Rhode Island Jewish Herald* and in *The Providence Journal-Bulletin* before writing many more in the association's journal.

Beginning in 1967, Segal served as RIJHA's second president. His daughter, Geraldine S. Foster, was made the organization's eighth president, becoming both its first woman and its only second-generation president. Foster's son and Segal's grandson, Harold, is as of this writing, the association's president, its twentieth. Unfortunately, no other descendant of incorporators has been active in the association's leadership. However, both children of the following incorporator have written articles for its journal.[30]

The association's second youngest incorporator was Prof. Israel J. Kapstein (1904–1983). Born in Fall River, "Kappy" lived in Boston before moving to Providence in 1916. Like David Adelman, he graduated from Classical High School and then Brown University in 1926.[31] As an aspiring writer, his closest friends included S. J. Perelman and Nathanael West (both members of the class of 1925), who would achieve significant literary recognition far beyond New England. After obtaining some writing gigs in New York City, Kapstein returned for graduate studies in English at Brown and earned his doctorate in 1933. He won some early recognition as a novelist and taught writing as well as literature, thereby becoming a beloved English professor on College Hill. In 1946, Kapstein became the first Jew to receive tenure at Brown, where he spent his entire academic career until retiring in 1969. Although nominally affiliated with Temple Emanu-El, a Conservative congregation on Providence's East Side founded in 1925, he became Rabbi Braude's close friend and colleague. As specialists in Hebrew and Aramaic translations, they won renown among Judaic scholars.[32]

Rabbi William Braude (1907–1988) was the youngest of the association's incorporators. Born in Lithuania, he immigrated as a teenager with his family to New York City but grew up in Denver. The son of an Orthodox rabbi who feared the disappearance of traditional Judaism, Braude earned his bachelor's degree at the University of Cincinnati before his ordination at HUC in 1931. A year later, following his first pulpit in Rockford, Illinois, he came to Providence's Beth-El, where Mattie Pincus took him under her wing. In 1934, Braude earned a master's degree and in 1937 a doctorate in religious studies at Brown. The university published his dissertation in 1940.[33] As Beth-El's rabbi, he also later taught in that department, helping pave the way for a generation of rabbinic scholars who would never be required to lead congregations. Long before his retirement in 1974, Rabbi Braude became Rhode Island's longest-serving congregational rabbi with a tenure of forty years. Rabbi Leslie Y. Gutterman, his associate and then his successor, having served forty-five years, established a new record.

Rabbi Braude was devoted to the congregation's library, and in 1967 it was named in his honor. He had played a key role in envisioning the new synagogue's design, in the search not only for a suitable architect but also an appropriate style. Rabbi Braude, who marched with Martin Luther King Jr. from Selma to Montgomery in 1965, was also a prolific writer. Between 1929 and 1985, he published eighty-six scholarly articles and reviews (in addition to many sermons and articles for general readers).

Infrastructure and Staff

So, in its early decades, where was RIJHA housed? Rumor has it that, in place of an office, David Adelman's car overflowed with myriad books and documents.

Since its founding, however, the RIJHA's official address was the John Brown House. Perhaps there was some space in an attic for storing files and a small reference collection. Otherwise, John Brown House was crammed with art, artifacts, furniture, books, manuscripts, offices, and staff.

During its earliest years, the association's membership records would probably have fit inside a briefcase.[34] By 1954, it had only forty-four dues-paying members. A year later, following the publication of the first issue of *The Notes*, it boasted more than 100 members. Many of the men, who could select from various levels of financial support, were pillars of the state's Jewish community. As for female members, most memberships were held in husbands' names; only a few widows and unmarried women were welcomed.

Finally, in 1963, RIJHA moved to a third-floor office in a younger building, a Victorian structure at 209 Angell Street (on the opposite, northern edge of the Brown campus). But why there? There's a simple Rhode Island explanation, which boils down to a commonly uttered phrase: "I know a guy." Since the mid-1930s, the building's owner had been Dr. Maurice Adelman, a prominent pediatrician and a Beth-El member. Married in 1929 to Eleanor Goldowsky, one of Seebert's two older sisters, Adelman was in fact his brother-in-law. Beatrice, the other Goldowsky sister, would serve as Adelman's office manager for a half-century. As a Brown graduate of 1916, Adelman had also been a member of Phi Epsilon Pi with a RIJHA founder, Arthur Levy.

Beginning in 1973, RIJHA's meetings were moved to the auditorium of the new Jewish Community Center (JCC) on Elmgrove Avenue (opposite Brown's football stadium and adjacent to its Marvel Gymnasium). Given the increased visibility and convenience for East Side residents, the association's membership reached 322 families and individuals. Members received complimentary issues of the journal, as did sixty-three Jewish and Rhode Island organizations. Nineteen copies of *The Notes*, mailed overseas, required a modest subscription fee.

In 1975, the association moved its operations from Angell Street to downstairs quarters within the Federation wing of the JCC complex. Two small spaces became available: an office and an adjacent storage area. Although RIJHA was not considered a beneficiary agency (and never became one), the Federation did not charge rent. The association's downstairs neighbor *was* a beneficiary agency, the Bureau of Jewish Education, which was led by a growing professional staff. Regrettably, despite similar goals, the bureau and association found very few ways to work together. Bureau staff members had a rather condescending opinion of the association's volunteers, and these volunteers felt that the staff had little interest in local or American Jewish history.

Even if these neighboring organizations had sought collaborative projects, there were probably financial impediments. Since its inception, RIJHA struggled, in this regard, to achieve its relatively modest goals. In 1954, for example, income was only $1,615, but it resulted in a balance of $1,000. The largest expenditures—for printing and rent at John Brown House—were about $600. Occasional speakers may have received honoraria, but volunteers did just about everything. Essentially, RIJHA was—and remains—a labor of love. Perhaps accordingly, through various waves of consolidation, the Bureau of Jewish Education's staff has shrunk.

Eventually, RIJHA's operating expenses improved, and several bequests were received. The association's annual budget is currently about $100,000, and its endowment now exceeds $900,000. In some ways, however, it has become a dowager organization.

In 1962, David Adelman and Seebert Goldowsky met with William G. McLoughlin, a professor of American history at Brown from 1954 until his death in 1992, to gain a deeper understanding of how the association could advance its research efforts. McLoughlin was a prolific author and editor who specialized in the history of American religion. He wrote two histories of the Ocean State: one for the American bicentenary, the other a decade later.[35] Unfortunately, a more comprehensive state history, long overdue, has not yet been published.

Prof. McLoughlin recommended that RIJHA engage one of his doctoral students, Freda Egnal, to compile a bibliography of all published and archival materials relating to Rhode Island Jewish history. This definitive project took nearly four years.

Egnal's first bibliography, focusing on materials found only within Brown University libraries, was published in the May 1963 issue of *The Notes* and ran twenty pages. Her second sweeping bibliography focused on materials belonging to other Rhode Island collections, such as libraries, Jewish organizations, synagogues, and a few prominent Jewish families. When published in the journal's November 1966 issue, it ran more than 200 pages.[36] Ms. Egnal, who earned a master of arts in teaching in 1965, identified nearly 1,000 items.

RIJHA steadily increased its efforts to assist researchers. In 1955, after the completion of the journal's first volume, consisting of four issues, an index was prepared. Then the number of issues was reduced to one per year. Each had its own index, and a cumulative index was published in 1987 to cover the first seven volumes. A second cumulative index was published in 1994 to cover the next seven. Occasionally, to guide researchers and writers, the journal also published short bibliographies of important and obscure new studies about Rhode Island Jewry.

The association's first regular employee was a part-time librarian. Dorothy M. Abbott, a retiree, had spent her career at the Providence Public Library. After serving RIJHA from 1967 to 1972, she received the title "librarian emerita." Ms. Abbott was a Methodist, but this was not entirely surprising, for Temple Beth-El's first professional librarian, Maryland Estes, who served from 1958 to 1981, was also not Jewish. Ms. Abbott was more instrumental than any of her successors in building its highly significant Judaica collection.

Ms. Abbott's successor was Eleanor F. Horvitz, whose title eventually became librarian-archivist. She served no fewer than thirty years, from 1972 until her retirement at eighty-three years of age. A Providence native, she had been an undergraduate at Brown's Pembroke College before moving with her husband to St. Louis and completing her degree at Washington University. After the couple returned to Rhode Island, she earned a master's at Brown and taught briefly in Providence's public schools.

Ms. Horvitz's basic tasks were building, cataloguing, and storing a vast archival collection, which included documents, photographs, Jewish newspapers, other published materials, two-dimensional ephemera, and a small number of artifacts and tchotchkes. Some of the obvious organizational records include Providence's General Jewish Committee, a forerunner of the Jewish Federation of Rhode Island; the Federation itself; and its subsequent transformation as the Jewish Alliance of Greater Rhode Island. With Ms. Horvitz's help, RIJHA also collected the records of many of the fundraising organizations' beneficiary agencies. Fortunately, the archives also include handwritten and printed records of numerous organizations that have disappeared. These include, for example, the Jewish Orphanage of Rhode Island, many small synagogues, and some burial societies. Records of some of the more colorful defunct social organizations include the Order of Hebraic Comradeship, Association of Parents of American Israelis, and Rhode Island Jewish Bowling Congress.

Eleanor Horvitz also became the most prolific contributor to the association's journal by writing or co-writing more than thirty articles, a record that I eventually surpassed. Her frequent collaborator was Geraldine Foster, the association's past president and a fellow Brown graduate and educator. Although a quiet and reserved person, Horvitz was more than eager to share her vast knowledge with researchers of all ages and levels of experience. Fortunately, her family's finances allowed her to serve the association on a voluntary basis.

RIJHA required clerical and administrative assistance on a part-time basis. Two fondly remembered office managers over many years were Caroline Gereboff and Evelyn Stepak. The longest serving office manager was Anne Sherman, whose upbeat tenure lasted from 1991 to 2015. Anne also contributed articles to *The Notes*.

Over many decades, RIJHA was able to achieve most of its goals without employing an executive director. In recent decades, two individuals with significant library experience were hired, but both soon resigned. It was evidently not easy working with volunteers, or perhaps vice versa. The association's current executive director as of this writing, Kate-Lynne Laroche, who earned a master's degree in history, previously served as its office manager. A non-Jew, she has a great deal to learn but is also eager to do so. Meanwhile, a new office manager, Jaime Walden, also not Jewish, ably assists with administrative tasks.

Most editors of *Rhode Island Jewish Historical Notes* have served as volunteers. The previous editor received an honorarium, as does the incumbent, but these are merely tokens of appreciation. The same is true with the previous and current graphic designers of the journal, Bobbie Friedman and Stephen Logowitz. Both are highly talented and accomplished professionals who have been more than generous with their expertise.

Heritage Harbor Museum

Reared by working-class parents in New Jersey and educated in the Midwest, Albert T. Klyberg came to the Rhode Island Historical Society as its librarian in 1968. Two years later he became its executive director. He retired in 1999, but his greatest professional and personal challenge still lay ahead.

Klyberg's weightiest academic accomplishment had been overseeing the publication of the papers of Rhode Island's great Revolutionary War general, Nathanael Greene. This project, which began in 1971, took thirty-four years and resulted in thirteen volumes.[37] Klyberg also oversaw the two-volume publication of Roger Williams's correspondence.[38]

In 1961, when still headquartered in the John Brown House and responsible for a few historic properties in rural parts of the state, the Rhode Island Historical Society acquired a former branch of the Providence Public Library on the city's East Side. This facility, built in 1874 as the Hope Street Methodist Episcopal Church, was further transformed into the society's study and research center. Consequently, Aldrich House, which had been donated by the Aldrich family to the society in 1974 and is only a short walk from its library, gained use as administrative offices and for the presentation of public programs and small, temporary exhibitions. John Brown House, although continually improved and upgraded, continued to serve as a museum of eighteenth- and early nineteenth-century decorative arts. Such use must have pleased the city and state's dwindling Yankee aristocracy, but it did little to reach the vast majority of Rhode Islanders, who descended from more recent immigrants or were immigrants themselves.

Consequently, in 1976, coinciding with the state's celebration of the country's bicentenary, Klyberg encouraged the formation of eighteen ethnic heritage subcommittees. RIJHA had already existed for twenty-five years, but he became an advisor to and an incorporator of the state's Black Heritage Society.

Similarly, Klyberg later became involved with the celebration of Rhode Island's French-Canadian history in the northern industrial town of Woonsocket, where many Jews, also associated with the textile business, had built a gorgeous new synagogue in 1961.[39] Thus, the Rhode Island Historical Society's first satellite museum, a cooperative venture with Woonsocket's municipal government, opened in 1997. In fact, the permanent and changing exhibitions center, given the dreadful name of "The Museum of Work and Culture," is housed in a former factory building once leased to a Jewish manufacturer.

But Klyberg, a true populist and proselytizer, sought to share a comprehensive understanding of Rhode Island history on a far larger and more dramatic scale. So, his next idea was creating Heritage Harbor, a high-tech, interactive museum for the state's residents as well as visitors from around New England and beyond. Although Heritage Harbor was a splendid and long overdue idea, the Historical Society's finances were modest—in fact, rather shaky.

Various commercial and industrial buildings in downtown Providence were considered for the proposed museum's home. A solution seemed to have been found in 1999, when the Narragansett Electric Company donated its outmoded Eddy Street generating plant to the Heritage Harbor Corporation. This vast and mighty structure, built between 1912 and 1925, offered approximately 260,000 square feet, including a turbine hall three stories high. Klyberg, who became the museum's acting director, and his supporters estimated that the cost of building Heritage Harbor would be $30 million, but the amount soon grew to $50 million, then even higher. Meanwhile, some generous gifts were pledged and others received from some of Rhode Island's larger corporations as well as many families and individuals—Jews among them.

A large degree of public financing would also be required, however. Unfortunately, in 2000 a state bond measure for $25 million was narrowly defeated. Two years later, a second measure, for only $5 million, was approved, but private fundraising faltered during the Great Recession.

Even before Klyberg's retirement as executive director, the Historical Society's board had lost confidence in the Heritage Harbor project, so it was spun off as an independent organization. Then, in 2002, to protect its assets and credibility, the Historical Society withdrew entirely from the project. Regrettably, some blame for this decision was placed on Klyberg's successor, Bernard Fishman, the first and only Jew to serve as the society's executive director until his departure in 2011. He knew museums rather well: in 1984, for example, he had become the founding director of the Jewish Museum of Maryland and guided it for fifteen years.[40]

Heritage Harbor, which became an affiliate of the Smithsonian Institution, also sought local partner organizations. The first two were the Black Heritage Society and RIJHA. Eventually, more than fifteen organizations signed on, and they were expected to raise funds for the museum's construction and operating costs as well as for their own office and storage areas. The consortium of ethnic organizations eventually included, for example, Rhode Islanders of Armenian, French, German, Irish, Italian, and Portuguese descent, and they were also invited to participate in a permanent exhibition known as "Cultural Crossroads."

Although guided by an experienced museum professional, the representatives of these ethnic groups, consisting mostly of idealistic volunteers, were expected to work democratically and, if necessary, collect artifacts on their own. I participated in the Crossroads group as a representative of RIJHA. After becoming the association's president in 2002, I served as a Heritage Harbor trustee for three years and later as a Historical Society trustee for a dozen years (through 2021). My service culminated when I briefly chaired the collections committee.

Eventually, the scale of the museum project was significantly reduced, such that Heritage Harbor would occupy only a small portion of a privately developed hotel complex. Many of Heritage Harbor's partner organizations, including RIJHA, withdrew from active participation, and others severed their ties. The entire project came to a halt in 2007. Ultimately, in 2009, Klyberg's dream of Heritage Harbor collapsed. While some of the significant funds that RIJHA had raised on behalf of Heritage Harbor were lost, other gifts remained in its endowment.

In 2014, a private developer purchased the former electric generating plant and, with considerable state funding, built entirely different spaces within it. When completed in 2017, these spaces were almost evenly divided between two institutions: a new nursing school cosponsored by the University of Rhode Island and Rhode Island College (another state institution) and administrative offices for Brown University.[41]

Alas, the Rhode Island Historical Society still lacks adequate space to display its permanent collection or changing exhibitions. Likewise, RIJHA, like many of Heritage Harbor's former partner organizations, cannot exhibit more than a fraction of its collection, and many materials are kept in an offsite storage facility. The state still lacks a venue or a method to educate most of its citizens about their shared past, and Rhode Island still does not require that its history be taught in public schools. Yet, a state law passed in 2016 does require instruction about the Holocaust and genocide.

Holocaust Museum and Memorial

Although its focus was only indirectly on Rhode Island, one of the partner organizations recruited to participate in Heritage Harbor Museum was the Rhode Island Holocaust Memorial Museum. In 1988, two years after its founding, the museum opened a memorial garden and a stone-clad facility within the Jewish Federation–Jewish Community Center's 1971 complex. While they represented very different visions and interpretations of Jewish history, leaders of the Holocaust Memorial Museum and RIJHA discussed ways to share space and work together as partners at Heritage Harbor. For better and worse, this never happened.

In 2007, never having succeeded in developing a notable collection, the Holocaust Museum shifted its emphasis and became the Rhode Island Holocaust Resource Center. While conducting annual memorial services, it focused on outreach to students and teachers—especially non-Jews. In 2013, after the Jewish Federation became the Jewish Alliance of Greater Rhode Island, and the JCC complex expanded to become the Dwares JCC, the Holocaust Museum acquired handsome upstairs quarters and was reborn as the Sandra Bornstein Holocaust Education Center.

But the state's Jewish tug of war between the condemnation of hatred and the celebration of freedom persists. In 2015, following an extensive fundraising campaign, the Rhode Island Holocaust Memorial, a diminutive sculptural ensemble, was dedicated within Memorial Park, near the Providence River and amidst World War and Korean War memorials. The Holocaust Memorial's miniature stone columns, representing the Six Million, are overshadowed by a gigantic stone pillar, topped with an allegorical figure, dedicated to the battles and victors of the First World War.

Memorial Park is located at a key symbolic juncture: only a five-minute, downhill walk from the John Brown House and only a five-minute, northerly walk to the First Baptist Meetinghouse in America (also known as "the Mother Church"), which was designed by Joseph Brown and completed in 1775. This also means that the Holocaust Memorial is no more than a ten-minute walk from the Roger Williams Spring, Justice Hahn's gift to the city.

The Association's Anthology

I grew up in Los Angeles, where, through its Jewish Federation, I met my wife, Betsey. We did not move to Providence until 1987, shortly after our first child was born. After living briefly in the Midwest, Betsey and I decided to live closer to her family or mine, and hers north of Boston looked inviting for a number of reasons. Following many years of teaching art history and conducting oral history interviews, I earned two more graduate degrees and began work as an administrator in federations. But I soon sought greater independence and more intellectual stimulation. Thus, I began undertaking a rich variety of historical projects for Jewish and secular organizations on a freelance basis.

Betsey and I joined RIJHA as soon as we moved to Providence, and I met many of its leaders and supporters through Temple Beth-El. But the organization seemed wary of transplants as well as younger people, so it took several years before I was invited to join its board (or, for that matter, the temple's board). Meanwhile, I had begun contributing articles to the association's journal. My first, published in 1994, was a shortened version of my study of Beth-El's modern architecture, which had appeared a year earlier in *American Jewish Archives Journal*.[42]

That year I was finally invited to join RIJHA's board, and eight years later I was elected its president. Having already served as president of Providence's Hebrew Free Loan Association, I had some sense of what I wanted to accomplish and how to go about it. My major goal was honoring the fiftieth anniversary of the association's journal, *The Notes*, which would occur the following year. My board supported the idea, but I was responsible for making it happen.

Rather than publishing a lengthy article or even a short book about *The Notes*, I thought of publishing an anthology of notable articles. The challenge was deciding which of the approximately 300 previously published articles were important and to whom.

Knowing that the journal's current editor, Leonard Moss, a retired English professor from Wheaton College, would probably not be interested in editing such a volume, my initial effort was to recruit somebody else. The obvious place to turn was the faculty of Brown University's distinguished Judaic studies program, which is actually part of the religious studies department. Over several decades, many prominent Brown professors—in numerous disciplines—had not only belonged to our association but became active board members and wrote many articles for the journal. The most obvious examples of professional involvement were sociologists,

Sidney and Alice Goldstein and Calvin Goldscheider, who also saw themselves as members and leaders of Rhode Island's Jewish community. Several editors of *The Notes* had also been professors: Albert Salzberg at Rhode Island College, George H. Kellner at the University of Rhode Island, and Michael Fink at the Rhode Island School of Design. Fink also became one of the journal's most prolific and stylish contributors. Nevertheless, a young professor at Brown, whose primary interest was French Jewry but who occasionally taught a course on American Jewish history, was not in the least bit interested in becoming the anthology's editor.

Consequently, I sought guidance from the obvious expert, Dr. Jonathan D. Sarna of Brandeis, who had delivered a significant lecture to the association in November 1994. His speech, "What's the Use of Local Jewish History?" was published in the 1995 issue of *The Notes*. Sarna happily suggested that the association seek guidance from his associate, Dr. Ellen Smith, a former librarian of the American Jewish Historical Society and the associate director of a Brandeis journalism program. She not only agreed to serve as editor but also helped persuade Sarna to publish the anthology in Brandeis's eminent series in American Jewish History, Culture, and Life.

A fundamental challenge facing the publication of the anthology was selecting a small number of articles to represent the hundreds previously published. Eventually, seventeen were chosen to represent three categories: communities, business and labor, and learning and leisure. The fourth category, "I Remember," represented dozens of first-person accounts, which quickly became essential to the journal's success by giving personal examples of broader trends.

It was also necessary to include within the anthology some examples of "lists"—more often the first examples of a phenomenon rather than the last. Such lists have guided historical research since the journal's first issue. The anthology's enumerations included Jewish-owned textile companies and a less extensive description of Jewish-owned farms. History buffs rather than experienced writers have typically assembled such lists. But scholars and professionals were well represented through the anthology's selection of articles. Indeed, several articles had been delivered as lectures at the association's annual meetings.[43] There was also space for two original introductory articles written by academicians, but in a non-academic style.[44]

In October 2004, *The Jews of Rhode Island* was co-published by the Rhode Island Jewish Historical Association, Brandeis, and the University Press of New England.[45] Jonathan Sarna spoke at the book's wonderful publication party. I too delivered celebratory remarks.

Having happily contributed in various ways, I was credited as the volume's co-editor. Perhaps my most enjoyable task was helping select about 100 photographs from more than 10,000 that I examined. Despite the creation of indispensable websites and the continuing use of online programs, I believe that the two national Jewish historical organizations remain deficient in their relative neglect of visual imagery in their journals.

Of course, my most practical responsibility was fundraising to underwrite the cost of producing 2,500 copies and to donate copies to every Jewish library, public library, and high school library in Rhode Island. Thanks to Prof. and Rev. Ernest Frerichs, the founder of Judaic studies at Brown, the anthology's largest donation came from the Dorot Foundation. Other notable donations were received from the Federation's Endowment Fund, the Rhode Island Foundation, and many RIJHA leaders. I lectured at numerous congregations, and most copies of the anthology were quickly purchased. Eventually, the entire edition sold out.

My Editorship

In 2003, following Leonard Moss's retirement as editor of *The Notes*, I needed to recruit his successor. There was no obvious candidate among authors of previous articles, and I tried unsuccessfully to entice a few acquaintances and strangers with some publishing experience. Then Stanley Abrams, the chair of RIJHA's publications committee, asked me to serve. For various reasons I was reluctant, but I said that I would give it a try. I suppose that, after editing nineteen annual issues and surpassing Dr. Seebert Goldowsky's record for longevity, I'm still trying. Professional and nonprofessional historians have far more to say. I keep a list of potential topics, which seems to grow rather than diminish.

One key to my success was the publication committee's decision, ultimately supported by the association's board, to increase expenditures on production costs. *The Notes* had to look and feel much better. This meant hiring a successful graphic designer to custom-design outside and inside covers as well as every other image and every page. After eleven issues, Stephen Logowitz succeeded Bobbie Friedman, and he too has become an excellent collaborator and colleague.

Another key to my success was welcoming articles about relatively recent occurrences in Rhode Island Jewish history—or putting aside the question of when our history begins (or resumes), or even, perhaps, what "historical phenomena" might be. I have learned to believe that almost all historical analysis is open to—or truly demands—reinterpretation. The purpose of such inquiry, however, is not to overturn conventions or strive for political correctness but to be far more imaginative and inclusive.

As a result, I have attempted to recruit many new writers, including Jewish and non-Jewish professors from many disciplines, as well as undergraduate and graduate students. The association continues to offer an annual financial prize to a student for a notable article, but there are, unfortunately, few submissions. A high school student could also submit an impressive essay, but this has not yet happened. At the other end of the age spectrum, the author of an article in a recent issue, a retired elementary school teacher, was ninety-seven years of age.

I happily encourage experienced writers to continue their submissions. But I am also pleased to occasionally republish an article from elsewhere that has not yet received the attention it deserves. Occasionally, I publish a reminiscence or a portion of a memoir by a deceased writer. In fact, there have been more than a few series of three consecutive articles by the same author; the record has been four. Several of these authors were Holocaust survivors, so *The Notes* has become an unacknowledged publishing arm of the Bornstein Holocaust Resource Center.

What has been my least enjoyable responsibility as editor? Surprisingly, it has not been writing more than 300 obituaries of association members. This is both an honor and a challenge that I enjoy. Rather, every four years it becomes an enormous task to index each volume of the journal. There is simply no high-tech shortcut. Almost every name, event, or phenomenon seems to matter, especially to individuals who may be conducting genealogical research—but boasting about ancestry was never RIJHA's goal.

Over nearly seven decades of publication, has our journal lost a broader focus, becoming burdened with trivia? I do not believe so. During the twentieth-first century, for example, the following major themes and focal points have endured: immigration to America and then migration to Rhode Island; financial hardship and prosperity; education; the professions; patriotism; Jewish congregations and organizations; Zionism; the arts; and recreation—among others. Thus far, however, few comparative studies have appeared placing Rhode Island within a regional or a larger context and, surprisingly, anti-Semitism has not been a prevalent theme.

One major omission in the journal's coverage has been spirituality. It is so much easier for a writer to discuss the glorious rise or sad decline of his or her congregation than the growth, withering, or rejuvenation of one's faith. And this may be as true for laypeople as for clergy. Generally, I have found that professional and nonprofessional historians, perhaps through their somewhat different perspectives and methodologies, have much to learn from one another. Yet, if the association had relied entirely on professional historians, its journal would never have emerged.

Yes, I would happily welcome the publication of a second anthology from *The Notes* (even if Prof. Jonathan Sarna's splendid Brandeis series no longer exists). During my tenure, the journal has been more productive than ever, publishing about 275 articles and about 1,700 photos—nearly 4,000 pages. Of course, I would also welcome the publication of a monograph covering the breadth and depth of Rhode Island Jewish history. Admittedly, however, the market for such a volume would be tiny.

The Future

RIJHA entered a new era in 2006, when it finally created its own website: www.rijha.org. The site has been redesigned many times in order to share the association's comprehensive understanding of Rhode Island Jewish history with local, regional, national, and, possibly, international researchers. Many wonderful resources have been posted, including a full run of

The Notes (except for each year's current issue); the association's occasional newsletter; its complete files of published obituaries; and a list of 400 oral history interviews (but not the actual recordings). The site also contains full runs of two discontinued newspapers: *Providence Passover Journal* and *Rhode Island Jewish Herald*, as well as announcements of upcoming meetings and a roster of association board members and staff. It may not be a flashy resource, but it is intended to be inviting.

The association has made other forays into contemporary educational or social technology. For example, in cooperation with the Rhode Island Council for the Humanities, the Rhode Island Historical Society, and Brown University's John Nicholas Brown Center, it recently launched its version of "Rhode Tour," which consists of a free mobile app and website for tours around the Ocean State.

Especially during the COVID pandemic, cyberspace has not only helped members of RIJHA stay in touch with each other and present some programs but has also led to some more ambitious Zoom meetings. For example, the Wyner Family Jewish Heritage Center at the New England Historic Genealogical Society, established in 2015 and headquartered in Boston, has brought together sister Jewish historical organizations from throughout the region. Surely, they will discuss and benefit from further collaborations. Ironically, the Wyner Center evolved after the departure of the American Jewish Historical Society (AJHS) from the Brandeis campus.

Unfortunately, that national body, which courageously initiated the study of American Jewish history and later served as an umbrella organization for smaller organizations around the country, no longer plays a leadership role. Instead, it works primarily to serve the needs of scholars and professional historians, although its website does serve researchers from multiple backgrounds.

One important way that RIJHA prepared for the future was by moving a second time, in 2018, within the Dwares Jewish Community Center, to larger, more adaptable, more comfortable, and far more visible quarters. This move to the former home of the Rhode Island Holocaust Education and Resource Center was made possible by a $263,000 capital campaign. The largest gift came from the Gertrude Regensteiner Revocable Trust.

Although deceased at the time of this gift, she and her immediate family had been Holocaust survivors. Other large gifts came from association leaders and members as well as the Jewish Alliance, which remains the association's generous and gracious landlord.

There is more wonderful financial news. At the time of its recent move, the association's endowment increased to more than $500,000. Through prudent management, it has continued to grow impressively to about $900,000.

But, in less conventional terms, will RIJHA's future be as bright as its past? Unfortunately, despite continuing accomplishments, membership has seriously declined to about 270 lifetime and annual members. Most members are elderly; "young" leadership would begin with individuals approaching grandparenthood. Indeed, the association's major challenge is identifying, encouraging, and educating two younger generations of leaders. No doubt many of Rhode Island's Jewish organizations face a similar challenge or peril.

Is there something especially confounding, burdensome, or illusory about Jewish life in the Ocean State? There are, of course, many fewer Jews than there were approximately ninety years ago—perhaps only 60 percent of those numbers. Fortunately, many young Jews are curious to explore a larger world, but many do not return after completing their studies or early work experiences. Fewer family businesses exist here than ever, and few are related to high-tech or expanding, international markets. Although the cost of housing in Rhode Island has increased significantly, it is considerably less expensive than in the larger cities of other states.

Fortunately, Rhode Island still offers many opportunities for individuals and families to become and remain Jewish, even as the number of synagogues has declined, and greater competition between Jewish and secular organizations for Jewish leadership and support exists. Yes, Rhode Island was and remains a rather quirky place. Simultaneously small and large, unified and divided, cosmopolitan and provincial, colorful and bland, it is forever denying, ignoring, and rediscovering itself.

It seems somewhat unlikely, however, that RIJHA could ever again attract such talented, accomplished, and driven leaders as its seven founders. What an unusual yet remarkable group of friends, colleagues, and visionaries they were. Could anybody have foreseen what the association has been able to accomplish, with quite limited resources, over a mere seven decades? Yet, when least expected, miracles do happen. RIJHA's success has been one such!

1. George M. Goodwin and Ellen Smith, eds., *The Jews of Rhode Island* (Waltham, MA: Brandeis University Press, 2004), Appendix B, 228–29.
2. For information about the recent lawsuit regarding the ownership of the *rimonim* housed at Touro Synagogue, see George M. Goodwin, "Wondrous *Rimonim*: Ownership, Holiness, Beauty, Rarity, and Value," *Rhode Island Jewish Historical Notes* (subsequently identified as *The Notes*) 17, no. 1 (2015): 130–59; Paul Berger, "America's Oldest Synagogue Wrestles with Court Battle and Its Own Decline," *The Notes* 17, no. 1 (2015): 160–67; "Shul v. Shul: Judge McConnell's Decision," *The Notes* 17, no. 2 (2016): 316–61; Mel A. Topf, "Introduction to the First Circuit Opinion," and "Decision in *Congregation Jeshuat Israel v. Congregation Shearith Israel*," *The Notes* 17, no. 3 (2017): 515–52.
3. It would be tempting to say that Jews, having departed one capital, were eventually attracted to another, but Rhode Island history, especially in view of its tiny size, is exceedingly complex. Providence, having been founded in 1636, was Rhode Island's first capital, but between 1681 and 1854, the capital rotated five times per year between Providence, Newport, Bristol, East Greenwich, and Kingston. Between 1854 and 1901, Providence and Newport served as the capital. Then in 1901, following the construction of a new State House, Providence became the only capital. The state's official name until 2020 was Rhode Island and Providence Plantations, when a ballot measure shortened it to Rhode Island.
4. Temple Beth-El in Providence has subscribed to AJHS's publications since their inception. For continuing reference and research purposes, the Temple also bound its copies.
5. On October 22, 1986, Nathan M. Kaganoff, AJHS's librarian, wrote to Temple Beth-El's leaders regarding the scope and quality of its archival collection: "I have visited several synagogues that have extensive archives and museums and I must say that I have never in all my experience visited a synagogue that has not as yet established its archives and has such a rich collection of materials as you have."

Letter in Beth-El archives.

6. George M. Goodwin, "Class of 1896: Three Pawtucket Lads at Harvard," *The Notes* 16, no. 2 (2014): 621–25.
7. Oscar Straus, *Roger Williams: The Pioneer of Religious Liberty* (New York: Century, 1894).
8. Rabbi Braude wrote eleven articles for *The Notes*. The two that Prof. Marcus acknowledged were: "Recollections of a Septuagenarian" (Part 1) 8, no. 3 (1981): 345–72 and (Part 2) 8, no. 4 (1982): 401–41. The second part was excerpted in RIJHA's 2004 anthology.
9. The nation's oldest, the Massachusetts Historical Society, founded in Boston in 1791, sought initially to collect materials on a national basis. Rhode Island's other predecessors were the New York Historical Society, founded in New York City in 1804, and the Maine Historical Society, founded in Portland in 1822, only two years after Maine had become a state through the Missouri Compromise.
10. In 1824, the Rhode Island Historical Society's "Southern Cabinet" was established in Newport. Nearly thirty years later it received its own state charter. In 1884, the society acquired a historic structure, the Seventh Day (or Sabbatarian) Meetinghouse, which had been built in 1730 to the east of where Touro Synagogue would be erected. In 1902, the Historical Society built a library extension adjacent to Touro. During the late 1960s, the Historical Society assumed ownership of and responsibility for another key religious structure, the Friends Meetinghouse, whose core was erected in 1699. Another significant development occurred in 1993, when the Historical Society opened a museum and a shop within the Brick Market, the second of three important buildings that Peter Harrison had designed in Newport. The Brick Market, completed in 1772, was once used as a town hall and is still owned by the municipality.
11. In 1979, Seebert Goldowsky became probably the first Jewish member of the society's publications committee. He chaired the committee from 1981 to 1984.
12. See Dietrich Neumann, ed., *Richard Neutra's Windshield House* (Cambridge, MA: Harvard Graduate School of Design, 2001).
13. For a detailed history of this property, see John Auwaerter and Karen Cowperthwaite, *Cultural Landscape Report for Rogers Williams National Memorial*, third draft (Boston: National Park Service, 2009), especially 32–41.
14. In 1867, Emma Lazarus, a summer visitor to Newport, had written a poem, "In

the Jewish Synagogue in Newport," which, when published four years later, also foresaw the rebirth of Newport's Jewish community. This was a contradiction of Henry Wadsworth Longfellow's poem, "The Jewish Cemetery in Newport," which he wrote in 1852 and published two years later. Ely Stock, a teaching associate in Brown's department of American civilization, reproduced and interpreted Longfellow's poem in an article: "Longfellow's 'The Jewish Cemetery at Newport,'" *Rhode Island History* (July 1961): 81–87. This was the first article with a Jewish focus that appeared in the journal since David Adelman's "Strangers: Civil Rights of Jews in the Colony of Rhode Island," which had been published in the July 1954 issue and will be cited later in my discussion. The third article was written by Sidney Goldstein, a prominent Brown sociologist: "The Providence Jewish Community After 125 Years of Development," *Rhode Island History* (April 1966): 51–57. I would like to thank Phoebe S. Bean, the Rhode Island Historical Society's librarian, for helping me identify these articles.

15. Morris Gutstein, *The Story of the Jews of Newport: Two and a Half Centuries of Judaism, 1658–1908* (New York: Bloch, 1936).
16. See Leon Hühner, *The Life of Judah Touro (1775–1854)* (Philadelphia: Jewish Publication Society, 1946) and Stanley F. Chyet, *Lopez of Newport: Colonial American Merchant Prince* (Detroit: Wayne State University Press, 1970).
17. George M. Goodwin, "The Politics of Preservation: How Touro Synagogue Became a National Historic Site," *The Notes* 18, no. 2 (2000): 177–207.
18. In 1952, the idea of the Three Chapels was conceived by a prominent Jewish architect, Max Abramovitz, who built extensively on the Brandeis campus. Jaya Kader, "The Three Chapels," in *An Architectural Celebration of Brandeis University's 50th Anniversary*, ed. Gerald S. Bernstein (Waltham, MA: Brandeis University Press, 1999), 30–33. (My article on Abramovitz's design of the Rose Art Museum follows.)
19. An early key study of Harrison's architecture was Carl Bridenbaugh, *Peter Harrison: First American Architect* (Chapel Hill: University of North Carolina Press, 1949). Bridenbaugh, whose specialty was colonial American history, taught at Brown between 1938 and 1942 and again between 1962 and 1969 as a University Professor. Largely as a result of his 1962 presidential address to the American Historical Association, however, he was considered an anti-Semite. See William Palmer, "Carl Bridenbaugh, American Colonial History and Academic

Antisemitism: The Paths to the 'Great Mutation,'" *American Jewish History* 98, no. 3 (2014): 153–74. Another early and still useful study of Harrison's importance is Antoinette F. Downing and Vincent J. Scully Jr., *The Architectural Heritage of Newport, Rhode Island, 1640–1915* (Cambridge, MA: Harvard University Press, 1952); a second, revised edition was published by American Legacy Press in 1982 (see 78–91). Downing, who lived on College Hill in Providence, was a founder of the Providence Preservation Society in 1956 and helped guide it for more than four decades. One fascinating but traditionally overlooked feature of Newport's Jewish cemetery is its gateway, designed in the Egyptian Revival style and erected in 1842. See George M. Goodwin, "The Gateway to Newport's Jewish Cemetery," *Rhode Island History* 67 (Summer/Fall 2009): 61–73.

20. The stamp also cites two phrases used in Seixas's letter to Washington and repeated in Washington's letter to the Hebrew congregation. A decade earlier, the Postal Service had approved the use of a Touro image, but it would have appeared on a postcard, which the Society of Friends rejected. On August 20, 1982, two days before the commemorative stamp was finally issued, the postmaster general, William F. Bolger, spoke at the reading of the Washington letter. See James H. Bruns, "Persistence Pays Off: The Touro Synagogue Stamp," *The Notes* 8, no. 4 (1982): 487–93.
21. The journal's first issue was mailed to association members using seven, three-cent stamps—each with a different historical image. The oldest stamp, issued in 1936 in honor of Rhode Island's Tercentenary, portrayed Roger Williams.
22. David C. Adelman, "Strangers: Civil Rights of Jews in the Colony of Rhode Island," *Rhode Island History* 13 (July 1954): 65–77.
23. Ibid., 65.
24. Goldowsky's article, "Local Jewish History: The Rhode Island Experience," *The Notes* 6, no. 4 (1974): 622–28, had actually been written as a speech, "Local Jewish History: The Rhode Island Experience," presented at a 1974 conference, "New Approaches to Local Jewish History," held at Ohio State University. The Academic Council of the American Jewish Historical Society, the Jewish studies program at Ohio State, the Ohio Historical Society, and the Columbus Jewish Federation cosponsored the conference. A surgeon, Goldowsky would become the biographer of Usher Parsons, an early Rhode Island surgeon, and the longest-serving editor of the *Rhode Island Medical Journal* (1961–1989). He was devoted to a factual

understanding of history—and just about everything else, including spirituality. Thus, his congregational rabbi, William G. Braude of Temple Beth-El, occasionally referred to him as "my favorite agnostic."

25. Seebert J. Goldowsky, *A Century and a Quarter of Spiritual Leadership: The Story of the Congregation of the Sons of Israel and David (Temple Beth-El) Providence, Rhode Island* (Providence, RI: Congregation of the Sons of Israel, 1989).
26. Goldowsky, "Local Jewish History: The Rhode Island Experience," 624. Adelman delivered his remarks at the association's first formal meeting, held on February 12, 1953, at the Rhode Island Historical Society's John Brown House.
27. Goldowsky, "Local Jewish History: The Rhode Island Experience," 624.
28. In 1874, this congregation merged with Sons of David to become Congregation Sons of Israel and David. In 1877, when it joined the Union of American Hebrew Congregations, it became one of the first Reform congregations in New England. In 1911, after erecting its second synagogue in South Providence, the congregation became widely known as Temple Beth-El.
29. Levy belonged to Brown's Jewish fraternity. See George M. Goodwin, "The Brothers of Phi Epsilon Pi," *The Notes* 14, no. 1 (2003): 127–47.
30. See Judith Kapstein Brodsky, "Kappy and Stella," *The Notes* 14, no. 2 (2004): 304–21; Jonathan Kapstein, "Captain John J. Kapstein, U.S. Army Air Force: In War and Peace," *The Notes* 17, no. 4 (2018): 664–80.
31. See Jay Barry, "Israel J. Kapstein of Brown," *The Notes* 14, no. 2 (2004): 281–303. This article was a shortened version of a chapter in the author's book, *Gentlemen Under the Elms* (Providence, RI: Brown Alumni Monthly, 1982), 94–109.
32. Two of Rabbi Braude and Prof. Kapstein's collaborative translations were *Pesikta-de-Rab Kahana: R. Kahana's Compilation of Discourses for Sabbaths and Festal Days* (Philadelphia: Jewish Publication Society of America, 1975) and *Tanna Debe Eliyyahu: The Lore of the School of Elijah* (Philadelphia: Jewish Publication Society of America, 1981). The first volume won the 1976 National Jewish Book Award for English translation. Rabbi Braude's earlier translation was *Pesikta Rabbati: A Translation from the Hebrew*, 2 vols. (New Haven, CT: Yale University Press, 1968).
33. The book was published as William G. Braude, *Jewish Proselytizing in the First Five Centuries of the Common Era: The Age of the Tannaim and Amoraim* (Providence, RI: Brown University Press, 1940). See "Bibliography of Selected Publications"

in Rabbi Braude's Festschrift: Herman J. Blumberg and Benjamin Braude, eds., *"Open Thou Mine Eyes . . .": Essays on Aggadah and Judaica Presented to Rabbi William G. Braude on His Eightieth Birthday and Dedicated to His Memory* (Hoboken, NJ: KTAV Publishing, 1992), xiii–xx. His eighth publication was a book review, consisting of five paragraphs, in the April 1943 issue of *Rhode Island History*. Perhaps this was an appropriate length for Samuel Broches's *Jews in New England* (New York: Bloch, 1942), a two-volume set that ran only 148 pages. Beth-El's spiritual leader did reveal some of his humorous side when he stated, "Now this reviewer is temperamentally incapable of excitement over candles, spermaceti and molasses with which many of the documents published in the Broches monograph deal. . . . But since he cannot follow the complexities of a simple business contract he is quite baffled by the give-and-take in letters exchanged among canny Jewish and Yankee traders," 67.

34. For more details about RIJHA's founding and evolution, see Geraldine S. Foster, "In the Beginning: How Our Association Grew and Took Root," *The Notes* 61, no. 2 (2012): 387–91.
35. William G. McLoughlin, *Rhode Island: A Bicentennial History* (New York: W.W. Norton, 1978); *Rhode Island: A History* (New York: W.W. Norton, 1986).
36. Freda Egnal, "An Annotated Critical Bibliography of Materials Relating to the History of the Jews in Rhode Island, Located in Rhode Island Depositories (1678–1966)," *The Notes* 4 (1966): 305–6.
37. Richard K. Showman, Margaret Cobb, Robert E. McCarthy, and Dennis M. Conrad, eds., *The Papers of General Nathanael Greene*, 13 vols. (Chapel Hill: University of North Carolina Press for the Rhode Island Historical Society, 1971–2005).
38. Glenn W. LaFantasie, ed., *The Correspondence of Roger Williams*, 2 vols. (Providence, RI: Brown University Press, 1988).
39. See George M. Goodwin, "Woonsocket's B'nai Israel," *Rhode Island History* 58 (February 2000): 3–21.
40. Fishman became the director of the Maine State Museum, in Augusta, where he continues to serve. A more recent Jewish member of the Historical Society's staff is Becca Bender, a film curator and archivist, who arrived in 2018. The newest Jewish member of the staff is Deborah Krieger, the exhibit and program coordinator at the Museum of Work and Culture in Woonsocket.

41. In 2011, Brown's Warren Alpert Medical School (named for its Jewish benefactor) relocated nearby, to a former jewelry factory, once one of the world's largest. It had been owned and operated by the Briers, a prominent Jewish family.
42. George M. Goodwin, "The Design of a Modern Synagogue: Percival Goodman's Beth-El in Providence, Rhode Island," *American Jewish Archives Journal* 45, no. 1 (1993): 31–71. I have published many articles on synagogue architecture.
43. At the association's annual meeting in 1999, for example, Albert T. Klyberg, the director of the Rhode Island Historical Society, offered: "A Rhode Island Historian Looks at the *Rhode Island Jewish Historical Notes.*" After examining every article published in the journal since 1954, he was the only historian or writer to render a comprehensive opinion. More generous than critical, he called the journal "a true Thanksgiving Feast." See *The Notes* 13, no. 1 (1999), 9.
44. The anthology included several appendices and other research aides including a timeline of Rhode Island Jewish history and a bibliography of notable references, with an abbreviated, topical guide to articles published in *The Notes*. No less important were the texts of two canonical letters penned in 1790: Moses Seixas's to George Washington and the president's reply.
45. Goodwin and Smith, eds., *The Jews of Rhode Island*.

3

Western States Jewish History Association

An Analysis

JONATHAN L. FRIEDMANN

The Western States Jewish History Association (WSJHA), as it came to be known in the 1980s, shares many traits with other Jewish historical societies. The association split from the Southern California Jewish Historical Society (SCJHS), which was formed in anticipation of the 1954 tercentenary celebration of the first Jewish community in what became the United States and the centenary of the Hebrew Benevolent Society, the first Jewish organization in Los Angeles. Its mission is to reconstruct, preserve, and disseminate a "collective memory" for Jews west of the Mississippi. Its archives, publications, and presentations are aimed at instilling a sense of local and regional pride. To that end, its research—like that conducted by many similar groups—centers primarily on heroic portrayals of successful ancestors, with little attention to character flaws or flawed characters.

However, as much as WSJHA represents the ethos and aims of Jewish historical societies—and is thus a worthy case study for this book—two aspects make it distinct. First, rather than organizing public events, offering community programs, or engaging in local advocacy, the main function of WSJHA has been the publication of articles in *Western States Jewish*

History (formerly *Western States Jewish Historical Quarterly*). This emphasis reflects the interests of Norton B. Stern (1920–1992), the quarterly's founding editor and a pioneer amateur historian of Jewish California. Stern conceived the journal as an outlet for his own extensive research and, through the years, he attracted articles from a cadre of mainly nonprofessional historians, the most prolific of whom was Stern's associate Rabbi William M. Kramer (1920–2004). In many ways, the association *is* the journal, and vice versa.

The second distinction is geographical. When WSJHA contentiously broke from the SCJHS in 1983, the new association positioned itself as "pan-local" or "pan-regional": rather than concentrating on one city or state, its net was cast across the American West, including the Midwest, and eventually spread to parts of Mexico, Canada, and the Pacific Rim. While this coverage is beneficial in terms of widening the scope of subjects and deepening the pool of potential readers and contributors, it is less successful in promoting community efforts or drawing attention to local or regional causes—tasks left to more localized and activity-oriented groups.

Western States Jewish History was published quarterly for five decades (1968–2018). Created by and for a lay audience, its articles generally display a "documentarian" or "data collection" approach, presenting facts with little analysis or contextualization. Favoring narrative over theory and clarity over jargon, the journal accomplished its goals of providing lay readers with little-known facts, highlighting achievements of ancestors, instilling a sense of place, and strengthening "Jewish pride." As appealing as this was to subscribers, trained historians tend to be dismissive or highly selective in their use of the quarterly's fifty volumes, which comprise a mixed bag of short biographies and location profiles, longer descriptive pieces, reprints of newspaper accounts and other primary sources, and an assortment of memoirs and reminiscences.

This scholarly-amateur divide will be examined in some detail. However, it is instructive to acknowledge the journal's nonprofessional goals and readership and the success of this approach in sustaining the publication over the decades. Moreover, the journal began at a time when academics generally ignored Jewish history in the American West. Without the painstaking work of Stern and his colleagues to piece together this history—however lacking by today's standards—we would know significantly less about the area's pioneer-era Jews and Jewish institutions.

WSJHA has made inroads into academia in more recent years. In the early 2000s, WSJHA entered formal relationships with local museums and academic institutions where its archives are currently housed. In 2013, the association created an online museum, the Jewish Museum of the American West, to make its research more accessible to historians and the general public. The slow march to academic status continues with *Western States Jewish History*, which was relaunched in 2020 as a peer-reviewed, biannual journal.

This chapter is divided into three sections. The first documents the formation, development, and agendas of the Southern California Jewish Historical Society, which began in 1952 and published *Western States Jewish Historical Quarterly* from 1968 to 1983. Section two documents the emergence of WSJHA, assesses the work of Stern and Kramer, and chronicles the quarterly's continuation as *Western States Jewish History*. The third section looks at how the journal has been received and utilized in lay and professional circles. What results is a view of WSJHA as a characteristic Jewish historical society, with all the passion, purpose, benefits, biases, pitfalls, and possibilities that such groups exhibit.

Southern California Jewish Historical Society

Ten men gathered at the Westwood, Los Angeles, home of Justin G. Turner on December 2, 1952.[1] Seemingly constructed to emulate a Jewish prayer quorum (*minyan*), the group's sacred task was the recovery, preservation, and dissemination of local Jewish history. Turner had three motivations for convening the group. First, he felt that local members of the American Jewish Historical Society (AJHS) should do more to encourage Southern Californians to join the national organization. Second, the group should actively gather historical records and firsthand testimonies of pioneer Jews of the area, only a few of whom were still living at the time. Third, the approaching tercentenary of Jewish communal life in America (1654–1954) and centenary of the founding of the Hebrew Benevolent Society of

Los Angeles (est. 1854) should be used to springboard the creation of a permanent group. Two months later, the nascent Southern California Jewish Historical Society (SCJHS) was recognized as a regional affiliate of AJHS.[2]

Justin G. Turner's eclectic interests, civic commitments, and affluence were illustrative of SCJHS's inaugural cohort. Born in Chicago in 1898, Turner earned a law degree from DePaul University and practiced in Chicago until 1943. His work with Town Investments, which had offices in Chicago and Los Angeles, brought him to Southern California, where in 1950 he founded Turner Investments in the Westwood neighborhood of Los Angeles. Biographical summaries describe Turner as an "attorney, investment executive, historian, author, and collector of Lincolniana [materials related to Abraham Lincoln]."[3] Each of these descriptors holds an array of activities, affiliations, and accomplishments. For example, his interest in Lincoln and the American Civil War led him to the editorial board of *Civil War History*, the presidency of the Manuscript Society and the Civil War Roundtable of Southern California, chairmanship of the Civil War Centennial Association of California and the Lincoln Sesquicentennial Association of California, vice presidency of the Lincoln Civil War Council, and honorary membership in the National Civil War Centennial Commission.[4] In April–May 1960, the San Francisco Public Library exhibited items from Turner's extensive collection of Lincolniana.[5] In January 1963, Turner organized a Los Angeles exhibit of materials pertaining to the role of Jews in the American Civil War, cosponsored by SCJHS and the Civil War Centennial Association.[6] His widely cited book, *Mary Todd Lincoln: Her Life and Letters*, co-authored with his daughter-in-law Linda Levitt Turner, is considered among the 100 essential Lincoln books—a significant achievement considering that more than 15,000 books and pamphlets have been published on Lincoln.[7]

Turner's antiquarian collecting went beyond America's sixteenth president. His autograph collection, maintained at the Library of Congress, includes notes, correspondences, memoranda, and printed materials relating to the signers of the Declaration of Independence as well as letters between Turner and President Harry S. Truman.[8] His photographs of Robert Louis Stevenson from his infancy to his call to the Scottish bar (c.

1875) were gifted to Yale University, along with related manuscripts, memorabilia, and printed materials.[9] In commemoration of Jewish Book Month in 1955 (November 15–December 15), Turner loaned rare *Haggadot* to the University of California, Los Angeles (UCLA) library for display.[10] He also acquired fragments believed to have originated from the Cairo Genizah.[11]

Turner recruited Marco R. Newmark as honorary president of SCJHS. Newmark's long list of Jewish and civic involvements rivaled that of his colleague. A descendant of a prominent Los Angeles pioneer family, Newmark held the presidency of the Southern California Historical Society, Federation of Jewish Welfare Organizations, Midnight Mission, and Los Angeles District of Zionist Organizations of America; directorship of the Conference of Christians and Jews, Jewish Home for the Aged, and Merchants and Manufacturers Association; and membership in various fraternal organizations. He also authored *Jottings in Southern California History* (1955) and, with brother Maurice, edited his father Harris's seminal memoir, *Sixty Years in Southern California, 1853–1913*.[12] Following in his family's well-connected footsteps, Newmark "was equally comfortable in a pew of a Roman Catholic Church, a pew of a Protestant Church, or in the Jewish Temple. He rallied to the cause of fellowmen, both Jewish and Gentiles, without discrimination in color or creed."[13]

Newmark was a link to Los Angeles's Jewish past. Turner, like many Angelenos, was a postwar transplant who had joined a wave of westward migrants led by thousands of war veterans and their families. As the city grew, the Jewish population kept pace, multiplying from roughly 70,000 in 1930 to over a quarter million by 1948. In 1951, some 330,000 Jews were living in Los Angeles, about 40 percent of whom had, like Turner, come from Chicago.[14] Uncovering, amplifying, and identifying with Los Angeles's Jewish history was emotionally and psychologically grounding for these new arrivals, especially as the city's Jewish character was not as visible as it was in some cities they left behind. By connecting with Newmark and discovering a century of Los Angeles Jewish contributions, Turner and the other SCJHS founders could proudly call the city "home."

In addition to Turner and Newmark, the inaugural officers included vice presidents Samuel Dinin, Aaron Riche, and Philip Louis Seman, treasurer

Peter Kahn Jr., recording secretary Julius Bisno, corresponding secretary Benjamin Dwoskin, financial secretary William R. Blumenthal, archivist Rudolph Lupo, and associate archivist Jacob Zeitlin.[15] Each of these men, some older and some younger, were prominent contributors to the city's cultural and Jewish institutional life from the 1920s through the 1980s.

Russian-born Samuel Dinin (1902–2005) received a doctorate from Columbia University and taught at the Jewish Theological Seminary before arriving in Los Angeles in 1945. He played a key role in developing agencies and resources for Jewish education, such as the Bureau of Jewish Education of Greater Los Angeles, University of Judaism (including as dean), Los Angeles Hebrew High School, and the Southern California campus of Camp Ramah. He was also editor of *Jewish Education* (1961–1970), which published thirty-nine of his articles between 1933 and 1993.[16]

Aaron Riche (1883–1979), a native of Poland, made his way from the East Coast to Los Angeles by 1930. His various commitments included president of Los Angeles B'nai B'rith Lodge 487, president of the B'nai B'rith Council, president of the Los Angeles Zionist District, co-founder and vice president of the Menorah Center, national committeeman of the Zionist Organization of America, member of the mayor's Olympic Committee (1932), executive vice chairman of the United Palestine Appeal of Los Angeles, co-founder of the United Jewish Welfare Fund, co-founder of the Los Angeles Jewish Academy, executive board member of the Jewish Publication Society, and co-founder and secretary of the Los Angeles Jewish Community Council.[17]

Polish-born Philip Louis Seman (1881–1957) held positions in Jewish organizations in New York, St. Louis, and Chicago before relocating to Los Angeles in the mid-1940s. He was a board member and taught education at the University of Judaism, served as literary editor of *Jewish Heritage* (Los Angeles), was associate editor of the *Youth Leaders' Digest*, and authored several books, notably *Jewish Community Centers in Action* (1921), *Education and the Jewish Community Life* (1924), and *The Jewish Community Center* (1926).[18]

Peter Kahn Jr.'s father, Peter M. Kahn (1878–1952), was a founder of the University of Judaism and a founding member of several Los Angeles institutions, such as the Jewish Consumptive Relief Sanitarium (a forerunner to City of Hope), the Jewish Community Council, the Los Angeles Jewish Academy day school, and the Jewish Community Library. When he died, Rabbi Jacob Cohn of Sinai Temple eulogized, "The father of the city is dead."[19] Kahn Jr. continued his father's legacy as vice president of the Southern California division of the American Jewish Congress, member of the Los Angeles Jewish Community Council's Committee on Jewish Population Study (1953), and patron of the Israel Philharmonic, among other affiliations.

Julius Bisno (1911–1983), a native of Tennessee, settled in Los Angeles in 1945. He served as national executive secretary of the B'nai B'rith Youth Organization, executive secretary of the Los Angeles Jewish Community Council, executive director of the United Jewish Welfare Fund, and executive secretary of the Jewish Community Foundation of Los Angeles. Like Turner, Bisno was a collector of manuscripts. In 1971, he donated items pertaining to Jews in American government and diplomatic services to the AJHS, and donated additional manuscripts the following year, some dating to the Revolutionary War.[20]

Ohio-born Benjamin Dwoskin (1919–2013) came to Los Angeles after World War II. He was the founding general manager of Mount Sinai Memorial Park and Mortuary (est. 1953), the country's largest synagogue-owned cemetery and mortuary. He was a contributor to the widely used handbook, *A Time to Mourn, A Time to Comfort: A Guide to Jewish Bereavement and Comfort.*[21]

William R. Blumenthal (1891–1974), a native Ohioan, served as executive director of the Los Angeles Jewish Federation, board member of the University of Judaism, president of the Beverly Hills Zionist District, vice president of the Western States region of the Zionist Organization of America, research director for *Wisdom* magazine, and board member of Sinai Temple, where he chaired the library committee in 1970 and contributed some 5,000 rare items to the library, including a 1540 Great Bible (the earliest authorized English translation). The rarities were valued at over $250,000 at the time.[22] Blumenthal was also president of the Los Angeles Fellowship for Jewish Culture, which published his *Jewish Question and Answer Book* in 1957.

Rabbi Rudolph Lupo (1887–1969) held pulpits in the Midwest and Portland, Oregon, before arriving in Los Angeles, where he directed the Peter M. Kahn Memorial Library of the Jewish Federation Council. Lupo is named in the opening credits of Cecil B. DeMille's *The Ten Commandments* (1956) as one of several religious scholars consulted during pre-production and production of the film.[23]

Jacob Zeitlin (1902–1987), an independent bookseller, poet, publisher, and book reviewer, arrived in Los Angeles from Fort Worth, Texas, in 1925 and opened a downtown bookshop in 1927. That same year, he published his first book of poems, *For Whispers and Chants*. In 1929, Zeitlin moved his shop to a more elaborate downtown building designed by Lloyd Wright (son of Frank Lloyd Wright), which became a hub for the city's intellectuals, some of whom joined Zeitlin in publishing *Opinion*, an influential but short-lived magazine (1929–1930).[24] In 1948, Zeitlin and his wife, Josephine Ver Brugge, moved the shop into a large red barn on La Cienega Boulevard, where they sold rare books, prints, and paintings. Zeitlin helped bring numerous collections to UCLA, including the Grunwald Graphic Arts Collection, and donated several manuscripts to the university's special collections department.

This accomplished group more than satisfied Jacob Rader Marcus's recommendation that local Jewish history societies include a rabbi, an educator, a historian, a publisher, and a lawyer.[25] Their various roles, connections, communal services, and intersecting commitments made them ideal candidates to form the first local chapter of AJHS,[26] and act as effective "public awareness" leaders.[27]

The SCJHS archive was initially located in the Jewish Community Library at the Los Angeles Community Council building, which opened in 1951 at 590 Vermont Avenue. This, too, was a natural fit. Not only did the building have offices for forty Jewish community agencies, but when the Community Council was formed in 1934—primarily in response to the rise of the Nazis and emergence of local sympathizers—Marco Newmark and Aaron Riche were among its founders. Julius Bisno, who became the Community Council's assistant executive secretary in 1945 and executive secretary in 1950, was instrumental in securing a place for the archives. In 1959, the Council merged with the Federation of Jewish Welfare Organizations, becoming the Los Angeles Jewish Federation Council. The organization would later become the Jewish Federation of Greater Los Angeles, with its offices at 6505 Wilshire Boulevard. Until 2009, that building housed the Peter M. Kahn Jewish Community Library, which contained the Julius Bisno Los Angeles Jewish Archives of SCJHS. The library and archive, comprising thousands of manuscripts, documents, community records, and photographs from the 1800s to the present, have since moved to American Jewish University, formerly the University of Judaism.[28] As of this writing, most of the materials are awaiting processing.[29]

Through SCJHS, Turner advocated for the preservation of local history and encouraged others to accumulate private letters and family records from prominent and lesser-known figures.[30] His correspondences with people such as Helen Keller and journalist Dorothy Thompson are of historical value.[31] This advocacy dovetailed with his efforts to preserve local history. In October 1952, two months before forming SCJHS, Turner delivered an address titled "Manuscripts and History" at the annual meeting of the American Association for State and Local History in Houston, Texas.[32] His commitment to the Jewish community, both local and national, was evident in his co-chairmanship of the B'nai B'rith Committee on Jewish Americana, trusteeship of the National Federation for Jewish Culture and the Jewish Publication Society, and service on the board of governors of the University of Judaism.

In conjunction with Los Angeles Jewry's centennial celebration in 1954, SCJHS reprinted the constitution and by-laws of the city's Hebrew Benevolent Society, copies of which it distributed at its annual meeting.[33] The document was doubly significant for Turner. Not only did the 1854 founding of the Hebrew Benevolent Society solidify the Jewish presence in Los Angeles, which had been minuscule and directionless since the first known Jew arrived in 1841,[34] but it was also aided by Solomon Nuñes Carvalho, a Charleston, South Carolina–born Jew of Sephardic descent who came west as a photographer with Colonel John Charles Frémont's fifth expedition.[35] Just the second Jew recorded to have crossed the Rocky

Mountains into California,[36] Carvalho arrived in Los Angeles in June 1854. During his three-month stay, Carvalho helped Sephardic brothers Joseph and Samuel Labatt, also originally from Charleston, organize the Hebrew Benevolent Society—the city's first chartered nonprofit charity.[37] Turner was a joint owner of Carvalho's 1865 oil painting, *Abraham Lincoln and Diogenes*, which was gifted to Brandeis University in 1958.[38] In a pamphlet commemorating Lincoln's sesquicentennial and the Brandeis gift, Turner wrote: "My interest in Solomon Nuñes Carvalho stems from two sources. First, he was the only Jewish personage of prominence who visited the West Coast in the early 1850s. Second, his portrait of Abraham Lincoln dated 1865, is the only known portrait of Lincoln by a contemporary Jewish artist."[39]

This statement, ostensibly connecting Turner's passions for Lincoln and Los Angeles Jewish history, reveals a bias shared by many local history organizations, Jewish and otherwise. Focusing on Carvalho as a "personage of prominence" set a template for the majority of papers and monographs the group would publish. Jews who "made it," especially financially, would be held up as exemplars of the Jewish experience in Southern California, usually with an accompanying impulse to overlook flaws of character or deed. While Turner and others called for the preservation of stories representing the range of Jewish "pioneers"—famous, unknown, and in between—their work largely centered on "great men," and, occasionally, "great women."

This approach had precedence in Los Angles history writing. For the nation's centennial in 1876, J. J. Warner, Benjamin I. Hayes, and Joseph Pomeroy Widney were commissioned to write a book-length history of Los Angeles.[40] Printed by Louis Lewin, a Jewish Prussian-born print shop proprietor, the volume unequivocally celebrated the city's population growth, economic development, and rise in national stature without a word on distasteful topics, blemishes, or unchecked violence, such as the infamous Chinese Massacre just five years earlier.[41] Unsavory subject matter would have reflected poorly on the city and its enthusiastic boosters. Decades later, in 1913, Jewish bandleader Abraham Frankum Frankenstein and clothing store owner F. B. Silverwood wrote "I Love You,

California," which eventually became the official state song.[42] The song was popularized by Mary Garden, who opined that it "[took] the kinks out of everyday business cares, and smooths, and makes straight perplexing social curves."[43] Among the uncomfortable "social curves" were the city's multiethnic history, widening economic inequalities, and increasing multiculturalism—all of which countered the boosteristic portrait of Los Angeles as an Anglo paradise. Historian Robert R. Dykstra called this attitude a "taboo on social conflict."[44]

Roseate tendencies are common among writers of local Jewish history, who often serve as defenders of their people and communities. For SCJHS, not only was instilling "tribal pride" an implicit goal, but most of the early officers and members were themselves Jewish men of prominence who sought out their own spiritual ancestors. Harvard historian Oscar Handlin cautioned against this habit in a 1948 article for *Commentary* magazine:

> [To] be written right, the history must be freed of the burden of a defensive attitude. It must cease to be apologetic; it cannot afford to be distorted by the necessity for justification. The approach must be open and unhackneyed. Leaving behind the respectably heroic individuals, it will rather seek the key to the past in the struggles of the great mass of humble men and women who tried to carry across the ocean a tradition embodied in a way of life.[45]

The third annual meeting of SCJHS, held in December 1956, featured an address by Rabbi Edgar F. Magnin, who had been rabbi of Wilshire Boulevard Temple since 1915, when it was called Congregation B'nai B'rith, and remained in that post until his death in 1984. (The congregation moved to Wilshire Boulevard in 1929 and was soon after renamed Wilshire Boulevard Temple.) Known as the "Rabbi to the Stars" and the "gentiles' favorite Jew,"[46] Magnin lived among movie moguls in Beverly Hills and was a familiar presence in the city's elite circles. In talks to service clubs and liberal organizations, radio appearances, and his regular column in the *Los Angeles Herald-Examiner*, "Dr. Magnin Says," the rabbi emphasized Jewish contributions in Los Angeles. In doing so, he bolstered Jewish audiences and acted as a "cultural broker" between Jews and non-Jews—goals shared by SCJHS.[47] Magnin, like Turner, was a model successful Western Jew.[48] However, unlike Turner, Magnin was a California native whose grandparents founded the San Francisco–based I. Magnin department store chain—a fact that made him all the more appealing to SCJHS members.

It was also announced at the 1956 meeting that a historical marker would be placed at the original site of Congregation B'nai B'rith at 218 South Broadway, built in 1873. The site was recognized as the first permanent home of Southern California's first Jewish congregation, which was incorporated in 1862. Identifying "first" Jews and "first" Jewish institutions would be a running theme of the society's projects, presentations, and publications. While Congregation B'nai B'rith undoubtedly deserves recognition as the first institution of its kind—or at least the first successful attempt[49]—one of the "Marcusian Laws" of Jacob Rader Marcus was to avoid claiming that someone or something was the first: "The minute that sentence was uttered, he would solemnly warn, someone would inevitably prove that there was another Jew who merited that historical distinction!"[50] Nevertheless, drawing attention to the presumed first Jew or first Jewish institution in a locality, especially if generations earlier, is an effective way of declaring "we have a history."

Furthermore, from its inception, Congregation B'nai B'rith/Wilshire Boulevard Temple attracted the city's "German Jews," a reference to status, wealth, and decorum that did not always or necessarily denote place of origin (a reality complicated by the nature of political structures in mid nineteenth-century Europe). Handlin observed that Yiddish- or German-speaking Jews in the United States before 1880 were often recognized as (or called themselves) "German," whether they hailed from Galicia, Posen, Prussia, Bavaria, Bohemia, Alsace, Holland, or someplace else.[51] In contrast to later Eastern European arrivals, who tended to settle in working-class neighborhoods—notably Boyle Heights (which, unlike many Los Angeles neighborhoods, did not have restrictive housing covenants prohibiting "non-whites")—the Jews of B'nai B'rith were, according to Neal Gabler, "by and large a moneyed bunch who regarded themselves as genteel and felt they had much more in common with other American elites than with their coreligionists."[52] During the early decades of the twentieth century, Hollywood Jews, who were largely "Eastern European in origin, German in attitude,"[53] also joined B'nai B'rith, adding to its reputation and appeal for those desiring a feel-good story of Los Angeles's Jewish past. These successful ancestors certainly merit attention and even celebration. Yet, the sanitized way their stories were typically told ignores class and cultural divisions between German Jews and Eastern European Jews, let alone broader ethnic and racial disparities embedded in California's "sociogenetic heritage."[54] Likewise, the accounts of Jews of Boyle Heights were most often told in isolation.[55]

Despite missed opportunities, research published by SCJHS was instructive in demonstrating the fluidity of the "German" label, revealing that many who passed as German Jews were in fact of Polish origin or descent and concluding that, in the American West, "Poles were both Germanized and Americanized."[56] These observations, drawn from city records, newspaper reports, and family histories, highlight the advantages of reinventing oneself as a "German Jew," as well as the likelihood that animosity toward later arriving Eastern Europeans was exacerbated by wealthy Germanized Polish Jews who refused to be associated with their "old fashioned," working-class brethren. Yet, while these correctives are valuable, they are still lacking from an academic history standpoint. The takeaway is that Polish Jews should also be counted among those who were successful in the American West. This leaves several questions unasked and unanswered: To what extent did these Polish Jews, many of whom hailed from Prussian-occupied lands, already view themselves as "German" before arriving in the United States? Was their reinvention voluntary, necessary, or a byproduct of achieving high social standing? Did attempts at self-Germanizing ever fail or cause misgivings? Was "German Jew" understood as an ethnic identity or merely as a euphemism, affectation, or "attitude," as Gabler suggests? Did ethnically German Jews make distinctions between themselves and affluent Germanic Polish Jews? Did these distinctions matter in cities like Los Angeles, with small Jewish populations (as compared to San Francisco)?[57] What did it mean to be "German" in America prior to the unification of Germany (1871)? Did the designation

"German synagogue" or "Polish synagogue" refer to demography or merely to the rite it followed? Did non-Jewish Polish immigrants exhibit similar patterns of identification? How did the Jews' ability to pass as "white" inform ethnic fluidity within Jewish communities?[58]

As noted, underlying such questions are insufficiently explored economic motivations and class divisions. The Germanic Jewish community habitually excluded "lesser Jews" from its social clubs and boards of directors. "Even the sick didn't mingle," writes Gabler, "because the Jewish medical community was divided between Kaspare Cohn Hospital, which had been established by the German Jews, and Mt. Sinai, which was supported by Eastern Europeans."[59] Rather than conjure images of a fractured Jewish community, accounts showcased successful acculturation to Anglo capitalist culture and collaborations between well-to-do Jews and Christians. However, there is little discussion of how wealthy Jews strategically supported certain Christian causes to win acceptance from Anglos but avoided less socially beneficial interreligious engagements, such as with Chinese temples or Black churches.[60] Similarly absent is discussion of the decline of (selective) Jewish-Christian activities in later decades of the nineteenth century. As the city's population expanded, churches became more insular, financially independent, and influenced by imported religious biases of Midwest Protestants.[61] Harris Newmark lamented the gradual rise of religious intolerance in his memoir:

> Speaking of social organizations, I may say that several Los Angeles clubs were organized in the early era of sympathy, tolerance and good feeling, when the individual was appreciated at his true worth and before the advent of men whose bigotry has sown intolerance and discord, and has made a mockery of both religion and professed ideals.[62]

Stephen Aron notes the proclivity of local Jewish history groups to glom onto rosy accounts. As a UCLA emeritus professor of history and current president and CEO of the Autry Museum of the American West, Aron is committed to bridging academic and public history. However, doing so requires digging deeper and sometimes asking uncomfortable questions:

> Beyond these founders of exceptional accomplishment, what can be said about the life stories of Jewish men of less substantive achievements and less substantial means? In what ways were their opportunities for economic, political, and social advancement more circumscribed? And what about the expectations and experiences of the founding mothers, daughters, and sisters of Jewish Los Angeles? These and other inquiries prompt new research that will build on what we know and bring us a still fuller picture of the beginnings of Jewish Los Angeles.[63]

Another unwritten rule of local history writing is to ignore or downplay unpleasant aspects of civic ancestors. In a lengthy and hypercritical review of *History of the Jews of Los Angeles* by Max Vorspan and Lloyd P. Gartner, published in the October 1970 issue of SCJHS's *Western States Jewish Historical Quarterly*, William M. Kramer and Norton B. Stern chided the book's surrender to a "self-deprecation motif that afflicts Jewish life."[64] The list of infractions included the "unhistoric" portrayal of banker Isaias W. Hellman as a "ruthless man,"[65] allusions to the "alleged shortcomings" of Abraham Blum, the third rabbi of Congregation B'nai B'rith,[66] identification of a Jewish woman as "the town prostitute,"[67] and brief comments on small-time criminals and shady businessmen who "were shunned by the prosperous and respectable."[68] Vorspan and Gartner surely regarded these details as responsible infusions of nuance and objectivity; but to Kramer and Stern they constituted "back-fence gossip" that sullied the Jews at large.

Kramer published a separate review (as Will Kramer) in the *Journal of the American Academy of Religion*.[69] That review is more general but just as relentless in its criticisms, confirming what others have observed about the pair: Stern was an assiduous researcher who prepared meticulous notes (such as those enumerated in the quarterly's review), while Kramer was an opinionated scribe with acerbic tendencies.[70] Whereas Stern frequently wrote articles and letters to editors correcting errors in the work of others,

Kramer painted history in broad strokes, teasing out useful lessons or allegories and occasionally making mistakes in the process.[71] For comparison, Stern later authored an article correcting "errors and omissions" in biographies of Judah L. Magnes, a prominent San Francisco–born rabbi and activist for whom Berkeley's Judaica museum was named (Magnes Collection of Jewish Art and Life, formerly Judah L. Magnes Museum). The article showcases Stern's close attention to even the smallest detail, as well as a generally forgiving tone.[72]

The review of *History of the Jews of Los Angeles* also points to early fissures at SCJHS. Max Vorspan, a rabbi and professor at the University of Judaism, was the society's archivist and served on the journal's editorial committee at the time the review was published. Stern was the journal's editor and his writing and research partner, William Kramer, was soon to become assistant editor. The scathing review, spanning twenty pages and dealing almost entirely with inaccuracies and misrepresentations (big, small, real, and imagined), was presumably published without Vorspan's consent. As such, it resembles the "back-fence gossip" the reviewers objected to finding in the book. The "Editor's Corner" section of the following issue stated that Vorspan "utilized the analysis" in a presentation at a meeting of SCJHS, and that "continuing dialogue will surely lead to a more profound understanding of the history of Western Jewry generally and of Los Angeles in particular." It was further hoped that "Professor Vorspan will contribute historical monographic studies to the Quarterly."[73] The anticipated studies did not materialize, perhaps reflecting a more permanent rift than Kramer and Stern realized, as well as the fact that the book—which grew from Vorpsan's doctoral dissertation—was essentially a "one-off" in a career dedicated to teaching history and holding leadership roles in the Conservative movement.[74] Vorspan's research would not appear in the journal until 1994, in the form of an updated essay on modern Los Angeles originally published in the 1990–1991 supplement to the *Encyclopedia Judaica*.[75] Perhaps tellingly, the biographical note at the end of that article states that Vorspan "published his doctoral dissertation on the history of Los Angeles Jewry" but does not name the book. More important, the journal's mainly lay subscribers must have been confused by the "academic debate" put forth in the unrelenting review, which was glaringly at odds with the journal's positive portrayals and folksy aesthetic.

Even with their tendency to cherry-pick "heroes" and paint partial portraits, local histories have nevertheless informed the broader reevaluation of American Jewish history, particularly in the area of periodization. The Jewish presence in America is conventionally anchored in three immigration streams: Sephardic (1654–1820), German states (1820–1881), and Eastern European (1881–1924).[76] These phases are challenged by records of individuals and communities who settled in various localities. For instance, the majority of Jews in New York by the eighteenth century were German or Polish; there was a Polish synagogue in Boston during the 1840s; and Central European Jews continued arriving during the Eastern European wave.[77] The scheme is further modified by regional realities. According to John Livingston, a Western United States revision would discard the Sephardic period and begin with the westward movement of Jews from the Eastern United States and Europe (1848–1890), followed by a decline of westward migration and rise of Eastern European populations in the Northeast and Midwest (1890–1941), and a second westward migration and renewal of the Jewish presence in the West (1941–present).[78] Such revisions are indebted to the work of amateur historians and historical societies, whose efforts, while typically narrow in focus and light on analysis, produce raw data for trained historians such as Livingston.

Other early accomplishments of SCJHS included dedicating Hellman Way on the campus of the University of Southern California in honor of Isaias W. Hellman, one of three men who donated land for the school (the others were Orzo W. Childs, a Protestant, and John Downey, a Catholic), and presenting Marco R. Newmark, SCJHS's honorary president, with a Los Angeles City Council resolution recognizing him as a member of a prominent pioneer family.[79] This was essentially a lifetime achievement award; Newmark died three years later at the age of eighty-one.

In 1960, SCJHS assisted in the research and publication of *The Jews of California: From the Discovery of Gold until 1880* by Rudolf Glanz (1892–1978), a Vienna-born and educated historian who, after his arrival in the United States in 1938, helped pioneer the field of American Jewish history.[80] This volume is arguably the earliest book-length treatment of the beginnings of California Jewry.[81] The aforementioned *History of the Jews of Los Angeles*, published in 1970, is perhaps the second (although more localized), and was similarly assisted by SCJHS. In a review of *The Jews of California*, Samuel Denin noted that Glanz did not have the same access to Los Angeles materials as Vorspan but nevertheless provided valuable insights into the nature and origin of Jewish immigration to California, Jewish life in San Francisco, Jewish involvements in the mining regions, interactions between Jews and non-Jews, and the roles Jews played in the state's social, economic, and political life.[82]

In 1962, Justin Turner became president of the Historical Society of Southern California, an organization he had served as vice president since 1957. By the 1960s, his role at SCJHS had changed to honorary president. Perhaps his most pertinent contribution to local Jewish history was his 1964 article, "The First Decade of Los Angeles Jewry: A Pioneer History, 1850–1860," which was reprinted as a 44-page booklet with images and manuscript reproductions, including the Hebrew Benevolent Society's constitution and by-laws.[83]

Western States Jewish History Association

SCJHS remained active through the 1960s with public exhibits and meetings featuring lectures by local professors and Jewish leaders. Toward the end of the decade, attention shifted to the publication of original research. Norton B. Stern, an optometrist, religious school principal (Beth Sholom Temple of Santa Monica), and pioneer amateur historian of Jews in the American West, approached the society with the idea of starting a quarterly journal.[84] He had apparently been looking for a venue to launch the project and saw SCJHS as a logical choice.[85] Coming in the exuberant aftermath of the Six-Day War and inspired by the decade's ethnic pride movements, the time seemed ripe for a journal whose implicit message was one of "Jewish pride." Starting with $500 and sponsorship from SCJHS, Stern would edit ninety-three issues before his death in 1992—the last one while seriously ill.[86]

October 1968 saw the first issue of *Western States Jewish Historical Quarterly*, copyrighted by SCJHS. Officers listed in the initial issue included six founders: Justin G. Turner, honorary president; William R. Blumenthal, president; Samuel Dinin, vice president; Aaron Riche, vice president; Benjamin Dwoskin, financial secretary; and Julius Bisno, treasurer. To them were added vice president Max Bay, a surgeon and past president of the Jewish Federation Council, vice president Rabbi Alfred Gottschalk, dean of the Los Angeles campus of Hebrew Union College–Jewish Institute of Religion (and later president of the HUC–JIR system, 1971–1996), archivist Max Vorspan, recording secretary Aviva Namir, and corresponding secretary Yolanda Frommer.

The journal's mission was almost identical to that of the Western Jewish History Center, established at the Judah L. Magnes Museum in Berkeley a year earlier. Although they did not formally collaborate, Stern shared a vision and drive with the center's founder, Seymour Fromer, a Bay Area educator who also co-founded the Magnes Museum with his wife, Rebecca Camhi Fromer, in 1962. (The word "States" was apparently added to the journal's title at the request of Fromer and historian Moses Rischin to distinguish it from a publication of the Western Jewish History Center.)[87] Fromer created the center "to collect, preserve, and provide access to archival and oral history documentation about the Jewish community in the American West."[88] Stern's journal was "dedicated to the discovery, collection, and dissemination of items and information pertaining to the Jewish experience in the American West."[89] The key distinction was that the Berkeley center was conceived, first and foremost, as a research archive, while Stern was almost singularly interested in publishing research articles. Stern and his partner, Rabbi Kramer, made regular trips to the Berkeley archive, and there was evidently no competition between the two projects.[90] Ruth Rafael, librarian and lead archivist at the center, indexed the quarterly journal issues when they arrived. She also contributed occasional updates on the center's acquisitions to the journal.[91]

Despite the titular aim of exploring the trans-Mississippi West, the first four issues (vol. 1) of *Western States Jewish Historical Quarterly* contain six articles on Southern California, six on Northern California, one on Arizona, and one on New Mexico. The California focus was as natural as it was necessary. Before Stern entered the scene, studies on California's

Jewish history were sparse, mostly obscure, and hardly known outside the region. In a paper surveying local Jewish history writing in the United States between 1946 and 1959, historian Abraham G. Duker dismissed California with a single sentence: "No research article has been published on California, with the exception of a biographical item."[92] In a footnote, Duker acknowledged the upcoming publication of Glanz's *The Jews of California*, calling it "a basic contribution to the history of the Jews in this area during the foundation years of the Jewish community of California."[93] This appraisal tells us more about Duker's unfamiliarity with California material than it does about regional history efforts. As a New York–based scholar, Duker exhibited an East Coast bias that permeated (and still permeates) the study of Jews in America. His appraisal of California Jewish history writing is contradicted by a more inclusive bibliography, compiled by Stern and Kramer for the *Southern California Quarterly*, that lists nineteen sources for the period of 1946 to 1959.[94]

In 1967, Stern published *California Jewish History*, an extensive annotated bibliography of over five hundred books, periodicals, and unpublished works covering the Gold Rush through the post–World War I period.[95] The book catalogues Stern's notes on sources he discovered at nineteen locations across the state: museums, archives, historical societies, colleges, universities, and public and private libraries. Although the volume contains over 500 entries, just a handful of the cited books deal exclusively with Jewish people, organizations, or institutions, such as a 1922 biography of Sacramento business and agricultural leader David Lubin.[96] More common are texts that make some reference, big or small, to Jews or Jewish activities in the state. Stern's annotations highlight these sections, as well as where the books could be found. For example, his summary of *My Seventy Years in California, 1857–1927*, the autobiography of J. A. Graves, a non-Jew, notes:

> These memoirs contain many references to Jews of both San Francisco and Los Angeles. It has photographs of several of these figures. The author was particularly close to the Hellman family. He succeeded Isaias W. Hellman as president of the Farmers and Merchants Bank

of Los Angeles. (See pages 89–96, 316–319, 425–430, etc.). SMPL, LAPL, NBS.[97]

The listed articles and unpublished works, totaling 167, focus more directly on Jews and Jewish activities. Mostly biographical in nature, the sources profile individuals, congregations, and organizations in different parts of the state. Two dozen articles are "in memoriams," while the rest are individual and group biographies, histories of synagogues, cemeteries, and businesses, and accounts of specific events and episodes. Roughly thirty of the articles were eligible for Duker's survey, having been published between 1946 and 1959, including a study of Jewish farming in California and essays on Jews of Los Angeles, Hollywood, and San Francisco.[98] Among the unpublished works are genealogical records, Stern's interviews and travel logs, and a handful of theses and dissertations, including Vorspan's doctoral dissertation, "History of the Jews in Los Angeles, 1850–1900" (1961). Reviewing the bibliography, Rev. Francis J. Weber, archivist for the Archdiocese of Los Angeles, affirmed key statements made in the book's introduction:

> Even a cursory reading of the titles in this handsomely bound volume will force agreement with the compiler's observation that "the story of the Jewish citizens of California yields a record in which we all can take pride." It is a saga which exhibits a rich historical heritage, civic awareness, responsibility and concern with values and meaning "which have not only contributed to their own fulfillment, but have given much to the well-being of our great State."[99]

Even if Duker had referenced all relevant sources located by Stern, his conclusion would still hold: "As for geographic areas, over half the items deal with the East; the Middle West and South follow with approximately one quarter each. Only a few articles relate to the Far West and South West."[100] At a 1986 conference on Jews in the American West, sponsored by the Rocky Mountain Jewish Historical Society, Marc Lee Raphael was still imploring historians of American Judaism to look "beyond New

York."[101] In a review of New York rabbi Arthur Hertzberg's 1989 book, *The Jews in America: Four Centuries of an Uneasy Encounter*, University of Oregon professor William Toll wrote: "[Hertzberg's] field of vision rarely strays west of the Hudson. . . . Descriptions of impacted neighborhoods, apartment living, and exclusively Jewish areas of second settlement in the Bronx or Brooklyn are taken as models of Jewish living which other cities presumably replicated on a reduced scale."[102] Hertzberg was seemingly unaware of San Francisco's 140 years of Jewish history (1849–1989) or that Los Angeles was home to the country's second largest Jewish population. Eighty issues of *Western States Jewish Historical Quarterly/Western States Jewish History* had been published by 1989, along with the journals, newsletters, and books of other Jewish history groups in the region. Their collective research challenged Hertzberg's claim that Jews who arrived in America were basically all poor, Eastern European, undereducated, and huddled around New York City.

General local histories also tended to ignore the Jewish presence. The Historical Society of Southern California, which was founded in 1883 and attracted SCJHS officers to leadership roles, began publishing its journal in 1884. Despite its longevity, *Southern California Quarterly* did not pay attention to the region's Jews until after Stern launched his journal. Before 1968, *Southern California Quarterly* had just one article devoted to a Jewish subject—Marco Newmark's essay on Congregation B'nai B'rith/Wilshire Boulevard Temple—and a few passing references to Jews in topical articles, such as city builders of Los Angeles and prohibition in Southern California.[103] (Newmark's essay, published in 1956, was among those that escaped Duker's notice.) As a corrective, Stern contributed five articles and four reviews of books on Jewish subjects to that journal between 1973 and 1992. His first paper, a biographical study of Los Angeles police chief Emil Harris (appointed in 1878), coauthored by Kramer, inspired SCJHS to replace Harris's tombstone at Home of Peace in East Los Angeles with one acknowledging his place in history.[104]

SCJHS's attempts to improve the historical record were not always successful. Stern complained about the "lack of knowledge and imagination" in the design of the California bicentennial medal (1969), commemorating the 1769 founding of the first Spanish mission and permanent settlement in Alta California.[105] The medal featured the California grizzly on one side and eight figures on the other: a Franciscan father, a Native American, a Mexican vaquero, an engineer, a frontiersman, a gold miner, a farmer, and a laborer. Missing, according to Stern, was the Jewish merchant and business leader, who supplied the needs, established financial institutions, and supported the development of the state: "Perhaps our Quarterly may in some modest measure help to create a better balanced historical understanding of the history of California and the West, than was deployed by those who approved the design of this medallion."[106]

Stern devoted countless hours to researching the Jews of early American California (1850–early 1900s) in both the northern and southern regions. Born in St. Paul, Minnesota, Stern grew up in Los Angeles, attended Santa Monica City College and UCLA, and graduated from the Los Angeles School of Optometry in 1943. A self-trained and self-styled historian, he first encountered the city's submerged Jewish history on the shelves of rare book shops in the early 1960s. He next searched for Jewish references in libraries and archives across the state.[107] Through visits to cemeteries and historic sites, interviews with pioneers and their descendants, and a close reading of temple records, newspapers, and business directories, Stern developed a reputation as a founding researcher of California's Jewish history and, through the journal, the broader American West.[108] He made five California road trips between 1966 and 1967, collecting whatever information he could from whatever sources he could find, both written and oral.[109] These "treasure hunts" were the foundation for decades of research and writing. A total of 397 articles authored or co-authored by Stern would appear in the quarterly, including posthumously published interview reports and reprints of some 200 local history columns written for the *San Francisco Jewish Bulletin* (1979 to 1983). This prodigious output makes up 20 percent of the journal's total content. Additionally, Stern authored, co-authored, or edited over a half dozen books related to California Jewish history.[110]

Aside from his medical vocation, synagogue work, and research avocation, Stern was president of Jewish Family Service of Santa Monica, a board member of the Santa Monica Community Chest, a member of the Landmarks Commission of Santa Monica, and a recipient of the Man of the Year Award from the Jewish War Veterans of Santa Monica and the Solomon N. Carvalho Award from SCJHS, among other activities and accolades. Despite his organizational involvements, Stern was not known as a "joiner" but rather as someone who marched to his own drum in a "single-minded pursuit of the stories and people of the western Jewish past."[111] His modest Santa Monica home had floor-to-ceiling bookshelves and drawers brimming with books, periodicals, historical records, documents, genealogical charts, and ephemera.[112]

The lead article in the first issue of *Western States Jewish Historical Quarterly*, published in October 1968, is a profile of Marco Newmark co-authored by Justin Turner and Norton Stern. It was a fitting start, bringing together three men who have each been called "the first Jewish historian of the Southland."[113] Like most articles the journal would publish over the next fifty years, it presents biographical details in a genial and straightforward manner, providing the reader an interesting and wholesome overview of the subject but offering little in the way of conceptual or contextual layers. As one historian observes, Stern's writings "were more 'accounts' than historical arguments, relying heavily on newspapers, genealogical lineages, and personal memories rather than philosophical beliefs about historiography or historical methodology."[114] Yet, the tireless work of sifting through sources, collecting tidbits and stories, and assembling them into a cogent, chronological narrative should not go unappreciated. Although leaving something to be desired from an academic perspective, the journal excelled at offering useful "building block articles" from which scholars could create more critical and comprehensive historical analyses.[115] Hasia Diner echoes this sentiment, giving special commendation to Stern's journal:

> Local and regional Jewish historical societies have played an important role in the collection and publication of many of these sources. Their archives are rich in primary materials. Moreover, the Jewish Historical Societies of Rhode Island, Michigan, Washington, DC, and New Haven

> have also published large amounts of material. While such articles and books may not quite match a standard of professional scholarship, they are an important and immensely rich basis for research and interpretation. The *Western States Jewish Historical Quarterly* is probably the best example of popular history serving multiple purposes and demonstrating the inextricable link between the "professional" scholar and the "amateur" buff.[116]

(Diner's comments appeared before the publication of the first issue of *Southern Jewish History* [1998], a journal of academic caliber. *Rhode Island Jewish Historical Notes* has also published scholarly studies.)

The Newmark article was Turner's only contribution to the journal. Articles from two other original officers, Aaron Riche and Philip Seman, appeared in later issues, although both are posthumous reprints.[117] Subjects slowly expanded through the first five years to include Arizona, Colorado, New Mexico, Montana, Nebraska, Kansas, and Hawaii. Rudolf Glanz wrote a handful of articles for the journal in the 1970s, covering the Jewish press in pre–Civil War America, the fur and gold rushes in Alaska, early Jews of Arizona, and Jews of the Sandwich Islands.[118]

William M. Kramer (1920–2004) joined Stern as associate editor of the quarterly in spring 1971. Kramer had been an editorial committee member for a little over a year, beginning with the January 1970 issue, and had contributed two articles along with the co-authored review of *History of the Jews of Los Angeles*.[119] Two hundred sixty-eight articles written or co-written by Kramer appeared in the quarterly over the next several decades, including reprints of 124 short pieces from his column "My Shtetele California," which ran in Southern California *Heritage* newspapers from April 1970 to May 1990.[120] Kramer's writings account for about 13 percent of the journal's total content.

Kramer was a man of many careers and hobbies. An ordained Reform rabbi, Kramer served Temple Israel of Hollywood and later Temple Beth Emet in Burbank and was the founding chair of the School of Education at the HUC–JIR campus in Los Angeles. He taught at UCLA, University of Southern California (USC), and the University of Judaism and was a professor of religious studies at California State University, Northridge. Kramer had "seven degrees," including a Doctor of Hebrew Letters from Hebrew Union College and licenses to practice law (he passed the bar in 1979) and marriage, family, and child counseling (granted in 1965), although he evidently had little or no formal training in history.[121] Sporting a "rabbinic beard" and a persona that matched the image, Kramer landed rabbi roles in films and television, notably on *L.A. Law*, *Unsolved Mysteries*, and *Life Goes On*, as well as advertisements for yogurt and bagels. As a collector, Kramer claimed to have "the largest private collection in English, including volumes and fugitive clippings, on Jews in art and Jews of the West."[122] He donated rare Judaica objects to the Skirball Cultural Center in Los Angeles and Magnes Museum in Berkeley, and German Expressionist paintings to the Los Angeles County Museum of Art. Kramer's varied interests and affiliations are documented in a binder of membership cards for some forty organizations, ranging from the Esalen Institute and Archaeological Institute of America to the Los Angeles Free Clinic and Burbank Interfaith Council.

While Stern was an avid and careful assembler of historical information, Kramer was more of a generalizer. Kramer took a homiletical view of the past, drawing out or playing up positive elements to inspire present-day Jews and improve the public's perception of the Jewish people. The research and writing partnership of Stern and Kramer yielded an impressive assortment of books and articles, and both men became vice presidents of SCJHS in the 1970s (Stern in 1970 and Kramer in 1977). During that period, the journal and society were essentially synonymous: the quarterly publication occupied most of the society's attention, energy, and financial commitments. As such, Stern and Kramer became the driving forces behind SCJHS in practice if not in name.

SCJHS's community initiatives were revived in the early 1980s under its new president, Pauline Hirsh, a trailblazer in the male-dominated field of Jewish organizational work and SCJHS's first woman president.[123] A longtime "nonpaid professional," Hirsh had worked with injured servicemen during World War II, opening her Sherman Oaks home as a Red Cross center, and in the late 1950s helped organize the San Fernando

Valley Child Guidance Clinic. She established and co-directed the Jewish Community Service Center, a volunteer referral and information program that reached out to seniors in the Fairfax area, was chairwoman of the United Jewish Welfare Fund's Women's Division and president of the Southern Pacific Coast region of Hadassah, besides being involved in the Jewish Federation's Speakers Bureau and Women's Division, later serving as the Jewish Federation Council's first female vice president. Through her work with SCJHS, she came to view her volunteer spirit as an inheritance.[124] "For the Jews of Los Angeles," she explained, "it was important to be part of the total community. They used their talents . . . their sensitivity to improve the quality of life for all in Los Angeles. On the whole, we are a people who care."[125]

Hirsh instituted a regular newsletter to inform locals of the group's activities and strengthened relations with "cooperating societies," which were listed on the inside cover of the journal.[126] She organized several projects around the Los Angeles bicentennial in 1981, commemorating the September 4, 1781, founding of El Pueblo de Nuestra Señora la Reina de los Ángeles by forty-four Spanish settlers. As part of the citywide celebrations, SCJHS mounted an exhibit of photographs and memorabilia at the Jewish Federation Council building and produced a pamphlet by Reva M. Clar, a regular contributor to the journal, featuring a decade-by-decade "capsule history" of Jewish life in Los Angeles and a map of Jewish sites.[127] The society also published Stern's edited book, *The Jews of Los Angeles: Urban Pioneers*, in conjunction with the city's bicentennial.

Three years later, Los Angeles hosted the 1984 Summer Olympics. SCJHS created an exhibit celebrating Jewish Olympic athletes. The display boasted, "since the first modern Olympics in 1896, Jews have been counted among the world's fastest, strongest, nimblest sports competitors in the world" and "have brought honor to themselves and to their country." Moreover, the exhibit proclaimed, these athletes "are a great source of pride to Jews everywhere."[128]

The quarterly began separating from SCJHS in the early 1980s. The officer list, which had appeared in the journal since 1968, started shrinking with the January 1977 issue (vol. 9, no. 4). By October 1979 (vol. 12, no. 1), only three officers were listed: president Hirsh and vice presidents Stern and Kramer.[129] The names of other board members were mixed in with ever-growing lists of "contributing editors" and "community consultants," signaling that Stern and Kramer increasingly saw the journal as an independent project that, while benefitting from SCJHS's sponsorship and subscription lists, was not guided by its board of directors. Rifts between the society and journal were deepened by the society's revitalized local efforts and the publication's emphasis on the entire American West.

In April 1983, Stern and Kramer created their organization, Western States Jewish History Association (WSJHA) and took the journal with them. According to the articles of incorporation, their main purpose was to continue publishing, although they occasionally gave lectures on related topics.[130]

> To publish a magazine and/or other scholarly, educational, and informational articles, journals, periodicals, publications, and literature concerning or pertaining to Jewish religio-communal and cognate studies, and to publish, distribute, or disseminate the magazine, and/or articles, journals, periodicals, publications, and literature published by the corporation to members of the general public, and to scholarly, educational, and religious groups who are interested in this subject matter.[131]

Tax-exempt status was granted on July 12, 1983. On the cover of the journal's next issue, published in October 1983 (vol. 16, no. 1), the name was abruptly changed from *Western States Jewish Historical Quarterly* to *Western States Jewish History*. Other features were kept the same, including format, layout, design, and the words at the bottom of the cover: "Founded by and published in cooperation with the Southern California Jewish Historical Society." Yet, the copyright was now under WSJHA, "a nonprofit corporation"—a legal designation SCJHS had never pursued, despite being over thirty years old.

Hirsh and the SCJHS board were dismayed by the incorporation of WSJHA and the changing of the journal's name. Even though Stern and Kramer were still board members of SCJHS, they apparently did not divulge their plans. Kramer, who had a reputation as "Wild Bill," was likely responsible for these behind-the-scenes maneuverings.[132] Stern was content to continue researching and writing, regardless of the journal's affiliation.

The situation came to a head in early December 1984. Stern and Kramer received a letter from Robert Louis Loeb, a pro bono attorney for SCJHS, claiming that they had unilaterally changed the journal's name without the society's knowledge, sent subscription solicitations for the "pirated" journal, and mailed offers for the sale of back issues of *Western States Jewish Historical Quarterly*.[133] The letter stated ten demands: (1) change the title to something "distinctly different" from the original; (2) change the journal's size, color, and format; (3) reset the numeration of the next volume to vol. 1, no. 1; (4) delete SCJHS as a sponsoring organization; (5) insert on the masthead page, "Not associated with the Southern California Jewish Historical Society"; (6) cease soliciting subscribers from SCJHS's lists; (7) return all back issues to SCJHS; (8) turn over all archival materials "of whatever type or nature" to SCJHS; (9) provide SCJHS an accounting of all monies received for the journal over the past five years; (10) turn over to SCJHS all funds received for solicitations and back issues. The letter continued that Stern and Kramer had "remained intransigent" despite good faith attempts by SCJHS to resolve these matters.

Stern and Kramer anticipated some of these objections. Beginning with the April 1985 issue of the retitled journal (vol. 17, no. 3), SCJHS was removed as a sponsoring organization and all other references to the society were erased. SCJHS officers and members were removed from the journal's list of editorial consultants and community advisors, although some with research interests, including Vorspan, stayed on. However, the title, numeration, and design persisted, and physical aspects would not change until the journal switched printers in 1992.[134] Most egregious was the insinuation that the pair had been keeping subscription funds and archival materials for themselves and had been doing so for years. Stern probably acquired documents, photographs, artifacts, and testimonies from individuals who expected them to go into the SCJHS archives but were instead kept at his home.[135] Possible financial improprieties are less clear, but given that subscriptions were the group's main revenue source and that other activities had been "moribund," this was a serious matter.[136] Still, the poor accounting and lack of transparency were likely not nefarious in nature. The society's structure was informal: there were no clear lines separating the society from the journal or determining where the funds were supposed to go.

Stern and Kramer had letters sent in response.[137] Signed by Michael B. Weisz, who worked at Fisher and Moest with Kramer, the letters argued that SCJHS only sought nonprofit status in response to WSJHA's incorporation:

> Out of whole cloth, your client invented ownership, and based on this nonexistent ownership, imagined a right to control, thereby causing grievous emotional harm though forewarned, interference with protective business advantage, and injury to reputation. This appears to be an ongoing campaign by both an individual or individuals and a now-incorporated institution.[138]

The letters, perhaps ghostwritten by Kramer, asserted that the journal was "never under the financial control" of the previously "unincorporated or informal group of individuals then conveniently known as the Southern California Jewish Historical Society," nor did SCJHS control editorial, archival, or printing aspects, which were headquartered at a separate location (Stern's home). Furthermore, the letter writer claimed, SCJHS only became interested in these matters after WSJHA incorporated and took the journal with it.

Hirsh authorized a formal complaint alleging trademark infringement and unfair competition, but this stalled in the draft stage.[139] She also sent a notice to SCJHS members in May 1984 detailing the perceived betrayal of the organization. WSJHA decided not to respond "in order to avoid fueling any flames of animous [*sic*], scandal or disunity to our already fragmented community."[140] Both sides eventually agreed that litigation was not advisable and that the matter should be resolved privately to "avoid any possible embarrassment to the historical and Jewish communities."[141] Fred Rochlin, an SCJHS board member and occasional contributor to the journal, was especially invested in maintaining civility, as he and his wife, Harriet, relied on Stern's archives and expertise for their studies of pioneer Jews in the American West.[142] For their part, WSJHA was prepared to offer research assistance to SCJHS "without fee or other consideration," so long as they were allowed to continue "serv[ing] the readership which it enjoyed since Vol. 1, No. 1."[143]

After Stern and Kramer left SCJHS, the society attempted a journal of its own, *Legacy: Journal of the Southern California Jewish Society*. However, the society remained focused on public programs, special exhibits, and community work, and just one volume was produced, spread over four years (1987–1990).[144] Three of the four issues are single-author monographs, including one by Hirsh on Jews in the Los Angeles apparel business.

In 1985, SCJHS was involved in the Fairfax Community Mural, painted on an exterior wall of Canter's delicatessen. Established in Boyle Heights in 1931, Canter's has occupied its current site, the former Esquire Theatre, since 1953. The seven-panel mural was painted by prolific Southern California muralist Art Mortimer with assistance from Steven Anaya and Peri Fleischman and additional help from Fairfax High School students and local senior citizens. SCJHS joined the youth department of the Jewish Federation and the Vitalize Fairfax committee in sponsoring the artwork, which depicts Jewish Los Angeles from the mid-1800s to 1985. Images include Congregation B'nai B'rith and its first rabbi, Abraham W. Edelman; the Newmark family; banker Isaias W. Hellman; the original Kaspare Cohn Hospital; police chief Emil Harris; Al Jolson from *The Jazz Singer* (1927); a notice for an anti-Nazi protest; the first Canter's location in Fairfax (1948); Dodgers pitcher Sandy Koufax; and other scenes and personalities familiar to readers of the quarterly.

Attorney, lay historian, and Los Angeles native Stephen J. Sass assumed the SCJHS presidency in 1989 and has continued in that role ever since. Operating under the adjusted name Jewish Historical Society of Southern California,[145] Sass has furthered the society's aims of communal investment and education. Activities have included cosponsored programs with the Chinese Historical Society of Southern California, exhibits at the

Autry Museum of the American West, Jewish history bus tours, oral history projects, hosting the AJHS annual conference (2008), and efforts to restore the historic Breed Street Shul in Boyle Heights (1923) and original building of Sinai Temple (1909), now home to the Pico Union Project, a multifaith cultural arts center and house of worship.[146] The society's 1996 documentary, *Meet Me at Brooklyn & Soto*, about the Jewish community of Boyle Heights between the 1920s and 1950s, aired on the local Public Broadcasting Service station (KCET) and more recently on Jewish Life Television (JLTV).[147]

Norton Stern died on March 14, 1992, at age 71. Kramer replaced him as the quarterly's editor on the next issue, published the following month (vol. 24, no. 4). A short while later, Kramer recruited David W. Epstein to assist with the publication of the journal. Epstein, who studied history in college and worked as a traveling manufacturer's representative, ran a typesetting business from his Woodland Hills home. He had developed working relationships with prominent local rabbis, explaining in a tribute to Kramer:

> I began producing *Western States Jewish History* for Rabbi Kramer in 1992, shortly after the death of his associate, Dr. Norton B. Stern. That same year I began to produce *The American Rabbi*, another journal published by the now late Harry Essrig. I was also publishing books. One of them, *How to Explain Judaism to Your Non-Jewish Neighbor*, was being written by Rabbi Edward Zerin. All this work was being done in my home.[148]

In contrast to Kramer and Stern, Epstein was not attracted to historical research, although he styled himself as a "storytelling historian" and promoted the journal through entertaining lectures at synagogues and Jewish organizations. Instead, he concentrated on the physical publishing, using his own company, Isaac Nathan Publishing, to produce the quarterly until spring/summer 2018. In addition to *Western States Jewish History* and *The American Rabbi*, he printed books for local Jewish leaders.[149] Epstein wrote just one research article for the journal, a look at DUNIE's, "St. Louis'

Foremost Jewish Restaurant and Delicatessen,"[150] as well as numerous introductions to special issues, tributes to Kramer, and updates on the association.

Epstein took a "big picture" approach, leaving detailed studies for others to pursue. "My personal focus," he wrote toward the end of his tenure, "was identifying ethical characteristics and patterns of behavior of the various pioneers around the West that was not possible within the area of local Jewish historical societies."[151] According to Epstein, these attributes fall into five categories forming the acronym "I HELP": integrity (I), knowledge of Jewish history (H), education (E), multi-language ability (L), and philanthropy (P). Of course, these traits were mostly shared by those who were upstanding and successful—that is, individuals considered worthy of being featured in the journal. The association's online Jewish Museum of the American West (jmaw.org), which Epstein created in 2013 and features over 600 "exhibits" mostly drawn from the first fifty years of the quarterly journal, is organized around these five traits, as is Epstein's self-published booklet, *Why the Jews Were So Successful in the West . . . and How to Tell Their Stories.*[152]

Following Kramer's retirement in 1998, Epstein became editor of the quarterly (beginning with vol. 30, no. 3). Gladys Sturman, a local Jewish activist and educator who studied history at the University of Judaism under Kramer, became publisher and editor in chief. Sturman and Epstein oversaw an impressive twenty-year run, which included eighteen double issues—consisting of single-author local histories; collected essays on neighborhoods and counties; compilations of newspaper clippings; themed anthologies on Sephardic Jews, Jewish women, and more; Stern's interview reports; and columns by Stern and Kramer. Throughout this period, the production of the journal was essentially a "one-man show," with Epstein working strenuously from his home to maintain the publishing schedule. This came with certain drawbacks, including the decision to publish virtually every submission (no matter the quality), the reprinting of older articles when new content was in short supply, and an abundance of typographical errors.

Sturman and Epstein became co-publishers of the journal in 2017, handing editorial duties to Donald H. Harrison, veteran publisher-editor of *San Diego Jewish World*. Plans were made to convert the quarterly into an open-access online journal with volume 51 (2018–2019). The journal instead ceased publication. In 2020, *Western States Jewish History* was revived as a biannual peer-reviewed academic journal, published by Texas Tech University Press. The relaunched journal is edited by Jonathan L. Friedmann, the current WSJHA president and professor of Jewish music history and dean of the Master of Jewish Studies Program at the Academy for Jewish Religion California, a transdenominational seminary in Los Angeles. The editorial board includes academics, archivists, research librarians, and genealogists with relevant specialties.[153]

Reception of the Journal

After completing the first volume of the quarterly, Norton Stern received a congratulatory note from rabbi and historian Bertram W. Korn.[154] Along with his subscription renewal, Korn wrote:

> Within one year you have clearly forged ahead to the highest level of local Jewish historical publications. Even taking into consideration the fact that there is a certain glamour about California which the area will probably never lose, whether for those in residence or far away, nonetheless you have managed to bring into print some remarkably interesting and important studies. I join students of Jewish history throughout the country in saluting you and in wishing you well in the years ahead.[155]

Korn later encouraged Kramer and Stern to soften their absolutist portrayal of pioneer Jews as noble heroes and come to terms with the existence of less savory characters and episodes. Korn's work on Jews in the South inevitably dealt with Jewish involvement in the slave trade, albeit with a philosemitic caveat that such Jews were an exception rather than the norm.[156] Kramer and Stern would argue similarly: "On balance, there have been relatively few 'warts' in Western Jewish history, but there are some and they sometimes make for informative and interesting history."[157] This concession, while still apologetic, diverges from their criticism of Vorspan and Gartner's mention of flawed Jewish Angelenos. Although Kramer and

Stern had occasionally alluded to violent episodes, synagogue scandals, and the like, they addressed these subjects directly in a 1981 article, "Some 'Warts' on the Face of Early Western Jewry."[158] The article begins on an introspective note:

> The history of an ethnic group when written and edited by those who identify with it, must constantly be examined to be sure it meets the standard of objectivity or contains an honest and open statement of bias. There is a strong tendency to be self-congratulatory and to stress the lives of those who can be role models. Since sub-cultures are played down in or are omitted from general histories, there is a tendency for ethnic history to attempt to make the picture more complete and in compensation to present itself in the best possible light.[159]

The authors attributed this realization to Korn, who understood the public relations and self-pride motivations for downplaying less morally admirable character traits, individuals, and incidents, yet nevertheless argued that American Jewry should not engage in self-censorship. Unfortunately, the promising opening reflection gives way to five accounts of a negative nature from California periodicals, dating from 1851 to 1880, with hardly any context or analysis. It is as though Kramer and Stern felt obligated to address Korn's recommendation but did so as minimally as possible.

The quarterly approached anti-Semitism in a similar manner. While historians, both lay and professional, have remarked on the rarity of anti-Semitism in the West during the pioneer period, especially when compared to elsewhere in the country, the "oldest hatred" was never completely absent. This is acknowledged in a handful of articles that reprint, in part or in whole, anti-Jewish editorials and newspaper accounts.[160] These brief pieces are couched in reminders that there was a "low level of anti-Semitic activity and feeling" and the reassurance that "the individual [Jew] could rise above it."[161] Although these observations are generally accurate, the way they are presented leaves the reader wondering about the impact of anti-Semitism on the lives of the people involved, how widely such accounts circulated among other Jews, how the incidents compared to prejudices faced by more overtly maligned populations (Hispanics, Native Americans, Blacks, and Chinese), and so on. Moreover, the trained historian seeks to understand *why* anti-Semitism was aberrational, not just *that* it was. Was anti-Semitism mitigated by the region's cosmopolitan makeup, the founding roles of Jews in Western towns, the small number of Eastern European Jewish immigrants in the early period, or other factors?[162] The cursory accounts, reliance on quotations and reprinted newspaper items, and lack of scrutiny suggest that these were anomalies of little consequence to the heroic narrative of Western Jewish pioneers.

Stern had already dismissed Jewish "villains" and anti-Semitism in his descriptive bibliography, published a year before the quarterly began. There, he assures readers that in the early period "noted for its violence and bloodshed, Jews were among the few stable elements of the population. Both their cultural heritage and their economic position made them a most desirable element in any locality, as noted by numerous writers."[163] Stern admits "there were a few villains,"[164] but frames them as outliers and oddities. In a similar vein, he writes that while "some anti-Semitism was encountered, as a whole, California was free of its most vicious evidences. In an area like San Francisco, with a substantial Jewish population from the earliest years, Jewish people were among the most civic and culturally minded and were in the forefront of those who helped to obviate the intolerance and hate so prevalent in the Old World."[165] Again, the possible reasons for this are not adequately explored.

Individual articles from *Western States Jewish Historical Quarterly* and *Western States Jewish History* are cited in a few dozen scholarly and semi-scholarly books, as well as a few hundred academic articles, theses, and dissertations. Typically, these sources cite historical details or individuals profiled in the journal as part of a larger analytical point, or use footnotes to locate primary documents, rather than relying on the journal for conceptual input. For example, Michael E. Engh's *Frontier Faiths: Church, Temple, and Synagogue in Los Angeles 1846–1888* incorporates supporting research from several articles by Stern and Kramer into a comparative history of the city's complex ethnic, ethnoreligious, and socioeconomic tapestry.[166] Fred Rosenbaum, who co-founded the Berkeley-based education center Lehrhaus Judaica with Seymour Fromer, made similar use of the quarterly in his book, *Visions of Reform: Congregation Emanu-El and the Jews of San Francisco, 1849–1999*.[167] Despite receiving a nasty review from Stern and Kramer for his earlier book on Oakland Jewry (resembling their review of *History of the Jews of Los Angeles*),[168] Rosenbaum came to respect their research ingenuity and attention to detail.

> [I]n conducting research for this project, I was struck again and again by the invaluable contribution they and their periodical have made to our understating of the pioneer period. It is something that, in the heat of the intellectual battles I had with them as a young man, I had not fully appreciated. The fact remains that in writing the first four chapters of this book, I made use of more than two dozen articles from their publication—many of them written by Stern and Kramer themselves.[169]

Again, Rosenbaum's gratitude is for their careful documentation and retrieval of obscure sources rather than their analyses or methodologies. Ava F. Kahn, who studied with Kramer as an undergraduate at Cal State Northridge, sums up the journal's usefulness to scholars in her book, *Jewish Voices of the California Gold Rush*: "Special thanks to the former editors of *Western States Jewish History* [Kramer and Stern] for publishing primary documents."[170]

While the total number of times the journal is cited is, on the surface, impressive, it is perhaps not as large as might be expected for a journal comprising 200 issues and well over 2,000 articles. At least five factors account for this relatively small impact in scholarly circles.

First, the articles are not equal in terms of depth, sophistication, or comprehensiveness. While some are lengthy studies of a person, place, or community, at times broken into several parts spread over several issues, others are interview reports, picture stories, and newspaper reprints spanning only a few pages. As a rule, articles that only scratch the surface are not likely to be cited.

Second and relatedly is the journal's inclusiveness. Instead of a peer-review process, the journal printed a disclaimer absolving the editors of "responsibility for statements of fact or of opinion made by contributors. Statements expressed by contributors are their own views and not necessarily the views of the editor or editorial committee." It is unclear how involved this "editorial committee" was during the journal's first few decades, but Stern's careful eye and encyclopedic knowledge were usually enough to improve articles and catch mistakes (although there were occasional errors, such as incorrect names or dates). Following Stern's death in 1992, the quality and type of articles the journal published became increasingly mixed, and typographical errors became more commonplace. These issues are red flags for scholars who might otherwise benefit from the information presented.

Third, in spite of the journal's mission and prolificity over the decades, Jewish life in the Western States remains an underappreciated subtopic of American Jewish studies. Several excellent books on the topic have been published, many of which appear in this chapter's endnotes, and interest has been growing in recent years. However, this seems to be a byproduct of the overall expansion of American Jewish studies. Indeed, writings on American Jews in the West are still far outnumbered by eastern-focused studies. Following the publication of the quarterly's first issue in 1968, Stern was reportedly asked, "Where are you going to find enough material for a second issue?"[171] He found no shortage of material, but the subject matter has struggled to penetrate the American Jewish consciousness. *Jews of the American West*, co-edited by Moses Rischin and John Livingston in 1991 and drawn from a conference called by Rischin and Fromer, was arguably the first scholarly volume on the subject: the first collection of essays by noted authorities, as opposed to the "mixed multitude" of amateurs and professionals that fill the pages of *Western States Jewish History*.[172] In that volume, Livingston calls the quarterly journal "quasi-scholarly but useful."[173] Yet, the anthology's chapters make little use of the journal. Shari Rabin's *Jews on the Frontier*, a more recent scholarly book on the topic, does not cite the journal at all, though the author may have discovered primary documents through mining the footnotes.[174] If scholars of Western Jewry have routinely underutilized the journal, it is no surprise that general studies of American Jewish history—which tend to gaze eastward—would consult it even less.

Fourth, by design, most articles in the journal appealed to its primary readership, providing popular histories for lay audiences. As a letter to subscribers stated: "We publish academic type articles, memories, and other types of histories."[175] While librarians and serious researchers were part of WSJHA's network of subscribers and contributors, the journal, like the SCJHS that launched it, maintained a public advocacy focus. Contextualizing and problematizing were out of place in accounts that, by and large, provided positive and mostly unblemished stories of Jewish immigrants and their descendants. The effectiveness of this popular appeal is attested by the fact that Michael Elias and Frank Shaw, screenwriters of the cowboy and rabbi comedy *The Frisco Kid* (1979), subscribed to the journal and drew inspiration from its accounts.[176]

Fifth, as the years went on, the journal seemed to revel in its nonacademic status. Epstein frequently committed "sins" against academic norms: misspelling author names and article titles in the tables of contents; inventing variant article titles for the table of contents; reprinting articles from earlier issues—usually with altered titles, sometimes more than once, and typically without stating they were published previously; not giving authors the opportunity to review typeset proofs; not having a copyeditor; and eschewing peer review despite listing several regional "editors" and "advisors" in each issue. The lay reader might excuse these lapses in quality control, but academics are not as forgiving.

Even so, the journal is occasionally credited in major books on Jews in the West. The preface to the 2000 edition of Fred and Harriet Rochlin's *Pioneer Jews: A New Life in the Far West*, first published in 1984, states that "*Western States Jewish History* has remained a vital source of scholarly and popular inspiration. . . . Through the years, its contributors have included historians, biographers, memoirists, journalists, and frequently its longtime editors, the late Dr. Norton Stern and Dr. Will Kramer, now retired."[177] *California Jews*, a collection of scholarly essays in the mold of *Jews of the American West*, notes that "the authors have taken advantage of the *Western States Jewish Historical Quarterly* (now *Western States Jewish History*), which has since 1968 published primary documents and articles that have brought California and the Western Jewish history out of the archives and into the light."[178] Along with written information, the book includes several photographs from the WSJHA archive.

Over the years, the quarterly attracted articles from only a handful of professional scholars. These include Marc Lee Raphael, Ava Kahn, Suzanne D. Rutland, David Dalin, Marc D. Angel, Stanley F. Chyet, and William Toll. In several cases, articles from professionals were written by request or taken from pre-published works, and rarely did they add value to the contributor's curriculum vitae. Some nonacademic historians used the journal as a springboard and primary outlet for their research. Reva M. Clar (1906–1977), a former ballet dancer and a descendant of Stockton, California pioneers, was the journal's contributing editor for over two decades. Through her numerous articles in *Western States Jewish History*, Clar became a noted authority on early Stockton rabbi-cantor Herman Davidson, Placerville pioneer Samuel Sussman Snow, the "girl rabbi of the American West" Ray Frank, and other figures. The side-by-side inclusion of articles by memoirists, genealogists, hobbyists, semi-professionals, and a few professionals suggests a philosophy of mutual engagement and information sharing. However, because no effort was made to bring contributors together outside of the printed page—perhaps with the goal of improving lay history writing (as some have advocated[179])—the overall quality is of an uneven assemblage.

In 1993 (vol. 25, no. 3), the journal began publishing in association with the Skirball Cultural Center, then located on the Los Angeles campus of Hebrew Union College–Jewish Institute of Religion. This constituted WSJHA's first formal attempt to partner with an academic institution. Kramer, who had recently taken over as editor, hoped that the Skirball would grant space for the WSJHA library when the center moved to its current building in 1996. This did not occur. However, WSJHA's academic partnerships expanded in 2007 (vol. 34, no. 3), when these words were added to the front cover: "Western States Jewish History partners with the Huntington/USC Institute on California and the American West & with the Autry National Center/UCLA Center for Jewish Studies."

These affiliations resulted from WSJHA's decision to divide its archives. Shortly after Kramer's death in 2004, Sturman and Epstein began sifting through the Kramer-Stern legacy. Aided by an $18,000 grant from the Jewish Community Foundation, a $10,000 donation from Sturman, and eleven volunteers from Congregation Shir Ami in Woodland Hills (served by Max Vorspan's son, Rabbi David Vorspan), Sturman led the herculean task of organizing and boxing materials from Kramer's large Westwood home, which included the library and archive inherited from Stern.[180] Sturman and Epstein recall: "We knew that each item would have to be examined and organized in some coherent fashion. Without organization, this massive collection would never be fully accessible to scholars, students, genealogists, and others."[181] Over the next few years, WSJHA donated 4,000 archival photographs (1880–1930) to the Autry Museum, rare journals, fragile ephemera, family albums, letters, film reels, and the like to the Huntington Library, approximately 1,400 books to the American Jewish University library, and roughly 300 boxes of historical papers to the Charles E. Young Library at UCLA. Smaller donations followed, including a box of Kramer's books to the Lincoln Memorial Shrine in Redlands, California; a copy of *Lawyers of Los Angeles: A History of the Los Angeles Bar Association and the Bar of Los Angeles County* (1959) to the California Judicial Center Library, San Francisco; the scrapbook of father and son actors Rudolph and Joseph Schildkraut to the special collections at USC; and additional materials to the Huntington Library and UCLA. While the decision to donate items to prestigious institutions has helped ensure their preservation and, in some sense, bolstered the field of Western Jewish history, the scattering of materials has also made them difficult to locate or access.

Epstein viewed these gifts as "a promise completed" to Kramer, who wanted the items to be recognized and preserved by institutions of stature.[182] Seemingly in keeping with tradition, SCJHS was not consulted regarding plans to separate and house the archives at the four locations. Its disappointed president, Stephen Sass, told the Los Angeles *Jewish Journal*: "Much of the material came from members of the Jewish community, and I hope [it] might stay within the community. I hope our organization can be involved and we can work together."[183] His hoped-for partnership did not come to pass.

At the dedication ceremony at UCLA in March 2009, Sturman and Epstein explained why they partnered with academic institutions. First was the issue of organization: "In addition to over a thousand books, we inherited some three hundred boxes of loosely sorted archival material. If these were to be useful for our journal or for historians and genealogists, this material would have to be examined and organized."[184] Second was the delicate condition of much of the material: "Every piece of paper had to be examined individually, often with a magnifying glass because the photo had faded or because the newspaper was fragile. Some of the newspapers dating back to the mid-1800s were too fragile to unfold. We set these aside for professionals to handle."[185] Third was the need for cataloging: "Each piece of paper had to be read thoroughly and labeled by the name of the subject, the name of the institution, the place and date."[186] Recognizing the role of professionals in preserving local and regional histories was significant. It acknowledged the resource and financial limitations of a "hobbyist" organization and affirmed the position of Marcus that information gathered by amateur historians provides an "important stone in building the story of the Jew in this land," which can be expanded by professional historians of American Judaism and can, in turn, inform the work of general historians of the United States.[187]

Caroline Luce, then a graduate student at UCLA and now associate director of the university's Alan D. Leve Center for Jewish Studies, was tasked with processing the portion of the archive given to the Charles E. Young Library. She was initially skeptical about the collection's potential value for scholars. As a budding "real" historian, she was wary of Stern and Kramer's piecemeal methodology, as well as their uncomplicated "Frederick Jackson Turner-esque frontier thesis," in which the open geography and social arrangements laid the groundwork for unhindered Jewish success. While there is some validity to aspects of this thesis, Luce notes that its triumphalist portrayal—along with a "whitewashed" view of the region's racial and ethnic diversity—is unsophisticated and incomplete by modern standards of history writing.[188] "Kramer and Stern came to seem passé as I became a stereotypical academic, criticizing and scrutinizing the work of anyone writing history from outside the ivory tower."[189] Yet, ultimately, the amount of research Stern and Kramer achieved, however basic their techniques or analyses, tempered Luce's self-described "snootiness," and she came to see the possibilities contained in the papers she catalogued.

Sturman and Epstein alluded to these possibilities at the UCLA dedication. In describing the WSJHA's philosophy, they noted how the journal excelled at bringing together biographies of well-known, semi-known, and little-known Jews of the American West, and how the assorted accounts testified to a vibrant Jewish presence in the region since the mid-1800s. Yet, as Sturman and Epstein conceded, individual stories are raw materials awaiting arrangement into a bigger, more nuanced, picture.

> Every individual creates history. One makes a purchase and a name and the date and the delivery address are recorded in a ledger. One joins a club and the name and office and date of admission are recorded. A name will appear in a local newspaper. All of this is as much a part of history as the life of Abraham Lincoln. History is but a record of daily lives. History is also considered geographically. There is a history of America, of California, of Arizona, of San Diego County, of a village, of a city, of a school district, or a religious organization, as well as a cultural history of the American Indian, the Latino or the Jew. History is written from the bottom up. When individual and local histories are carefully compiled and written, they create a picture of life in a given period and at a given place, and their value justifies the patience and labor involved.[190]

Conclusion

From its inception, the quarterly journal took a celebratory approach, frequently presenting interesting facts and details but rarely scratching beneath the heroic surface. "Contributions" and "contributors," especially in the areas of business, banking, real estate, and politics, comprise many of the articles, with several prominent individuals, such as Isais Hellman, Kaspare Cohn, and San Francisco journalist Isidor Choynski, as repeat subjects. The pioneer period, loosely defined as the mid-1800s to the early 1900s, takes up much of the journal. Accounts of successful people and the "firsts" in various fields most often appear as hermetically sealed narratives, untainted by flaws of action or character, silent in regard to other Jews who were not as successful, fortunate, or virtuous, and untouched by wider developments of Jewish or general history. For example, only four are centered on Jewish-Christian interactions, nine address Jewish-Chinese relations, and one focuses on Jews and Blacks.[191] In each case, the story is positive or at least positively told. Just a handful of essays broach the sensitive subject of anti-Semitism, and they generally frame such animosity as anomalous—a view seemingly informed by Turner's "frontier thesis." Few comparisons are made with developments among Jews located elsewhere, both globally and in the United States.

Still, whatever conceptual or methodological objections scholars may have, the sheer number of topics and personalities covered by the quarterly is unquestionably impressive. Over 2,000 articles were published during the journal's fifty years as a quarterly. Many are richly referenced and of significant length, drawing on public records, diaries, directories, newspapers, photographs, minutes, letters, and the like. Among the longer works are thirty-one two-part articles, fourteen three-part articles, three four-part articles, two five-part articles, and one seven-part article. However, the majority are less meticulously researched and span just a few pages. These include sixty-four "picture stories" of various kinds (i.e., pictures with captions); the "Western Picture Parade" series, which ran from vol. 8 (1975) to vol. 24 (1982); sixty interview reports; twenty-one collections of newspaper clippings; numerous reprints of historical newspaper reports; 200 columns by Stern that originally appeared in the *San Francisco Jewish Bulletin*; and 124 columns from Kramer's *Heritage* newspaper series, "My Shtetele California." While this breakdown reveals some of the journal's shortcomings and missed opportunities—most of which can be excused as "coming with the territory"—there are intrinsic benefits to locating and presenting relevant historical data and accurate chronologies of the subjects explored, even if broader connections, developments, or implications are overlooked or only lightly treated.

Despite its goal of documenting Jewish life in the American West, the journal has devoted the majority of its pages to California. This is largely a consequence of the California-centrism of its founders and WSJHA's roots in SCJHS. Additionally, several western states and regions have their own Jewish historical societies with their own publications (journals and/or newsletters), making *Western States Jewish History* at best a second choice for authors in those areas. In contrast, there is no Jewish historical journal dedicated specifically to California. Relatedly, writers of local or regional Jewish history are sometimes motivated to "correct the historical record" by highlighting the role of Jews—a task arguably better served through publishing in the journals of general historical societies, such as the *Southern California Quarterly*. At the same time, serious Jewish scholars tend to aim for a wider audience of peers, publishing articles of local, state, and regional interest in well-regarded national or international Jewish journals, including the *Jewish Quarterly Review*, *American Jewish History*, *The American Jewish Archives Journal*, and *Modern Jewish Studies*.

During its initial fifty-year run (1968–2018), the journal published 1,382 pieces dealing with California locations, personalities, and experiences: 502 on the San Francisco Bay Area; 479 on Greater Los Angeles; 181 on Northern California; 174 on Southern California; and forty-six on California in general. In comparison, only sixteen focus on Alaska, fifty-three on Arizona, forty-six on Colorado, twelve on Hawaii, four on Idaho, seven on Illinois, six on Kansas, two on Louisiana, three on Minnesota, five on Missouri, eleven on Montana, twenty-one on Nebraska, nineteen on Nevada, twenty on New Mexico, fifteen on North Dakota, three on Ohio, twelve on Oklahoma, twenty-eight on Oregon, three on South Dakota, sixty-one on Texas, fourteen on Utah, fifty on Washington, and nine on Wyoming. The Midwest as a region has six, the Southwest has four, the Western States have seventy-two, the United States as a whole has nineteen, Canada has 100 (general ten, Alberta fourteen, British Columbia sixty-seven, Saskatchewan four, Winnipeg one, and Yukon four), Mexico has eighteen, and the "Pacific Rim, etc." has thirty-four (general two, Tahiti two, Australia five, New Zealand five, China eleven, Japan four, India two, Philippines one, Brazil one, and Panama one).

In a handful of articles two locations take up equal or nearly equal space: Los Angeles and San Francisco (eight); Southern California and

San Francisco (two); California and Oregon (one); Southern California and Arizona (one); San Francisco and Texas (one); San Francisco and New Mexico (one); San Francisco and Mexico (one); San Francisco and British Columbia (one); Nevada and Utah (one); Colorado and Utah (two); and Arizona and New Mexico (two).

Aside from the intended audience of those who take pride in family and communal history, celebrate Jewish achievements, and/or seek to localize their Jewish identities, the assorted articles contain potentially useful building blocks for academic studies. The journal's ambitious scope, which looks beyond what is normally considered the Western United States, is itself an interesting statement: "The West" as an idea or ideal, rather than a strictly geographic designation. This inclusiveness and the absence of a strenuous review process allowed authors to explore topics and lay groundwork in areas that professional historians might not otherwise consider. Along these lines, Gladys Sturman, who served as publisher and editor in chief from 1998 to 2017, encouraged readers to see themselves as historical figures, assuring them that they need not be expert writers to add to the collective portrait:

> *Western States Jewish History* is interested in all kinds of history. We invite readers to submit personal recollections of their early years in the West. Very often these present a picture that adds valuable insight into life in a specific area or time period. For those of you whose first response is, "I can't write," let us assure you that we will be happy to edit your article. We need information, not eloquence.[192]

The association's online Jewish Museum of the American West includes a similar notice, complete with a form for visitors to fill out.[193] This strategy agrees with Avi Decter's assessment that museums should engage visitors by encouraging them to tell their own stories in relation to the exhibits.[194] Such an approach is well suited for an online museum, where content can be expanded with ease and without brick-and-mortar concerns for space, schedules, or funding.

It remains to be seen how longtime subscribers will react to the journal's recent relaunch as a peer-reviewed publication, which introduces the critical analysis, contextualization, and academic standards that such publications demand. In an attempt to bridge the popular-scholarly divide—or, more properly, to serve "two masters"—the association is maintaining its lay-oriented museum and supporting popular book projects, while at the same time professionalizing the journal and producing academic volumes.[195] This two-pronged effort represents a possible way of pursuing local and regional Jewish history that is both academically rigorous and accessible to the public.

It is also yet to be determined how the academy will respond to the revamped journal and expanding inroads into professional history writing. On the one hand, *Western States Jewish History* is a journal with a long history and, with it, some level of name recognition. On the other hand, for better or worse, those familiar with the title might assume it is still the journal it used to be. Developing a reputation as a publication of consistently high quality and exacting standards will take some time. The hope is that movement in that direction will not alienate longtime readers but will succeed in engaging both laypeople and professionals in the history of Jews in the American West.

1. Joining Justin G. Turner were Morris Bernstein, Julius Bisno, William R. Blumenthal, Samuel Dinin, Lawrence P. Frank, Rabbi Leonard Greenberg, Rabbi Rudolph Lupo, Marco Newmark, and Jacob Zeitlin.
2. Julius Bisno, "Southern California Jewish Historical Society," *Publications of the American Jewish Historical Society* 42, no. 4 (1953): 420–21.
3. "Justin George Turner Papers: Finding Aid," Huntington Library (Online Archive of California), http://pdf.oac.cdlib.org/pdf/huntington/mss/turnerj.pdf.
4. "The Society's New President, Justin George Turner," *Newsletter: The Historical Society of Southern California* 1, nos. 1–2 (1962): 6–7.
5. *A Display of Lincolniana from the Collection of Justin G. Turner* (San Francisco: San Francisco Public Library, 1960). See also *Lincolniana: A Catalogue of Historic Autograph Letters and Documents from the Justin G. Turner Collection of Americana* (Los Angeles: Occidental College, 1957); *Ordeal of the Union: Civil War Manuscripts and Documents* (Los Angeles: University of Southern California, 1963).

6. "Jewish Role in American Civil War Depicted in Los Angeles Exhibit," *Jewish Telegraph Agency*, January 2, 1963.
7. Justin G. Turner and Linda Levitt Turner, *Mary Todd Lincoln: Her Life and Letters* (New York: Alfred Knopf, 1972). The book collects every known letter written by Mary Todd Lincoln, along with a contextualizing biography placed in between the letters. Michael Burkhimer, *100 Essential Lincoln Books* (Nashville: Cumberland, 2003), 171–73. *Look Away*, a play by Jerome Kilty based on the Turners' book, debuted at New York City's Playhouse Theatre on January 7, 1973.
8. The Justin G. Turner Autograph Collection, Library of Congress, Washington, DC, contains 650 items. Exhibits from this collection are catalogued in *The Signers of the Declaration of Independence: A Loan Exhibition of Manuscripts by the Signers, from the Justin G. Turner Collection* (Los Angeles: Los Angeles County Museum, 1955), and *Early Americana: A Loan Exhibition of Original Manuscripts of the Period 1630–1800 from the Justin G. Turner Collection to Commemorate the 170th Anniversary of the Signing of the United States Constitution, Sept. 17, 1787; Sept. 16–Oct. 13, 1957* (Los Angeles: California Museum of Science and Industry, 1957).
9. Gift of Justin G. Turner, 1958, Edwin J. Beinecke Collection of Robert Louis Stevenson, Yale University Archive.
10. "From the Librarian," *UCLA Librarian* 9, no. 4 (1955): 24.
11. Morris Lutzki, *Catalogue of Geniza Fragments (now British Library ms. Or. 13,153): from the Collection of Justin G. Turner* (London: Hebrew Section, Oriental and India Office Collections, The British Library, 1994).
12. Harris Newmark, *Sixty Years in Southern California, 1853–1913*, ed. Maurice H. Newmark and Marco R. Newmark (New York: Knickerbocker, 1916); Marco R. Newmark, *Jottings* in Southern California History (Los Angeles: Ward Ritchie, 1955). The brothers re-edited *Sixty Years in Southern California* for its second edition in 1926, and Marco edited, indexed, and annotated a third edition in 1930 (Maurice died in 1929).
13. Ana Begue de Packman, "Marco Ross Newmark," *Southern California Quarterly* 41, no. 4 (1959): 296.
14. Max Vorspan and Sheldon Teitelbaum, "Los Angeles," *Encyclopedia Judaica*, vol. 13, 2nd ed. (New York: Macmillan Reference, 2007), 197.
15. Julius Bisno, "The Third Annual Meeting of the Southern California Jewish Historical Society," Publications of the *American Jewish Historical Society* 46, no.

2 (1956): 120.

16. The first volume of *Jewish Education* was published in 1929. The name was changed to *Journal of Jewish Education* in 1994.
17. "The Los Angeles Jewish Community Council," in *Southwest Jewry*, vol. 3, ed. Joseph L. Malamut (Los Angeles: Los Angeles Jewish Institutions and Their Leaders, 1957), 23.
18. Marco R. Newmark, "Dr. Philip Seman," *The Historical Society of Southern California Quarterly* 41, no. 1 (1959): 79.
19. Erik Greenberg, "Peter 'Pete' Kahn: Los Angeles Jewish Leader, 1878–1952," *Western States Jewish History* 38, no. 1 (2005): 20.
20. The Julius Bisno Collection, housed at the American Jewish Historical Society's Center for Jewish History in New York, includes correspondences and autographed photographs from Jewish members of the United Nations, cabinets of US presidents, US Supreme Court, and US governors, senators, representatives, diplomats, philanthropists, and Jewish organizational leaders.
21. Ron Wolfson, *A Time to Mourn, A Time to Comfort: A Guide to Jewish Bereavement and Comfort* (Woodstock, VT: Jewish Lights, 1996).
22. "Names in the News," *Jewish Post* (Indianapolis), January 16, 1970.
23. Also consulted for *The Ten Commandments* were William C. Hayes of the Metropolitan Museum of Art, New York, Labib Habachi of the Department of Antiquities, Luxor, Egypt, and Keith C. Seele, Ralph Marcus, and George R. Hughes of the Oriental Institute, University of Chicago.
24. See Kevin Starr, *Material Dreams: Southern California through the 1920s* (New York: Oxford University Press, 1990), 305–33.
25. Jacob R. Marcus, *How to Write the History of an American Jewish Community* (Cincinnati: American Jewish Archives, 1953).
26. Justin G. Turner, "Southern California Jewish Historical Society," in *Southwest Jewry*, vol. 3, ed. Joseph L. Malamut (Los Angeles: Los Angeles Jewish Institutions and Their Leaders, 1957), 194.
27. Stephen Sass, interview by authors, July 24, 2020.
28. Collections in the archives of the Jewish Historical Society of Southern California (formerly Southern California Jewish Historical Society) include those of the Jewish Community Library of Los Angeles, Jewish Federation Council, Julius Bisno Archival Collection, Los Angeles Jewish Community Council, B'nai B'rith

Messenger, and more, as well as materials covering various synagogues and neighborhoods, such as Boyle Heights. Sivan Siman-Tov, archivist for Jewish Historical Society of Southern California, email to author, October 13, 2020.

29. The SCJHS photograph collection has been processed and will be partially digitized, and a finding aid will be online in the near future.
30. "Activities of the Society," *Southern California Quarterly* 43, no. 3 (1961): 358–59. For example, see *A Catalog of Historic Letters, Books and Documents from the Private Library of Justin Turner*, Exhibited at the State University of Iowa Library, May 1–May 27, 1954 (Iowa City: University of Iowa, 1954).
31. Letter from Justin Turner asking Helen Keller about John Greenleaf Whittier, September 26, 1960, Helen Keller Archive, American Foundation for the Blind, Arlington, VA; Dorothy Thompson letter to Justin G. Turner, September 12, 1958, Perkins Autograph Collection, Ella Strong Denison Library, Scripps College.
32. Justin G. Turner, "Manuscripts and History," paper presented at the American Association for State and Local History at Houston, Texas, October 24, 1952.
33. Constitution and By-Laws of the Hebrew Benevolent Society of Los Angeles, California (Los Angeles: Southern California Jewish Historical Society, 1954). The original document, held at the Bancroft Library, University of California, Berkeley, was printed in 1855. The society also published Souvenir Program: First Annual Meeting and Installation, Thursday, February 4, 1954 (Los Angeles: Southern California Jewish Historical Society, 1954).
34. Jacob Frankfort was the first known Jew to reside in Los Angeles, arriving with the Rowland-Workman exploratory party in 1841. Eight men with Jewish surnames appear in the city census of 1850. Max Vorspan and Lloyd P. Gartner, *History of the Jews of Los Angeles* (San Marino, CA: Huntington Library, 1970), 4–6.
35. For a recent biography, see Sophie Greenspan, *Westward with Fremont: The Story of Solomon Carvalho* (Philadelphia: Jewish Publication Society, 2018).
36. Carvalho was preceded by Emanuel Lazarus, who entered California in 1826 with the Jedediah S. Smith party. Morris U. Schappes, *A Documentary History of the Jews in the United States, 1654–1875* (New York: Schocken, 1950), 670.
37. *California Inventory of Historic Resources* (Sacramento: California Department of Parks and Recreation, 1976), 210. See Ava Kahn's introduction to Solomon Nunes Carvalho, *Incidents of Travel and Adventure in the Far West with Colonel Fremont's Last Expedition* [1856] (Lincoln: University of Nebraska Press, 2004).

38. *Abraham Lincoln and Diogenes* was presented to Brandeis University by Mr. and Mrs. Justin G. Turner, Mr. and Mrs. Maurice Turner, and Mr. and Mrs. John J. Mack. It is housed at the Rose Museum of Brandeis University.
39. Justin G. Turner, *A Note on Solomon Nuñes Carvalho and his Portrait of Abraham Lincoln* (Los Angeles: Plantin, 1960).
40. J. J. Warner, Benjamin I. Hayes, and Joseph Pomeroy Widney, *An Historical Sketch of Los Angeles County, California* (Los Angeles: Louis Lewin and Co., 1876), also known as *Centennial History of Los Angeles.*
41. On October 14, 1871, a mob of some 500 Angelenos, spurred by racial resentment, attacked, robbed, and murdered between seventeen and twenty residents of Chinatown along Calle de los Negros. It has been described as the largest mass lynching in American history. See Scott Zesch, *The Chinatown War: Chinese Los Angeles and the Massacre of 1871* (New York: Oxford, 2012). Harris Newmark included a chapter on the massacre in his memoir, *Sixty Years in Southern California, 1853–1913,* ed. Maurice H. Newmark and Marco R. Newmark (New York: Knickerbocker, 1916), 421–36.
42. The State Legislature passed a resolution designating it as California's state song in 1951. California Government Code section 421.7 states, "'I Love You, California,' a song published in 1913 with lyrics by F. B. Silverwood and music by A. F. Frankenstein, is an official state song."
43. Mary Garden's words appeared in a letter to F. B. Silverwood, which was printed on the back cover of the sheet music for "I Love You, California." See Josh Kun, ed., *Songs in the Key of Los Angeles: Sheet Music from the Collection of the Los Angeles Public Library* (Santa Monica: Angel City, 2013), 63.
44. Robert R. Dykstra, *The Cattle Towns* (New York: Alfred A. Knopf, 1968), 361–64.
45. Oscar Handlin, "Our Unknown American Jewish Ancestors: Fact and Myth in History," *Commentary,* January 1, 1948, 110.
46. Neal Gabler, *An Empire of Their Own: How the Jews Invented Hollywood* (New York: Anchor, 1989), 277.
47. Ferenc Morton Szasz, *Religion in the Modern American West* (Tucson: University of Arizona Press, 2001), 76.
48. Magnin was himself the subject of several articles published in *Western States Jewish History,* most of them authored or co-authored by Rabbi William M. Kramer, whose career and interests in many ways mirrored those of Rabbi Magnin,

although Kramer was not in the same league as the "Rabbi to the Stars." The short articles originally appeared in Kramer's weekly column, "My Shtetele California," printed in Southern California *Heritage* newspapers from 1970 to 1990. William M. Kramer and Reva Clar, "Rabbi Edgar F. Magnin in Stockton (1914–1915): Rehearsal for Los Angeles," *Western States Jewish History* 17, no. 2 (1985): 99–121; William M. Kramer and Reva Clar, "Rabbi Edgar F. Magnin and the Modernization of Los Angeles Jewry, Part I," *Western States Jewish History* 19, no. 3 (1987): 233–51; William M. Kramer and Reva Clar, "Rabbi Edgar F. Magnin and the Modernization of Los Angeles Jewry, Part II," *Western States Jewish History* 19, no. 4 (1987): 246–62; William M. Kramer and Reva Clar, "Los Angeles Rabbi Edgar Magnin's 1906 San Francisco Earthquake-Fire Memories," *Western States Jewish History* 27, no. 3 (1995): 143–45; Norton B. Stern and Benjamin Efron, "Rabbi Edgar F. Magnin: Summary of an Interview at Wilshire Boulevard Temple, Los Angeles, California, February 18, 1966," *Western States Jewish History* 41, no. 3 (2009): 547–50; William M. Kramer, "The *Los Angeles Times* Noted Rabbi Magnin's Arrival," *Western States Jewish History* 42, nos. 2–3 (2010): 15–16; William M. Kramer, "Rabbi Magnin Answers," *Western States Jewish History* 42, nos. 2–3 (2010): 40; William M. Kramer, "Magnin Regarding Colleges," *Western States Jewish History* 42, nos. 2–3 (2010): 46; William M. Kramer, "The Life of Edgar Magnin, Part I," *Western States Jewish History* 42, nos. 2–3 (2010): 141–42; William M. Kramer, "The Youth of Edgar Magnin, Part II," *Western States Jewish History* 42, nos. 2–3 (2010): 143–44; William M. Kramer, "Young Magnin, Part III," *Western States Jewish History* 42, nos. 2–3 (2010): 145–46.

49. An earlier effort, Congregation Beth El, was conceived in 1861 but quickly vanished.
50. Gary P. Zola, "To Our Readers," *The American Jewish Archives Journal* 42, no. 2 (2010): vii.
51. Handlin, "Our Unknown American Jewish Ancestors," 104. See John Geipel, *Mame Loshn: The Making of Yiddish* (London: Journeyman, 1982), 6; Marion Aptroot, *Yiddish Language Structures* (Berlin: De Gruyter, 2013), 108–12.
52. Gabler, *An Empire of Their Own*, 270.
53. Ibid., 271.
54. Kevin Starr, *California: A History* (New York: Modern Library, 2005), 305.
55. See *Western States Jewish History* 43, nos. 3–4 (2011), a special issue titled *Boyle*

Heights: Recollections and Remembrances of the Boyle Heights Community in Los Angeles, 1920s–1960s, edited by Abraham Hoffman.

56. Norton B. Stern and William M. Kramer, "The Major Role of Polish Jews in the Pioneer West," *Western States Jewish Historical Quarterly* 8, no. 4 (1976): 344.
57. See Ellen Eisenberg, Ava F. Kahn, and William Toll, *Jews of the Pacific Coast: Reinventing Community on America's Edge* (Seattle: University of Washington Press, 2009).
58. On the subject of Jewish "whiteness" in America, see Karen Brodkin, *How Jews Became White Folks and What That Says about Race in America* (New Brunswick, NJ: Rutgers University Press, 1998) and Eric L. Goldstein, *The Price of Whiteness: Jews, Race, and American Identity* (Princeton, NJ: Princeton University Press, 2019).
59. Gabler, *An Empire of Their Own*, 271.
60. Michael E. Engh, *Frontier Faiths: Church, Temple, and Synagogue in Los Angeles, 1846–1888* (Albuquerque: University of New Mexico Press, 1992), 98–100.
61. Ibid., 99.
62. Newmark, *Sixty Years in Southern California*, 383.
63. Stephen Aron, "Jewish Los Angeles in the Making: The Early Pioneer Merchants and Bankers," *Western States Jewish History* 38, nos. 3–4 (2006): 2.
64. William M. Kramer and Norton B. Stern, "The Study of Los Angeles History: An Analytical Consideration of a Major Work," *Western States Jewish Historical Quarterly* 3, no. 1 (1970): 53.
65. Ibid. Vorspan and Gartner do not use the phrase "ruthless man" but rather call him a "strong, ambitious man." *History of the Jews of Los Angeles*, 42.
66. Kramer and Stern, "The Study of Los Angeles History," 53. See Vorspan and Gartner, *History of the Jews of Los Angeles*, 98.
67. Kramer and Stern, "The Study of Los Angeles History," 53. See Vorspan and Gartner, *History of the Jews of Los Angeles*, 83.
68. Kramer and Stern, "The Study of Los Angeles History," 53.
69. Will Kramer, "Review of *History of the Jews of Los Angeles*," *Journal of the American Academy of Religion* 40, no. 1 (1972): 133–34.
70. Stephen Sass, interview with editors, July 24, 2020; Caroline Luce, "Western States Jewish History Special Collections: Reflections," *Western States Jewish History* 41, no. 3 (2009): xix.

71. Luce, "Western States Jewish History Special Collections," xviii. Some of Stern's travel notes were archived at the Western Jewish History Center and now in Bancroft collections.
72. Norton B. Stern, "Judah L. Magnes of Oakland: Errors and Omissions in His Life Story," *Western States Jewish History* 17, no. 4 (1985): 352–57.
73. Norton B. Stern, "The Editor's Corner," *Western States Jewish Historical Quarterly* 3, no. 2 (1970): 124.
74. "Rabbi Max Vorspan, 86; Scholar and Historian," Los Angeles Times, June 16, 2002.
75. Max Vorspan, "Los Angeles 1970 to the Present: An Encyclopedic Essay," *Western States Jewish History* 26, no. 2 (1994): 127–44. The article contains some updates and expansions. Vorspan contributed one more article to the journal, a witty reflection titled "How the 'Vest Was Von': An Irreverent Account of the Conservative Jewish Occupation of Los Angeles," *Western States Jewish History* (1997): 219–30.
76. Among other sources, the three conventional phases are restated and reaffirmed in Jacob Rader Marcus, "The Periodization of American Jewish History," *American Jewish Historical Society* 47, no. 3 (1958): 1–9.
77. Handlin, "Our Unknown American Jewish Ancestors," 105.
78. John Livingston, "Introduction," in *Jews of the American West*, ed. Moses Rischin and John Livingston (Detroit: Wayne State University Press, 1991), 19–20.
79. Julius Bisno, "The Third Annual Meeting of the Southern California Jewish Historical Society," *Publications of the American Jewish Historical Society* 46, no. 2 (1956): 120–21; Turner, "Southern California Jewish Historical Society," 195; Justin G. Turner, "In Memoriam: Marco Newmark," *California History* 39, no. 2 (1960): 175–76.
80. Rudolf Glanz, *The Jews of California: From the Discovery of Gold until 1880* (New York: Waldon, 1960). For a summary of Glanz's life, writings, and accomplishments, see Lloyd P. Gartner, "Rudolf Glanz (1892–1978)," *American Jewish History* 69, no. 2 (1979): 270–73.
81. Abraham G. Duker, "An Evaluation of Achievement in American Jewish local Historical Writing," *Publications of the American Jewish Historical Society* 49, no. 4 (1960): 217.
82. Samuel Dinin, "*The Jews of California* – Review," *The California Historical Society Quarterly* 41, no. 1 (1962): 162–63.

83. Justin G. Turner, "The First Decade of Los Angeles Jewry: A Pioneer History, 1850–1860," *American Jewish Historical Quarterly* 54 (1964): 123–64; Justin G. Turner, *The First Decade of Los Angeles Jewry: A Pioneer History, 1850–1860* (Philadelphia: Press of Maurice Jacobs, 1964).
84. In the years leading up to the founding of the quarterly journal, Stern taught several adult community courses in Los Angeles, including "The Jewish History of California," through the Reform movement's Union of American Hebrew Congregations College of Jewish Studies. Kramer also taught a course, "The Historical Development of Jewish Ethics," for that program. "New School for Jewish Adults Opens," *Los Angeles Times*, January 29, 1966.
85. Stephen Sass, interview with editors, January 27, 2021.
86. Harriet Rochlin, "Norton B. Stern: Pioneer Western Jewish Historian and Founding Editor of the First *Western Jewish Historical Quarterly*," *Western States Jewish History* (1998): 218.
87. Ava F. Kahn, correspondence with authors, November 18, 2020.
88. "Magnes History," The Magnes Collection of Jewish Art and Life, https://magnes.berkeley.edu/research/magnes-history.
89. Homepage, Jewish Museum of the American West, http://www.jmaw.org/.
90. Fred Rosembaum, interview with editors, October 9, 2020. Fromer and Kramer may have discussed moving the journal to the center around the time of Kramer's retirement in 1998. Ava F. Kahn, email to author, October 22, 2020.
91. For instance, Ruth Rafael, "Selected Acquisitions, Western Jewish History Center, Judah L. Magnes Memorial Museum," *Western States Historical Quarterly* 6, no. 2 (1974): 234; 8, no. 1 (1975): 92.
92. Duker, "An Evaluation of Achievement," 217. The article cited is J. Solis-Cohen Jr., "A California Pioneer: The Letters of Bernard Marks to Jacob Solis-Cohen (1853–1857)," *Publications of the American Jewish Historical Society* 44, no. 1 (1954): 12–57.
93. Duker, "An Evaluation of Achievement," 218.
94. William M. Kramer and Norton B. Stern, "Archival Sources for the History of Religion in California, Part II: Jewish Religious Archives and Ethnic Histories," *Southern California Quarterly* 72, no. 3 (1990): 275–89. Kramer and Stern updated the survey in two parts: "A Guide to California Jewish History, Part I," *Western States Jewish History* 24, no. 4 (1992): 378–83; "A Guide to California Jewish

History, Part II," *Western States Jewish History* 25, no. 4 (1993): 325–58.

95. Norton B. Stern, *California Jewish History: A Descriptive Bibliography* (Glendale, CA: Arthur H. Clark, 1967). Following the release of Stern's *California Jewish History*, Seymour Fromer hired Sara G. Cogan to compile annotated Jewish bibliographies of the Mother Lode, San Francisco, and Los Angeles. Stern is listed as a source for those volumes. Sara G. Cogan, *Pioneer Jews of the California Mother Lode, 1849–1880: An Annotated Bibliography* (Berkeley: Western Jewish History Center, 1968); *The Jews of San Francisco & the Greater Bay Area, 1849–1919: An Annotated Bibliography* (Berkeley: Western Jewish History Center, 1973); *The Jews of Los Angeles, 1849–1945: An Annotated Bibliography* (Berkeley: Western Jewish History Center, 1980).

96. Olivia Rossetti Agresti, *David Lubin: A Study in Practical Idealism* (New York: Little, Brown, and Co., 1922).

97. Stern, *California Jewish History*, 45. J. A. Graves, *My Seventy Years in California, 1857–1927* (Los Angeles: Times-Mirror, 1929). SMPL = Santa Monica Public Library; LAPL = Los Angeles Public Library; NBS = Norton B. Stern private library.

98. Jacob M. Maze, "Jewish Farmers in California," *Jewish Farmer* 51, no. 5 (1958): 83–84, and 52, no. 5 (1959): 71–80; Irwin Soref, "The Jewish Community of Los Angles in Retrospect," *Reconstructionist* 18, no. 15 (1952): 8–12; Martin Hall, "The Jews of Los Angeles," *Chicago Jewish Forum* 16, no. 4 (1958): 223–27; Ben B. Seligman, "They Came to Hollywood: How Jews Built the Movie Industry," *Jewish Frontier* (July 1953): 19–29; and Earl Raab, "There's No City Like San Francisco: Profile of a Jewish Community," *Commentary* 10, no. 4 (1950): 369–78.

99. Francis J. Weber, "Review of *California Jewish History: A Descriptive Bibliography*," *Southern California Quarterly* 49, no. 4 (1967): 464.

100. Duker, "An Evaluation of Achievement," 243.

101. Marc Lee Raphael, "Beyond New York: The Challenge to Local History," in *Jews of the American West*, ed. Moses Rischin and John Livingston (Detroit: Wayne State University Press, 1991), 48–65.

102. William Toll, "Review of Jews in America: Four Centuries of an Uneasy Encounter," *American Jewish Archives Journal* 45, no. 2 (1993): 255.

103. Marco Newmark, "Wilshire Boulevard Temple: Congregation B'nai B'rith, 1862–1947," *Southern California Quarterly* 38, no. 2 (1956): 167–84; Wendell E.

Harmon, "The Bootlegger Era in Southern California," *Southern California Quarterly* 37, no. 4 (1955): 335–46; and Margaret Romer, "Pioneer Builders of Los Angeles: Part II," *Southern California Quarterly* 43, no. 3 (1961): 342–49, which mentions the Jewish heritage of Isaias and Herman Hellman.

104. Norton B. Stern and William M. Kramer, "Emil Harris: Los Angeles Jewish Police Chief," *Southern California Quarterly* 55, no. 2 (1973): 163–92. SCJHS presented the new tombstone for Emil Harris in 1973, in conjunction with the article's publication.

105. Mission San Diego de Alcalá, the first of twenty-one Franciscan missions built between 1769 and 1833, was founded on Presidio Hill by Father Junípero Serra, in today's San Diego.

106. Norton B. Stern, "The Editor's Page," *Western States Jewish Historical Quarterly* 2, no. 1 (1969): 62.

107. Rochlin, "Norton B. Stern," 219.

108. Gladys Sturman and David Epstein, "Postscript: The Western States Jewish History Archives," in *A Cultural History of Jews in California*, ed. Bruce Zuckerman, William Deverell, and Lisa Ansell (West Lafayette, IN: Purdue University Press, 2009), 49.

109. Abraham Hoffman, "Dr. Norton B. Stern: A San Francisco Treat in Jewish History," *Western States Jewish History* 41, no. 1 (2008): x.

110. Books by Norton B. Stern include *California Jewish History*; *Mannie's Crowd: Emmanuel Lowenstein, Colorful Character of Old Los Angeles* (Glendale, CA: Arthur H. Clark, 1970); *Baja California: Jewish Refuge and Homeland* (Los Angeles: Dawson, 1973); *Jews in Early Santa Monica: A Centennial Review* (Los Angeles: Jewish Federation Council of Greater Los Angeles, 1975); *The Birth of Modern Los Angeles Jewry* (Santa Monica, CA: Stern, 1977); *San Francisco's Artist: Toby E. Rosenthal* (Northridge: California State University, Northridge, 1978), co-authored with William M. Kramer; *Morris L. Goodman: The First American Councilman of the City of Los Angeles* (Santa Monica, CA: Lipton, 1981), co-authored with William M. Kramer; *The Jews of Los Angeles: Urban Pioneers* (Los Angeles: Southern California Jewish Historical Society, 1981).

111. Sturman and Epstein, "Postscript," 49.

112. Stephen Sass, interview with editors, July 24, 2020.

113. Justin G. Turner and Norton B. Stern, "Marco Ross Newmark, 1878–1959: First

Jewish Historian of the Southland," *Western States Jewish Historical Quarterly* 1, no. 1 (1968): 3–8.

114. Luce, "Western States Jewish History Special Collections," xvi.
115. William Deverell, "Organizational and Spiritual Leadership," *Western States Jewish History* 38, nos. 3–4 (2006): 207.
116. Hasia R. Diner, A Time for Gathering: The Second Migration, 1820–1880 (Baltimore, MD: Johns Hopkins University Press, 1992), 292.
117. Aaron Riche, "Zionism in Los Angeles on Its Twenty-Fifth Anniversary," *Western States Jewish History Journal* 23, no. 1 (1991): 31–34, reprinted from Jewish National Fund of Los Angeles, Jubilee Number 1902–1927, ed. George Saylin (Los Angeles: Jewish National Fund, 1927); Philip L. Seman, "The Jewish Community in Mexico City, 1924–1935," *Western States Jewish History* 43, no. 1 (2011): 176–90, reprinted from *The Reflex* 6, no. 4 (1935).
118. Rudolf Glanz, "Where the Jewish Press was Distributed in Pre-Civil War America," *Western States Jewish Historical Quarterly* 5, no. 1 (1972): 1–14; "Notes on the Early Jews of Arizona," *Western States Jewish Historical Quarterly* 5, no. 4 (1973): 243–56; "The Jews in the Sandwich Islands," *Western States Jewish Historical Quarterly* 6, no. 3 (1974): 177–87; "From Fur Rush to Gold Rushes: Alaskan Jewry from the Late 19th to the Early 20th Centuries," *Western States Jewish Historical Quarterly* 7, no. 2 (1975): 95–107. Two posthumous reprints were also published: "Jews and Chinese in America," *Western States Jewish History* 38, no. 2 (2006): 112–32, reprinted from *Jewish Social Studies* 16, no. 3 (1954); and "The 'Bayer' and the 'Pollack' in America," *Western States Jewish History* 45, no. 1 (2012): 73–94, reprinted from *Jewish Social Studies* 17, no. 1 (1955).
119. William M. Kramer, "Tree Art in Western Jewish Cemeteries," *Western States Jewish Historical Quarterly* 2, no. 2 (1970): 91–100; and "'They Have Killed Our Man But Not Our Cause': The California Jewish Mourners of Abraham Lincoln," *Western States Jewish Historical Quarterly* 2, no. 4 (1970): 187–216.
120. Kramer's "My Shtetele California" columns were printed in *Western States Jewish History* 42, nos. 2–3 (2010), edited by David W. Epstein.
121. William M. Kramer, "My Life of Careers," *Western States Jewish History* 30, no. 3 (1998): 202. This paper, commemorating Kramer's fifty years in the rabbinate, was presented at the Central Conference of American Rabbis' 105th Annual Convention, Chicago, Illinois, May 30, 1994.

122. Ibid., 203.
123. Stephen Sass, interview with editors, July 24, 2020.
124. "Jewish Federation Council to Honor Pauline Hirsh," *Los Angeles Times*, November 23, 1981.
125. Marylouise Oates, "Driving Force Behind Jewish Exhibit," *Los Angeles Times*, April 20, 1981.
126. The *Southern California Jewish Historical Newsletter* was printed seasonally from 1980 to 1986. The July 1980 issue of Western States Jewish Historical Society (vol. 12, no. 4) lists the Western Jewish History Center of the Magnes Memorial Museum in Berkeley as a "cooperating society." The Texas Jewish Historical Society was added in July 1981 (vol. 13, no. 4).
127. "Periodical Reflections," *Western States Jewish Historical Quarterly* 13, no. 4 (1981): 377.
128. Southern California Jewish Historical Society Newsletter (Summer 1984): 1. See Peter Levine, Ellis Island to Ebbets Field: Sport and the American Jewish Experience (New York: Oxford University Press, 1993), 216–17.
129. The journal listed Pauline Hirsh as "Mrs. Leo Hirsh."
130. Historical talks by Stern received press attention during the 1970s but seem to have tapered off during the 1980s. See, for example: "Historian to Give Talk," *Los Angeles Times*, November 15, 1973; "Historian to Speak," *Los Angeles Times*, April 8, 1974; "Lecture on Jews," *Los Angeles Times*, May 12, 1974; "Romance of the Jews," *Los Angeles Times*, January 16, 1976; "Talk on 'Early Santa Monica,'" *Los Angeles Times*, November 11, 1976; "Jews of Wild and Wooly West," *Los Angeles Times*, October 23, 1977; and "Series on Los Angeles Jews to Begin with Pioneers," *Los Angeles Times*, February 2, 1981.
131. Articles of Incorporation, Western States Jewish History Association, April 5, 1983.
132. Stephen Sass, interview with editors, July 24, 2020.
133. Robert Louis Loeb, letter to Norton B. Stern and William M. Kramer, December 3, 1984.
134. The journal's format changed with vol. 25, no. 1 (1992), when it began printing through Isaac Nathan Publishing, run by David W. Epstein. Until that point, the format remained consistent through a series of publishers: Lorrin L. Morrison (1:1–4:4); Westland Printing (5:1–21:4); no press indicated (22:1–23:3); Bristol

Press (23:4–24:1); Capitol Press (24:2–24:3); and Westland Printing (24:4).

135. Stephen Sass, interview with editors, July 24, 2020.
136. According to Michael B. Weisz, letter to Robert Louis Loeb, December 11, 1984, "the publication functioned and prospered during periods when the other faction of the unincorporated group was, for all practical purposes, moribund." Minutes from the WSJHA annual meeting on July 9, 1985, indicated that "paid circulation was slightly under 800," a figure that included 132 renewed subscriptions from SCJHS members. The number of people who subscribed to the journal before the organizations split is unclear.
137. Michael B. Weisz, letter to Robert Louis Loeb, December 11, 1984, and January 3, 1985.
138. Weisz, letter to Loeb, January 3, 1985.
139. Stephen Sass, interview with editors, July 24, 2020.
140. Minutes from Western States Jewish History Association Meeting, July 1, 1984.
141. Michael B. Weisz, letter to Robert Louis Loeb, April 1, 1985, states, "Drs. Stern and Kramer have advised me that they remain in touch with their friend, Mr. Fred Rochlin, and so channels are always open for them to discuss any projects which will benefit their common interests and that of their two separate organizations to advance the historical study of Western Jewry."
142. Harriet Rochlin and Fred Rochlin, *Pioneer Jews: A New Life in the Far West* (Boston: Houghton Mifflin, 1984), x, acknowledge Stern, "a one-man research center on the pioneer Jews, [who] read the entire manuscript and most kindly pointed out errors and oversights."
143. Weisz, letter to Loeb, January 3, 1985.
144. "History of the Jewish Presence in Hollywood: From Cowboy to Corporate Leader," *Legacy: Journal of the Southern California Jewish Historical Society* 1, no. 1 (1987); Pauline Hirsh, "Two Pair Pants Come with This Coat, a Perfect Fit: History of the Jews in the Southern California Apparel Business," *Legacy: Journal of the Southern California Jewish Historical Society* 1, no. 2 (1988); Norma Pratt Fain, "Women Moving Forward: Dreamers, Builders, Leaders: A History of Jewish Women in Southern California," *Legacy: Journal of the Southern California Jewish Historical Society* 1, no. 3 (1989); and Lynn C. Kronzek, "Fairfax: A Home, a Community, a Way of Life," *Legacy: Journal of the Southern California Jewish Historical Society* 1, no. 4 (1990).

145. Southern California Jewish Historical Society is the society's legal name, although it does business as (DBA) the Jewish Historical Society of Southern California. The name change was suggested in the 1980s by Morton Silverman, of Manilow and Silverman Mortuary, who said that people looking for a Jewish organization in the phone book would find it more easily.
146. See Community Outreach Program: Reuse Alternatives (Los Angeles: Breed Street Shul Project, 2003).
147. Ellie Kahn, *Meet Me at Brooklyn & Soto: Celebrating the Jewish Community of East Los Angeles* (Teaneck, NJ: Ergo Media, 1998), DVD.
148. David W. Epstein, "One Special Memory of Rabbi William M. Kramer," *Western States Jewish History* 37, no. 1 (2004): 9.
149. For example, Samuel A. Kunin, *Circumcision: Its Place in Judaism, Past and Present* (Woodland Hills, CA: Isaac Nathan, 1998) and Michael Isaacson, *Jewish Music as Midrash: What Makes Music Jewish* (Woodland Hills, CA: Isaac Nathan, 2007).
150. David W. Epstein, "DUNIE'S—The Missing Delicatessen, Somewhere in the West," *Western States Jewish History* 30, no. 3 (1998): 256–61.
151. David W. Epstein, "The Times, They Are a Changing," *Western States Jewish History* 49, no. 4 (2015): 4.
152. David W. Epstein, *Why the Jews Were So Successful in the West . . . and How to Tell Their Stories* (Woodland Hills, CA: Isaac Nathan, 2007).
153. As of this writing, the editorial board of the reconstituted *Western States Jewish History* includes: Jonathan L. Friedmann, editor (Academy for Jewish Religion California and Western States Jewish History Association); Judith S. Pinnolis, reviews editor (Hebrew College); Marc Dollinger (San Francisco State University); Victoria Fisch (Jewish Genealogical Society of Sacramento); Tamar Frankiel (Academy for Jewish Religion California); Aaron Fruchtman (California State University Long Beach); Joel Gereboff (Arizona State University and Academy for Jewish Religion California); John F. Guest (Western States Jewish History Association); Abraham Hoffman (Los Angeles Valley College); Jason Schulman (John Jay College); Mark Abbott Stern (independent researcher); Wynne Waugaman (University of Southern California); and Hollace Ava Weiner (Fort Worth Jewish Archives).
154. See, for example, Bertram W. Korn, *American Jewry and the Civil War* (Philadelphia: Jewish Publication Society, 1951).

155. Norton B. Stern, "The Editor's Page," *Western States Jewish Historical Quarterly* 2, no. 1 (1969): 62.
156. Bertram W. Korn, "Jews and Negro Slavery in the Old South, 1789–1865," *Publications of the American Jewish Historical Society* 50, no. 3 (1961): 151–201.
157. William M. Kramer and Norton B. Stern, "Some 'Warts' on the Face of Early Western Jewry," *Western States Jewish Historical Quarterly* 14, no. 1 (1981): 82.
158. For earlier examples, see two articles by Norton B. Stern, "A San Francisco Synagogue Scandal of 1893," *Western States Jewish Historical Quarterly* 6, no. 3 (1974): 196–203, and Norton B. Stern, "A Murder to be Forgotten," *Western States Jewish Historical Quarterly* 9, no. 2 (1977): 176–85.
159. Kramer and Stern, "Some 'Warts' on the Face of Early Western Jewry," 82.
160. Norton B. Stern and William M. Kramer, "Anti-Semitism and the Jewish Image in the Early West," *Western States Jewish Historical Quarterly* 6, no. 2 (1974): 129–40; David A. D'Ancona, "An Answer to Anti-Semitism: San Francisco, 1883," *Western States Jewish Historical Quarterly* 8, no. 1 (1975): 59–64; Grove L. Johnson, "A Gentile Reproves an Anti-Semite: Fresno, 1893," *Western States Jewish Historical Quarterly* 9, no. 4 (1977): 299–300; and Robert J. Chandler, "A Stereotype Emerges," *Western States Jewish History* 21, no. 4 (1989): 310–12.
161. Stern and Kramer, "Anti-Semitism and the Jewish Image in the Early West," 129, 139–40.
162. Livingston, "Introduction," 22. A few scholars addressed anti-Semitism in the American West in a more nuanced way, including Todd M. Kerstetter, God's Country, Uncle Sam's Land: Faith and Conflict in the American West (Urbana and Chicago: University of Illinois Press, 2006), 21–22, which distinguishes between "covert" and "overt" anti-Semitism.
163. Stern, *California Jewish History*, 13.
164. Ibid.
165. Ibid., 14.
166. Engh, *Frontier Faiths*.
167. Fred Rosenbaum, *Visions of Reform: Congregation Emanu-El and the Jews of San Francisco, 1849–1999* (Berkeley: Judah L. Magnes Museum, 2000).
168. William M. Kramer and Norton B. Stern, "A Jewish History of Oakland: A Review Essay," *Western States Jewish Historical Quarterly* 9, no. 4 (1977): 371–77.
169. Rosenbaum, *Visions of Reform*, xvii.

170. Ava F. Kahn, ed., *Jewish Voices of the California Gold Rush: A Documentary History, 1849–1880* (Detroit: Wayne State University Press, 2002), 26. She has also stated that much of her research on the West could not have been completed without the footnotes in the journal. Kahn, email to author, October 22, 2020.
171. Gladys Sturman, "A Letter from the New Editor," *Western States Jewish History* 30, no. 3 (1998): 197.
172. Moses Rischin and John Livingston, eds., *Jews of the American West* (Detroit: Wayne State University Press, 1991). In a bibliographical essay for *California Jews*, 187–88, Ava F. Kahn and Marc Dollinger write, "This 1991 collection of essays was the first scholarly work to acquaint readers with Jews in the far West. Its introduction and eight chapters were written by authorities of local history."
173. Livingston, "Introduction," 19.
174. Shari Rabin, *Jews on the Frontier: Religion and Mobility in Nineteenth-Century America* (New York: New York University Press, 2017). This point is also made in Ava F. Kahn, "Review of *Jews on the Frontier*," *Journal of Jewish Identities* 12, no. 2 (2019): 230–31.
175. David W. Epstein and Gladys Sturman, Letter to subscribers to *Western States Jewish History*, June 2016.
176. "Editor's Page," *Western States Jewish Historical Quarterly* 12, no. 2 (1980): 191.
177. Harriet Rochlin, preface to the 2000 edition. Rochlin and Rochlin, *Pioneer Jews*, vi.
178. Ava F. Kahn and Marc Dollinger, "Introduction: The Other Side," in *California Jews*, ed. Ava F. Kahn and Marc Dollinger (Hanover, NH: University Press of New England, 2003), 2.
179. See Joel Gereboff, "Integrating Local Jewish Historical Societies and Public History," *Shofar* 13, no. 3 (1995): 62–63.
180. Tom Tugend, "Western Jewish History Collection Gets Broken Up among Local Academic Institutions," *Jewish Journal of Greater Los Angeles*, February 16, 2007.
181. Sturman and Epstein, "Postscript," 49.
182. David W. Epstein, "To Rabbi William M. Kramer: A Promise Completed," *Western States Jewish History* 47, no. 1 (2014): 80.
183. Tugend, "Western Jewish History Collection Gets Broken Up."
184. Gladys Sturman and David W. Epstein, "Dedication of WSJH Archives, UCLA, March 3, 2009," *Western States Jewish History* 41, no. 4 (2009): xi.

185. Ibid., xii.

186. Ibid.

187. Marcus, *How to Write the History of an American Jewish Community*, 28–29.

188. Luce, "Western States Jewish History Special Collections," xvi.

189. Ibid.

190. Sturman and Epstein, "Dedication of WSJH Archives," ix.

191. For Jewish-Christian relations, see Julius Eckman, "Jewish Lecturing to Christian Groups: An 1872 View," *Western States Jewish History* 17, no. 2 (1985): 156–59; George Fisher, "Religious Equality in California, 1862," *Western States Jewish History* 20, no. 1 (1987): 73–76; Michael E. Engh, "'Charity Knows Neither Race nor Creed': Jewish Philanthropy to Roman Catholic Projects in Los Angeles, 1856–1876," *Western States Jewish History* 21, no. 2 (1989): 154–65; Deborah Y. Bachrach, "Christian Science and Jews in Minnesota: Background for Early Concerns," *Western States Jewish History* 50, no. 2 (2018): 33–50. For Jewish-Chinese relations, see Reva Clar and William M. Kramer, "Chinese-Jewish Relations in the Far West: 1850–1950, Part I," *Western States Jewish History* 21, no. 1 (1988): 12–35; Reva Clar and William M. Kramer, "Chinese-Jewish Relations of the Far West: 1850–1950, Part II," *Western States Jewish History* 21, no. 2 (1989): 132–53; "A Letter and a Jewish Article in Chinese," *Western States Jewish History* 26, no. 2 (1994): 112; E. P. Stein, "General Two-Gun Cohen: Morris Abraham Cohen, the Chinese Connection, 1887–1970, Part I," *Western States Jewish History* 32, no. 1 (1999): 4–21; E. P. Stein, "General Two-Gun Cohen: Morris Abraham Cohen, the Chinese Connection, 1887–1970, Part II," *Western States Jewish History* 32, nos. 2–3 (2000): 162–83; Leo J. Rain, "Dr. Jacob Rosenfeld: A Jewish Commander in a Chinese Army, 1903–1952," edited by Malgert Cohen, *Western States Jewish History* 33, no. 4 (2001): 291–302; Rudolf Glanz, "Jews and Chinese in America," *Western States Jewish History* 38, no. 2 (2006): 112–32; William M. Kramer, "Chinese-Jewish Moh-ist," *Western States Jewish History* 42, nos. 2–3 (2010): 30–31; Nan Abrams, "The Greenwalds of Humboldt County: The Emerald Opiate Ring and the Case of the Chinese Certificates," edited by Victoria Fisch, *Western States Jewish History* 43, no. 2 (2011): 101–15. For Jewish-Black relations, see William Levy, "A Jew Views Black Education: Texas, 1890," *Western States Jewish History* 8, no. 4 (1976): 351–60.

192. Gladys Sturman, "History Takes Many Forms," *Western States Jewish History* 37,

no. 2 (2005): 98.

193. "Submissions," Jewish Museum of the American West, http://www.jmaw.org/submissions/.

194. Decter, *Interpreting American Jewish History*, 214.

195. On the popular side, current WSJHA president Jonathan L. Friedmann recently produced *Jewish Gold Country* (Charleston, SC: Arcadia, 2020) and *Jewish Los Angeles* (Charleston, SC: Arcadia, 2020). On the academic side, Friedmann and WSJH vice president John F. Guest published a scholarly study, *Songs of Sonderling: Commissioning Jewish Émigré Composers in Los Angeles, 1938–1945* (Lubbock: Texas Tech University Press, 2020).

4

Southern Jewish Historical Society

MARK K. BAUMAN

Early Efforts

In 1892, a group of businesspeople, lawyers, and rabbis established the American Jewish Historical Society.[1] By the mid-1950s only a very few academic scholars, including Salo Baron, Oscar Handlin, and Jacob Rader Marcus, joined the ranks of such amateur historians. Of these, only Marcus, the head of the American Jewish Archives and widely considered the dean of American Jewish historians of his generation, incorporated southern Jewish history into his work, although his students Bertram W. Korn, Malcolm Stern, and Stanley Chyet would do so as well.

Such was the immature nature of the broader field when Saul Viener and Louis Ginsberg launched the first Southern Jewish Historical Society (SJHS) in Viener's home in Richmond, Virginia, on January 13, 1957, after sending a letter that solicited participants on December 28, 1956. This small meeting led to rapid expansion of membership from many southern cities and as far north as Philadelphia. Viener and Ginsberg sought a concrete organization to follow Richmond's participation in the 1954 tercentenary commemoration of the first group of Jews who settled in what later became the United States. Viener had been deeply involved in the celebration, and both men were members of the American Jewish Historical Society. Although he pursued a business career, Viener had earned a master's degree in history and gave presentations and wrote articles on history besides being deeply active in promoting Jewish history organizations. A resident of Petersburg, Ginsberg had written a history of the Jews of Virginia.[2]

This first society launched the *Journal of the Southern Jewish Historical Society*, first edited by Marilyn S. (Mrs. David J.) Greenberg. Sadie Engelberg, chair of the history department at John Marshall High School in Richmond, edited the third and long-delayed final issue. Almost all the officers of the society and the editor and board of the journal were amateur historians and also members of Jewish families who had lived for generations in the region. With the exception of Ginsberg, all the officers lived in Richmond, and the society ultimately housed its papers at the Congregation Beth Ahabah archives, also in Richmond.

The first issue of the journal featured a foreword by Jacob Rader Marcus, then president of the American Jewish Historical Society. Marcus had encouraged the creation of a journal in a speech at the society's first conference held at the Valentine Museum in Richmond. This issue also included articles by historian and rabbi of a Norfolk, Virginia, congregation Malcolm H. Stern, the staff members of the Valentine Museum in Richmond (on acquisitions to the SJHS collection initially housed there), and genealogists and amateur historians Thomas J. Tobias of Charleston, South Carolina, and Harry Simonoff of Miami, Florida. As Viener later observed, Simonoff "did not believe in footnotes. We could not prevail upon him to provide footnotes, so we went ahead and printed the article."[3]

In his foreword, Marcus noted the importance of southern Jewish history for a greater understanding of American Jewish history. He observed, "It is imperative that the story of the old be retold, correctly, and in proper perspective, that the magic of the new be captured while it is young and vital and everpresent."[4] Marcus's statements reflected the mission of the society: to preserve, record, and learn from the Jewish history of the region. In keeping with the sense and reasoning behind the tercentenary commemoration, the knowledge held importance for scholars and laypeople, Jews and non-Jews. Will Herberg's *Protestant—Catholic—Jew: An Essay in American Religious Sociology* appeared in 1955, suggesting a pluralistic society overcoming the anti-Semitism of previous decades.[5] Providing a positive Jewish history for Jews and non-Jews that traced Jewish longevity and contributions in the American South perfectly fit the era.

Although Marcus urged the society to venture beyond filiopietistic depictions, it typically failed to do so. Of the three issues that appeared in November 1958, October 1959, and November 1963, none exceeded thirty-six pages in length. Somewhat typical were reminiscences in the second issue by Emilie V. Jacobs concerning her father, Rev. George Jacobs, who served congregations in Philadelphia and Richmond. Jacobs was in her eighties, and the article developed after she and her sister Virginia Jacobs displayed family memorabilia on the 100th anniversary of their parents' wedding. Shortly after the last publication, the society ended its existence, apparently because of a financial shortage. By that stage, also, relatively few people (the exact number is unknown) had remained involved and most of them lived in and around Richmond.[6]

Few academic historians displayed interest in American Jewish history prior to the 1970s, when a new cadre rejuvenated the field. Interest in the history of the Jewish South was part and parcel of the broader national trend. During the latter 1960s and early 1970s, books by Eli N. Evans, Harry Golden, and Leonard Dinnerstein fostered interest in southern Jewish history.[7] Consequently in 1976, as the United States celebrated the bicentennial of the Declaration of Independence, Viener worked closely with Bernard Wax, executive director of the American Jewish Historical Society (AJHS), to convene the board of trustees of AJHS in Richmond. The National Foundation of Jewish Culture, the Richmond Jewish Community Council, and the department of history of Virginia Commonwealth University, through the intervention of historian Melvin I. Urofsky, lent additional support to the meeting. Urofsky joined Viener to co-chair this meeting.[8] Scholars and laypeople attended and gave presentations. Invitations had been issued, but the meeting was also open to the public through advertising and word-of-mouth. Milton J. and Rosemary Krensky of Chicago were sufficiently impressed to underwrite the publication of *Turn to the South*, a collection of presentations from the meeting edited by Urofsky and Nathan M. Kaganoff, librarian and editor of AJHS. This second anthology in the field was dedicated to Mrs. Krensky's father, Bernard C. Ehrenreich, rabbi of a congregation in Montgomery, Alabama, during the first half of the twentieth century and the subject of the first article in the volume.[9]

The anthology reflected the state of the field and the nature of the society at the time. Far superior in quality to the articles in the earlier society's journal, authors represented a mixture of amateurs and professional scholars in American and American Jewish history, American studies, and sociology. Most pursued southern Jewish history tangentially to their regular specialties. Nonetheless, Urofsky, Evans, Stern, Arnold Shankman, and Abraham Lavender made additional contributions through the years, and Stephen J. Whitfield remains a force in the field today. Lawrence H. Fuchs's foreword, Urofsky's preface, and many of the articles supported the southern Jewish distinctiveness school of historiography, first developed by Golden and Evans a few years earlier.[10]

The distinctiveness school began by questioning what made the southern Jewish experience different, and typically juxtaposed German Reform life in the region with the experiences of East European Jews in the twentieth-century New York metropolitan environment. Contrasts were inevitable. Jews in the South owned, bought, and sold slaves far later than in the North. They supported the Confederacy and Lost Cause imagery. Classical Reform held greater sway and, with it, opposition to Zionism. Southern Jews, fearful of anti-Semitism as such a tiny minority, acculturated to regional mores and did not speak out on controversial issues. Yet, Jews contributed disproportionately to the economy, culture, and philanthropic causes in what this school designated as the least anti-Semitic region in the country.

The Modern Southern Jewish Historical Society

With the enthusiasm generated by this conference, during spring 1977 Viener, Louis Schmier, Abram Kanof, and David Goldberg met at the airport in Raleigh, North Carolina, and signed the documents that formally established a new Southern Jewish Historical Society. Kanof, a past president of AJHS, served as host/acting chair and Viener appeared on the document as the society's first president. Then a graduate student at the University of North Carolina, Goldberg later attained a PhD in history from Louisiana State University but followed a career as an appraiser and estate sale director in New Orleans, and Schmier taught at Valdosta State College (later University), specialized in the history of the Jews in southwest Georgia, and served as secretary of the organization from 1985 until 1991.[11]

The first conference of the society convened in Raleigh in April 1978. About 150 attendees, mostly laypeople, listened to a variety of presentations. Jack Coleman succeeded Viener, who became chair of the AJHS board, the next year. A second collection of essays derived from conference presentations appeared in 1984.[12]

Since the Raleigh conference, SJHS has met in virtually every southern state, as well as in Cincinnati at the American Jewish Archives.[13] A conference in Memphis led to the creation of the Memphis and Mid-South Jewish Historical Society.[14] This society hosted additional SJHS conferences, as have Jewish historical societies in Maryland, North Carolina, South Carolina, Virginia, Texas, and Washington, DC. Occasionally, universities have also acted as meeting places or hosts. By convening in various locations, members gain knowledge of local history and explore sites of Jewish historical interest. Local historical activity is also stimulated.

SJHS maintains a close working relationship with the Institute of Southern Jewish Life (ISJL) in Jackson, Mississippi. Three of the historians at ISJL, Mark I. Greenberg, Stuart Rockoff, and now Josh Parshall, have been very active in the society (Rockoff is a past president and Parshall is vice president/president-elect as of 2021). ISJL sponsored a SJHS conference, as did its predecessor, the Museum of the Southern Jewish Experience. A similar positive relationship is developing with the new Museum of the Southern Jewish Experience (MSJE) in New Orleans. Historians associated with SJHS serve as advisors for the museum, and SJHS president Jay B. Silverberg launched a recent endowment fundraising effort that resulted in substantial donations to SJHS, MSJE, and the Jewish studies program at Tulane University.During the switch to Zoom presentations in light of COVID-19 restrictions, SJHS and Breman Jewish

Heritage Museum in Atlanta cosponsored a speaker series that attracted audiences reaching over five hundred from across the United States and Europe. Sandy Berman, the museum's original archivist, served as the primary source section editor of *Southern Jewish History*. Jeremy Katz, her successor at the museum, oversees the exhibit and movie review section of the journal.[15]

SJHS also closely interfaces with universities in several ways. Society conferences have been cosponsored and taken place at Emory, the University of Alabama, the University of Texas, the College of Charleston, Vanderbilt, and other institutions. Officers, society and editorial board members, journal peer-reviewers and authors, conference presenters and featured speakers, and recipients of grants and awards come from college and university ranks throughout the country and even overseas. In 2022, for the first time the society sponsored two panels at the AJHS Biennial Scholars' Conference.

SJHS outreach to these state and local historical societies, museums, and Jewish studies programs falls under the society's dual mission to encourage scholarship in the field and to disseminate information to academic and lay audiences. The level of these activities has been virtually unique; no other organization including AJHS has exerted similar effort and obtained similar positive results. The Scott and Donna Langston archival grant program, active participation of numerous archivists and museum professionals, the encouragement of individuals to donate materials to archives, and publications in the journal have fostered the development and expansion of archives and museums in the region.

Conferences

Fundamental differences exist between the more scholarly programs of SJHS and those less academic on the state society level concerning the qualifications of the speakers and the scholarly nature of presentations. Besides venturing beyond local subject matter, presentations at SJHS conferences are more likely to consider historiography and place materials in broader contextual frameworks. Whereas local historical conferences tend to highlight speakers with ties to local communities and their subject matter, interaction at SJHS is more likely to take place between academic presenters and laypeople related to individuals discussed in the papers or knowledgeable about the events depicted that occurred in their communities. These exchanges often stimulate the speakers in a fashion not common at typical historical society conferences.[16]

Many outstanding historians of American Jewish history have served as featured conference speakers. In 2020, a partnership developed among SJHS, Atlanta's historic Temple (the Hebrew Benevolent Congregation), and the Breman Museum to support a speakership in honor of Janice Rothschild Blumberg, a past president of the society who has participated in and written about southern Jewish history. With a major donation to the society endowment, a new Lawrence Kanter speaker gave an inaugural lecture virtually in 2022. The Helen Marie Stern Memorial Fund sponsors a cultural event at conferences and has helped fund speakers and the society's journal.

Regardless of the quality of the panels and speakers, some laypeople occasionally complain that there are too many academic sessions. On some occasions local historical societies hosting conferences have also attempted to press for less academically oriented local speakers and for more time for local tours with fewer slots for academic programs. Yet, as former society president Bruce Beeber commented to this author, he prefers more sessions and the ability to miss some if they become too exhausting. When lesser quality and/or filiopietistic speakers give presentations, both laypeople and scholars in the audience typically give negative reviews.[17] Some conflict has also occurred between the society and host communities over fundraising and planning expectations for conferences. This tension has gradually been overcome with the society's adjusting its expectations for funds being remitted to the society and other accommodations.

Publications

Solomon Breibart edited the society's original newsletter from 1981 to 1990 with historian Arnold Shankman in charge of "mini-articles."[18] Helen Silver followed Breibart as editor. This newsletter contained material on society conferences and news as well as short historical articles. It became more professional under the editorship of Leonard Rogoff, and then of Adam Mendelsohn and Bryan E. Stone, and now of Deborah Weiner, all trained historians well published in the field. Renamed *The Rambler* in 1996, it appears several times a year in a format designed by a professional.[19] Articles highlight society and member news and advertise the annual conference as well as the activities of local organizations. Short book and exhibit reviews, items concerning archives, and shorter historical pieces fill its pages.

In 1996, a committee chaired by University of South Carolina historian Belinda Gergel and Memphis archivist Patricia LaPointe conducted a survey and presented a report the following year at the annual meeting concerning the establishment of a new history journal. With the strong support of Samuel Proctor and Sol Breibart, among others, the membership voted to approve the new undertaking. Yet the outgoing treasurer, Arthur "Bud" Whitehill, voiced qualms about the society's ability to support this endeavor financially. Wax countered that he would step in as treasurer, help with fundraising, and agree to resign if a deficit persisted after three to five years caused by publication costs. Historian Mark K. Bauman agreed to serve as editor and past president Rachel Heimovics, touting experience in professional publishing, signed on as managing editor. Because of Whitehill's warning, these editors assumed the unusual role of journal fundraisers beyond their regular editorial duties. For about twenty years the Lucius N. Littauer Foundation of New York and the Gale Foundation of Texas provided substantial funding beyond society dues. When the missions of these foundations changed, other foundations and individuals came forward to fill the void. In 2021, SJHS president Jay Silverberg solicited a $200,000 addition over a five-year period to the society endowment from Dr. Lawrence J. Kanter, which will end the editors' roles as fundraisers. Personal contacts proved crucial in every case of foundation and estate funding.

Mentorship has served as an unofficial core value of the society and its membership. When Heimovics began researching how to produce the journal, Proctor served as her mentor based on his experience as the longtime editor of the *Florida Historical Quarterly*. He provided entrée to a printer that he used for his journal who has served as the printer for *Southern Jewish History* since the beginning of its publication. In turn, Heimovics (now Braun) mentored Bryan Edward Stone, her successor, during a three-year transition. She continues to serve as an unofficial advisor and one of four or five outside proofreaders.

From the onset, Bauman determined that this would be an annual, peer-reviewed journal. Well-written and researched articles would forward the understanding of southern and therefore American Jewish history while also being accessible to the broader lay readership. He recommended the simple name, *Southern Jewish History*, which the society board approved.

Published in 1998, the first volume of the journal featured an article, "Why Study Southern Jewish History?" by Gary P. Zola, executive director of the American Jewish Archives and author of an important book and articles in the field.[20] Other articles were written by a graduate student researching a dissertation on Texas Jewish history,[21] a historian delving into North Carolina Jewish history, a nurse tracing the story of two nurses during and after World War I, an eighty-four-year-old amateur historian writing about a politician and community activist in Virginia, and a recent Tulane PhD on two women who represented divisions within the New Orleans Jewish community. This mixture of graduate students, beginning and senior academics, amateurs, and scholars with backgrounds outside of history continues, as does the tremendous variety of subject matter. Beyond the South and throughout the United States, the journal has drawn authors from Canada, France, Germany, Great Britain, Israel, Japan, and South Africa. Subfields are almost too numerous to mention: social and cultural history, economic and business history, history of religion, race relations, military and architectural history, women's history, etc.[22]

Attempting to maintain the academic standards of *American Jewish History* and the *American Jewish Archives Journal*, the top journals in the broader field, is not always easy. Fewer manuscripts are submitted, so that the editor constantly solicits potential articles. It is not unusual for authors to revise multiple times even before manuscripts are of sufficient quality to send to peer reviewers. Bauman often has to take a hands-on approach to editing, reorganizing, analyzing, and providing historical context and historiography to bring manuscripts up to par. Yet the journal has encouraged scholars and scholarship in the field and made sound history accessible to the academic and lay readership. Articles originally published in the journal have been republished in monographs and anthologies and become mainstays on reading lists for a growing number of courses in southern Jewish history.[23]

At the onset, Bauman established an editorial board whose members serve five-year terms of office. Through the years, junior and senior scholars (some of the most renowned in southern and American Jewish history), archivists, genealogists, gifted amateurs, and a college president made key policy decisions and helped the journal grow. Ideas from this board, the SJHS board, and managing editors Rachel Heimovics and Bryan Edward Stone led to the creation of book, exhibit, movie, and website review sections, a primary source section, and the newest section on memoirs/autobiographies, each of which is under the supervision of a section editor.[24]

Grants and Awards

SJHS provides a variety of grants and awards to support and encourage sound scholarship. Awards for the outstanding article in the journal and the best book in the field, both published over four-year intervals, rotate on a two-year cycle. The outstanding career service award is named for the late Saul Viener and one for outstanding career scholarship in the field is named for the late Samuel Proctor. The awards committee also bestows an honor roll award for outstanding service to the society. Annually a society committee distributes funding for project research and completion.[25]

Some programs have met only temporary success and thus have been discontinued. A short-lived speakers' bureau through the society website essentially became moribund from a lack of leadership. A student essay contest featured winners who later gained their doctorates and published extensively in the field, yet this program was discontinued because of a paucity of submissions. Nonetheless, outreach to and inclusion of undergraduate and graduate students has burgeoned through grants, publications in the society journal, and presentations at conferences, in addition to greatly reduced dues for student memberships. For students, the society offers a welcoming and well-known presence. During the mid-1980s, Tom Sokolosky-Wixon chaired a society historic sites committee while cataloging Jewish burial locations in Mississippi. Again, this effort proved to be short-lived.[26]

Administration

The society's website, www.jewishsouth.org, includes information on the society and its officers, grants and awards programs, conferences, and the history journal and *Rambler* newsletter. Also included is an extensive bibliography maintained by Adam Meyer, a professor in the Jewish studies program at Vanderbilt University.

Volunteers largely manage the activities of SJHS. Although the majority of SJHS members are interested and knowledgeable laypeople, presidents have been split almost equally between laypeople and academic scholars.[27] The society is also almost unique among Jewish historical societies in having non-Jews as members, presenters, board members, and presidents. In this and other ways SJHS stresses its identity as a historical society rather than as a Jewish organization, although conferences often make provisions for Shabbat services and for people who maintain the dietary laws.

Board members and presidents are elected for two-year terms with eligibility to be reelected for an additional two years. The secretary and treasurer positions are also elective but without similar time limitations. The treasurer submits and oversees the finances of the society including the annual budget, checking account, and the endowment housed with the Richmond Jewish Federation. Only one president has resigned as a result of inability to fulfill the responsibilities of the position. The journal and *Rambler* editors, past presidents, and Bernard Wax (until his passing in 2022) serve on the board as ex officio members. The officers and board oversee the budget and fundraising, select conference locations, work with local host committees, and otherwise manage the society's affairs. Committees with chairpeople chosen by the officers and board supervise grants and awards, finance and development, membership, nominations, and conference programs. Only the journal and *Rambler* editors receive small stipends. Barbara Tahsler is the only individual who could be characterized as paid staff—and an indispensable one at that. Former president Beryl Weiner arranged for her to oversee membership on a part-time basis while she served as his administrative legal assistant. She has continued to work for the society since he passed away.[28]

The Southern Jewish Historical Society and Changes in the Field

When the society was established, only Louis Schmier pursued the study of southern Jewish history as his primary focus. Then Mark Bauman joined him in this concentration in 1978. Few graduate students—Carolyn Lipson-Walker, Bobbie Malone, Marc Cowett, Steven Hertzberg, and Gary Zola—wrote dissertations in the field until a turning point began during the mid-1990s. At that stage and since a growing number of graduate students and academics have written numerous dissertations, articles, and books on the subject and turned to it as their major research endeavor. Jewish studies programs in southern universities have expanded exponentially, as have courses and academic positions in the field and the number of university presses willing to publish books in the field. SJHS helped foster this multilayer surge through its conferences, grants, and journal, but especially through its welcoming environment and network. Conversely, the society has benefited from the growing number of scholars who participate in programs, as officers of the society, and as conference program chairs and members of host committees, besides working with and for the society journal and contributing to its pages.

As previously indicated, during the 1970s the prevailing image was of a distinctively different southern Jewish history unique from that of other sections of the country. Many scholars continue to follow that school and have expanded upon it. Yet, during the early 1990s, Lee Shai Weissbach, studying the small towns of Kentucky, challenged this prevailing paradigm. His study of small-town Jewry, the standard in the field of American Jewish history, continued to maintain his position that Jews living in small towns throughout the country behaved in remarkably similar ways.[29] Bauman expanded on this concept with his *The Southerner as American: Jewish Style* and additional works. In brief, Bauman argued that, although some variations appear from region to region, when comparing similar Jewish communities—port cities, small towns, and commercial versus industrial cities—similarities far outweighed differences. Moreover, local environments were as likely to impact on Jews as regional factors. Weissbach, Bauman, and others argue that a major problem arises when comparing Eastern European Jewish life in the New York metropolitan area with almost anywhere else in the country except similar industrial cities.[30]

This debate rages on at SJHS conferences, with some society policy statements, and in the pages of *Southern Jewish History*. Yet few articles in the journal adhere to the distinctiveness school. In 2013, Hasia Diner, a New York University history professor, chaired a society committee to award the best article in the journal from the previous four years. She subsequently commented to the journal editor concerning the paucity of articles with particularly southern themes. Neither the society nor the journal take an explicit stand on the historical debate that provides fertile fodder for academic discourse.

There is nothing specifically southern about the society beyond subject matter, unless one can gauge a broader level of hospitality—a proposition other regional societies would readily challenge. It also makes no effort to create an image of ideal or actual Jews in the American South beyond attempting to depict Jews and Judaism in the region with historical accuracy. An editorial board member recently commented to the journal editor about the disparate images of the Jewish South in the last several issues of *Southern Jewish History*. Numerous articles stress the positive roles of rabbis during the long Civil Rights era. Juxtaposed with these are essays showing Jews adhering to Lost Cause mythology and glorifying Judah P. Benjamin, one of the first Jews in the United States Senate and later a Confederate who served in three cabinet positions for his friend Jefferson Davis. Attorney Daniel Weinfeld's observation reflects well on the society, an organization that supports scholarly research that depicts southern Jewish history critically—even as its historians agree to disagree over interpretation.

The leadership of its dedicated, informed amateurs and professional academics, the scholarly quality of its conferences and journal, its outreach to state and local institutions, and its broader roles in nurturing a growing cadre of scholars and scholarship and moving the study of southern Jewish history forward set the Southern Jewish Historical Society above and apart from its predecessor and from other regional Jewish historical societies. It is an ever-evolving, twice constituted organization. With a dramatically growing endowment and stable organizational structure, this should remain the case for the foreseeable future.

1. The author thanks Rachel Heimovics Braun, Leonard Rogoff, Jay B. Silverberg, Bryan Edward Stone, Bernard Wax, and Stephen J. Whitfield for their helpful comments and corrections.
2. Saul Viener, "Roots of the Southern Jewish Historical Society: The Recollections of Saul Viener," *Southern Jewish Historical Society Newsletter* (July 1982): 2–3; Eric L. Goldstein, "Making History: An Interview with Saul Viener," *Southern Jewish History* 10 (2007): 39–88; Mark K. Bauman, "Editor's Note on History and Memory," *Southern Jewish History* 10 (2007): 23–24; Louis Ginsberg, *History of the Jews of Petersburg, 1789–1950* (Petersburg, VA: privately published, 1954); Louis Ginsberg, *Chapters of the Jews of Virginia, 1658–1900* (Petersburg, VA: privately published, 1969).
3. Viener, "Roots of the Southern Jewish Historical Society," 2. Harry Simonoff later wrote *Jewish Participants in the Civil War* (New York: Arco, 1963).
4. Jacob Rader Marcus, "Foreword," *Journal of the Southern Jewish Historical Society* 1, no. 1 (1958): 3.
5. Will Herberg, *Protestant—Catholic—Jew: An Essay in American Religious Sociology* (New York: Doubleday, 1955).
6. Viener, "Roots of the Southern Jewish Historical Society," 2. Copies of the original journals can be found in the SJHS Collection at the Jewish Heritage Collection, Addleston Library, College of Charleston. Solomon Breibart encouraged SJHS to place its records at the College of Charleston and served as a liaison with the college. On Thomas J. Tobias, see Harlan Greene and Dale Rosengarten, "In Distinguished Company: A Profile of Solomon Breibart," *Southern Jewish History* 7 (2004): 3–4.
7. Harry Golden, *Our Southern Landsman* (New York: Putnam, 1974); Eli N. Evans, *The Provincials: A Personal History of the Jews in the South* (New York: Free Press,

1973); Leonard Dinnerstein, *The Leo Frank Case* (New York: Columbia University Press, 1968); Leonard Dinnerstein and Mary Dale Palsson, eds., *Jews in the South* (Baton Rouge: Louisiana State University Press, 1973).

8. Urofsky, an expert on Zionism, had begun his extensive writing on Louis Brandeis, whose family resided in Kentucky. He later published numerous works on the Supreme Court, Supreme Court justices, and individual rights and freedoms. Viener was an extremely kind and persuasive individual. He likely got Urofsky involved in SJHS and influenced the academic's later foray into Virginia Jewish history and the Levy family's involvement in restoring Monticello. See Melvin I. Urofsky, *Community and Commonwealth: The Jewish Experience in Virginia* (Charlottesville: Virginia Historical Society, 1997); *The Levy Family and Monticello, 1834–1923* (Chapel Hill: University of North Carolina Press, 2002).

9. Bernard Wax, "Ruminations about the SJHS," *Southern Jewish History* 10 (2007): 1–2; Goldstein, "Making History," 71–2, 74; Eli N. Evans, "Reflections on the Past and Future of the Southern Jewish Historical Society," *Southern Jewish History* 10 (2007): 89–92. On this and following, also see Nathan M. Kaganoff and Melvin I. Urofsky, eds., *Turn to the South: Essays on Southern Jewry* (Waltham, MA: American Jewish Historical Society and Charlottesville: University of Virginia Press, 1979). The first anthology was a collection of previously published essays, Dinnerstein and Palsson, eds., *Jews in the South*. On Viener's background, interests, and leadership in Richmond's tercentenary celebration, see David Weinfeld, "Two Commemorations: Richmond's Jews and the Lost Cause During the Civil Rights Era," *Southern Jewish History* 23 (2020): 77–123. For the impact of the conference on Stephen J. Whitfield and his commitment to writing southern Jewish history, see Deborah R. Weiner, "A Sense of Connection to Others: A Profile of Stephen J. Whitfield," *Southern Jewish History* 7 (2004): 58.

10. Golden, *Our Southern Landsman*; Evans, *The Provincials*; Janice Rothschild Blumberg, "The Distance Traveled: Reminiscences of Twenty-Five Years in SJHS," *Southern Jewish History* 10 (2007): 13.

11. Mark K. Bauman, "Revisiting History," *Southern Jewish History* 10 (2007): 25–26. On Louis Schmier's leadership, see Blumberg, "The Distance Traveled," 14. David Goldberg's thesis at UNC investigated Jewish mayors in southern cities from the last decades of the nineteenth into the first decades of the twentieth century. His LSU dissertation was "The Jews of Dryades Street, New Orleans, 1920–25," a

somewhat unusual topic for the era in that it dealt with the Eastern European Orthodox community.

12. Bauman, "Revisiting History;" Samuel Proctor and Louis Schmier with Malcolm Stern, eds., *Jews of the South: Selected Essays from the Southern Jewish Historical Society* (Macon, GA: Mercer University Press, 1984). Proctor, the sixth president of SJHS, was a distinguished professor of history at the University of Florida. Like so many other participants at the time, he wrote a few articles on southern Jewish history but concentrated outside of the field (in his case, on Florida history). Proctor also encouraged his graduate students Canter Brown Jr. and Mark I. Greenberg to work in the field of southern Jewish history. Several conference presentations during the mid-1970s led to Mark K. Bauman and Berkley Kalin, eds., *The Quiet Voices: Southern Rabbis and Black Civil Rights from 1880s to the 1990s* (Tuscaloosa: University of Alabama Press, 1997).
13. A full list of conference locations is available at Southern Jewish Historical Society, https://www.jewishsouth.org/past-conferences, accessed August 24, 2021.
14. Blumberg, "The Distance Traveled," 17–18.
15. In 2021, Jeremy Katz accepted the position of archivist at Hamilton College in New York but continues as section editor.
16. For a personal note about this interaction and how it differs from typical historical conferences, see Stephen J. Whitfield's comments in Weiner, "A Sense of Connection to Others," 63–64.
17. Copies of most of the programs and occasional conference audience evaluations are available in the SJHS Collection. Laypeople comprise the substantial majority of membership. Most of these are sophisticated and well-educated senior citizens who appreciate sound scholarship that is free of jargon and accessible. On early conflicts over the quality of speakers and disagreements over scholarship, see Saul J. Rubin, "The Pioneer Period of the SJHS (1976–1983)," *Southern Jewish History* 10 (2007): 6–7. As Rubin put it (p. 7), "This remains a contemporary issue—the tension between popularists and scholars."
18. Greene and Rosengarten, "In Distinguished Company," 14; Adam Mendelsohn, "An Interview with Bernard Wax," *Southern Jewish History* 17 (2014): 141; Rubin, "Pioneer Period," 8. David Goldberg informally circulated society news before the creation of the newsletter.
19. Wax, "Ruminations," 2; Bernard Wax, "Postscript: Reminiscences and

Observations," *Southern Jewish History* 17 (2014): 147. Copies of many of the newsletters are available in the SJHS Collection.

20. Gary P. Zola, "Why Study Southern Jewish History?" *Southern Jewish History* 1 (1998): 1–21.
21. Bryan Edward Stone ultimately wrote and edited books on Texas Jewish history and other articles for the journal, as well as becoming the journal's managing editor.
22. A full listing of the journal articles is available at www.jewishsouth.org. All volumes can be downloaded for free with the exception of the last two that are available for nominal payments.
23. See Stephen J. Whitfield, "The Achievement of Mark K. Bauman," *Southern Jewish History* 20 (2017): 1–32; Scott M. Langston and Bryan Edward Stone, "Teaching Southern Jewish History: A Dialogue," *Southern Jewish History* 15 (2012): 1–40.
24. The names of editorial board members and section editors are available in the individual journal volumes.
25. For information on these grants and awards, see the society website, www.jewishsouth.org.
26. Files in author's possession and at the SJHS Collection; Blumberg, "The Distance Traveled," 18.
27. For a partial list up to and including 2007, see "Conferences and Presidents," *Southern Jewish History* 10 (2007): 27.
28. On the voluntary nature of the leadership, see Wax, "Ruminations about the SJHS," 4.
29. Lee Shai Weissbach, *Jewish Life in Small-Town America* (New Haven, CT: Yale University Press, 2005). For a more recent example of the southern distinctiveness school, see Marcie Cohen Ferris and Mark I. Greenberg, eds., *Jewish Roots in Southern Soil* (Waltham, MA: Brandeis University Press, 2006).
30. Mark K. Bauman, *The Southerner as American: Jewish Style* (Cincinnati, OH: American Jewish Archives, 1996). See also Mark K. Bauman, ed., *Dixie Diaspora: An Anthology of Southern Jewish History* (Tuscaloosa: University of Alabama Press, 2006) and *A New Vision of Southern Jewish History* (Tuscaloosa: University of Alabama Press, 2019) (this includes a reprint of *The Southerner as American: Jewish Style* and a historiography essay first published in *American Jewish Archives Journal* 59 [2007] that traces the issues and publications involved in this debate). See also

Mark K. Bauman, "Regionalism," in *Oxford Handbook of American Jewish History*, eds. Michael Cohen and Shari Rabin (New York: Oxford University Press, forthcoming) for a broader discussion of regionalism in American Jewish history. In this last essay, Bauman points to the difficulty of defining the states within regions. Until recently, *Southern Jewish History* defined the South as the former states of the Confederacy—Alabama, Arkansas, Florida, Georgia, Mississippi, North and South Carolina, Texas, and Virginia—plus Maryland and Washington, DC. In 2021, after a strenuous debate within the editorial board, Oklahoma and Delaware were added.

5

Our Star Is Rising

Jewish Historical Society of Michigan's Pivot to Relevance

CATHERINE CANGANY

Like so many Jewish institutions, Jewish Historical Society of Michigan (JHSM) began as a *minyan*. As the immediate past president, Risha B. Ring, PhD, likes to say, the founders were "ten history nerds seated around a card table." Indeed, JHSM's first location was founder Allen A. Warsen's living room. A high school history teacher and director of a religious school, Warsen had been vocal since Detroit's 250th anniversary in 1951 about the need for a local Jewish historical society. Three years later, when the Detroit Historical Museum crafted an exhibit to celebrate the tercentenary of Jewish people in what is now the United States, Warsen renewed his call, hoping a leading Jewish organization would step forward. When none did, he spearheaded it himself, founding JHSM on Sunday, June 21, 1959.[1]

The timing of JHSM's creation was deeply significant to Michigan's Jewry. As in so many other Jewish communities, in the wake of the Shoah, the 1950s was a decade of extraordinary development for Michigan's Jews: new religious schools, new synagogues, new hospitals and centers—all as the majority of the community continued its northwest migration out of Detroit and into the suburbs. The reasons for the migration are complex, rooted in racism, anti-Semitism, and socioeconomics, and are not exclusive to Jews. But even today, many Jewish seniors are uncomfortable talking about the full range of push-pull factors that motivated the community's exodus. But the move and the rebuilding did encourage the community to look inward and articulate the importance of understanding and preserving history, culture, and belief. That included creating a historical society.[2]

Michigan's Jewish history began in the early 1760s, when Jewish fur traders and merchants moved into the forts at Michilimackinac (at the top of the Lower Peninsula) and Detroit. While the area was under French authority, non-Catholics had been forbidden from settling there. But immediately after the British took control in 1760, Jews arrived, motivated by the novel economic opportunities and the pathway to naturalization. Between the opening of the Erie Canal in 1825, railroads first laid in the 1830s, and statehood in 1837, many people caught "Michigan fever." The land became more accessible and more lucrative: statewide fishing, mining, and lumber industries took hold. Jewish peddlers, shopkeepers, and merchants were at the forefront of the commercial ventures that supported these industries. By the dawn of the Civil War, Jewish communities were established across Michigan's Upper and Lower Peninsulas.[3]

Jewish people have lived in the state's largest population center, Detroit, since 1762. With the exception of Michilimackinac and a colony of Jews who settled in Ann Arbor briefly in the 1840s, Michigan's highest concentration of Jews always has been in Metro Detroit, which JHSM calls home. As elsewhere in the United States, Detroit's Jewish population expanded exponentially in the late nineteenth century. When Henry Ford doubled wages to offer his employees $5 a day in 1914, Jewish laborers joined the assembly lines, keen for a monetary boost into the middle class. Ford and other employers supported temperance, urging prohibition at the state level, which began in 1917. The city's proximity to Windsor, Ontario, spurred Detroit's Jewish criminal mob of bootleggers, the Purple Gang, to smuggle in liquor from Canada. Although the gang disintegrated during the 1930s, the community stigma of being related to "Purples" persists. Today, 62 percent of Metro Detroit's Jewish adults are locally born, making the community markedly connected, interconnected, and engaged.[4]

JHSM's 1959 founding minyan was composed of what Allen Warsen termed "a number of Jewish intellectuals." They feature professors (of Hebrew, anthropology, education, and Russian), administrators of synagogues and religious schools, an architect in Albert Kahn's firm, and fellow history teachers—including colleague Richard Leland, who remembers Warsen flagging him down at school one day and asking for five dollars. Without hesitation or any idea of the purpose, Leland handed over the money. Warsen then congratulated him on becoming a founding member of JHSM. That early contribution worked Leland right into a job: he was elected JHSM's first treasurer.[5]

In its establishment, JHSM had a high-profile advocate in scholar-rabbi Jacob Rader Marcus, who had helped found the American Jewish Archives at Hebrew Union College in 1947. Twelve years later, Marcus recognized that the field of American Jewish history was still young and understudied. On hearing the news of JHSM's creation, he sent along his personal endorsement, praising the founders for their recognition that "local research" would help bring the unwieldy subject into "sharp focus." These efforts would produce "valuable contributions to our understanding of Jewish life in America . . . and advance a discipline whose cultural value to the American Jew is potentially incalculable."[6]

Together, the founders agreed to four aims, in line with the functions of historical societies across the globe: to promote the study of and research in Michigan Jewish history, publish periodicals for recording and interpreting that history, preserve historical materials, and create and maintain a repository for them. The first and second of those aims have carried through the entirety of JHSM's existence. All the organization's programmatic and publication undertakings have been and continue to be designed to promote the study of and research in Michigan's Jewish history—through lectures, conferences, tours, curricula, and periodicals. In that sense, the mission has not changed in sixty-three years.[7]

Bus, walking, and site tours have long been JHSM mainstays. Mostly Metro Detroit focused, or day trips from Metro Detroit, they have been offered with regularity to students, families, and seniors since the 1980s. Bike tours were added in the 2010s. Whether public historical overviews or private and customized, these tours appeal particularly to audiences looking for nostalgia and *l'dor v'dor* (intergenerational) opportunities to share family history. JHSM's passionate volunteers—many of whom have lived these experiences themselves—are ideal for providing visits to neighborhoods and public high schools that were once overwhelmingly middle class and Jewish and are now poor and Black. It is easy to critique the organization for seeming to encourage poverty tourism. But JHSM also works closely with the Black community, through programming partnerships, joint bus tours, and support of Black organizations.[8]

Volunteers continue to play a special and vital role in JHSM's programming and management today, as docents, event chairs, supporters, and directors, which includes a board of eighteen members, plus active past presidents. But in the last twenty years, as JHSM has continued to grow, the organization has professionalized. In 1990, it hired its first part-time administrative assistant. Nine years later, it hired its first publications editor, who became JHSM's first part-time director in 2003. With the hiring of the organization's first trained historian in 2018, the position expanded to full time. This marked a significant step forward in JHSM's commitment to offering professional-quality undertakings.[9]

Since 2018, lecture programs have largely been outsourced to professional historians, showcasing academic research and moving away from the filiopietism that often characterizes the work of history enthusiasts. Taking a lead from the 1959 founders, JHSM today strives to be as supportive of and appealing to scholars as it does the general public. A sizeable network of academics, and their graduate and advanced undergraduate students, are involved in our publications and programming. Recent lecturers include Jonathan Sarna (Brandeis University), Marc Dollinger (San Francisco State University), Lila Corwin Berman (Temple University), Pamela S. Nadell (American University), Rachel B. Gross (San Francisco State University), and Annelise Heinz (University of Oregon). Our speaker roster also features public historians, working in archives, architecture, museums, libraries, and the government. Recent speakers include Erin Einhorn (NBC News), Craig Wilson (Mackinac State Historic Parks), Louis Miller (William L. Clements Library), and Laura Miller (architectural preservationist). With speakers like these, the quality of our programming has increased substantially, as have our public discussions about how professional historians "do" history, why it takes so long to produce, how it differs from local history, and why it matters in theory and practice.

Engaging with scholars necessarily means facing hard historical truths. Marc Dollinger and Mary-Elizabeth Murphy (Eastern Michigan University) have spoken candidly to our audience about Jews, racism, and civil rights—including Jewish acts of racism and Jewish resistance to civil rights—to challenge a persistent local belief that Michigan's Jews have always been allied with the Black community. Notably, Erin Einhorn (NBC News) has revealed Jewish ties to Detroit's segregation wall, built in 1941 to separate a new, white neighborhood from an existing poor Black neighborhood. The wall was a condition of the Federal Housing Administration's deal with the developer: If the wall was built, the new neighborhood's white buyers would be eligible for loans and mortgage guarantees. Jews lived on either side of the Birwood Wall, in varying degrees of awareness and with a range of views on it. There was even a Jewish developer who contemplated building a second, similar wall, before being cried down by other Jews. Comparable programs have addressed the history of Zionism and German American Jews' reluctance in the early twentieth century to jeopardize their gains in the United States with vocal support for Israel. These truths are not easy to hear—and they go against decades of community stories and community belief. But we feel strongly about connecting scholars with the general public to mainstream the research and strip away discomfort in talking about difficult issues.[10]

Programs of this caliber and incisiveness have occurred mostly during the COVID-19 pandemic and mostly virtually. Adding Zoom to our repertoire increased our programming by 40 percent and membership by 13 percent. It also has substantially enlarged our program participation, drawing viewers from twenty-seven states, plus Canada, Israel, and Washington, DC. We anticipate offering some virtual programming (or virtual options for in-person programming) for the foreseeable future, to continue engaging with our far-flung supporters.

Zoom has also made it possible for us to be a less Detroit-centric organization—a problem JHSM has had since 1959. Although Western and Northern Michigan have small, vibrant Jewish communities, until recently it has been a challenge to engage routinely with them. With Zoom, we are able to be more deliberate about featuring historians from these regions and offering programs that are more geographically inclusive and that contribute non-Detroit perspectives. Recent lectures have focused on communities across the entirety of Michigan, including Iron Mountain, Grand Rapids, Sault Ste. Marie, South Haven, and Benton Harbor.

These ties far exceed the in-person connections JHSM has cultivated over the last seven decades. In 1964 we worked with the Michigan Historical Commission and the Mackinac Island State Park Commission to place a historic marker at Fort Michilimackinac commemorating Ezekiel Solomons, the first known Jewish settler in what is now the state of Michigan. More recently, in 2016 we hosted a "Michigan Women Who Made a Difference: Jewish Voices Conference" in Grand Rapids, in partnership with the city's Temple Emanuel. More than 100 general-public attendees were drawn from all sides of the state to hear sessions led by academics. In October 2023 we will offer a fall color bus tour of Northern Michigan's synagogues and other Jewish sites. We anticipate that it will draw participants from the entire state.[11]

This higher-quality and geographically inclusive programming is also possible because of our renewed commitment to high-quality publications. We find that great research feeds great events. Since March 1960, JHSM has published a well-regarded journal, *Michigan Jewish History* (*MJH*). At its outset, articles were contributed by knowledgeable public historians, many of whom had serious publication credits to their names, including Irving I. Katz, Irving I. Edgar, Rabbi Emanuel Applebaum, and Paul Masserman. The journal was meant to appeal to both academic and general audiences. Over time, the balance shifted to more accessible topics and content, including creative writing and oral history. Since 2018, the balance has been recalibrated to the founders' vision. Although those more accessible components are still included, as of the fall 2020 issue, *MJH* is now peer-reviewed—to attract higher-quality work and academic authors' consideration. We also offer an annual $2,000 best article prize, to favor and promote cutting-edge research and writing that rings with clear significance and relevance.[12]

But we know there is still work to do. At JHSM's fiftieth anniversary in 2009, membership stood at nearly 1,000. That number has generally persisted, despite many new members joining each year. Part of this is attrition: Like most historical societies, JHSM appeals primarily to seniors. Within that demographic, we overwhelmingly attract Ashkenazic Michigan Jews who grew up in northwest Detroit, just prior to the community's relocation to the northwest suburbs. As we replace members each year, we note that we are not appealing widely to individuals outside that population, including young and middle-aged adults, families, Jews of color, and Sephardim, among others. These challenges are not unique to JHSM. But if we do not solve them, we run the risk of eventually making the organization irrelevant.[13]

To grow and diversify our audience and increase our visibility in the Jewish community and beyond, in 2020 JHSM developed a Community Outreach, Relations, and Engagement (CORE) Committee. CORE's origins lie in a November 2018 collaboration with The Henry Ford, particularly its Museum of American Innovation. The one-day event, "The Henry Ford . . . THROUGH A JEWISH LENS," began with a sold-out lecture to 600 people by Steven Watts, PhD, author of *The People's Tycoon: Henry Ford and the American Century*,[14] the biography recommended by The Henry Ford. Watts spoke about "Henry Ford and the Jewish Question," a frank appraisal of the motor magnate's anti-Semitism and the continued power of anti-Semitism today. Following Watts's talk, attendees moved to the museum floor to tour a dozen pop-up exhibits, highlighting examples of Jewish innovation in the museum's collections. Featured items included a Rapid bus (engineered by Max Grabowsky in 1906), IBM's original logo (drawn by graphic designer Paul Rand in 1956), and a "chair in a box" from about 1940 (crafted by furniture designer Nathan Lerner). Detroit Symphony Orchestra Associate Concertmaster Kimberly Kennedy closed out the evening by playing a selection of works by Jewish composers on one of Henry Ford's Stradivari violins.[15]

Two years in the making, this collaboration has put JHSM on the map and inspired us to form CORE, to seek out strategic partnerships with other peer and "aspirational peer" organizations, including the Albert Kahn Legacy Foundation, Anti-Defamation League, Coalition for Black and Jewish Unity, Detroit Urban League, Flint Institute of Arts, Ford Piquette Avenue Plant, Hazon, Interfaith Leadership Council, JCRC/AJC, Sholem Aleichem Institute, and Zekelman Holocaust Center, in addition to Jewish federations, synagogues, and organizations across the state.

We have also been at greater pains to use social media and digital platforms to engage with Jewish Michiganians of all ages. Our Facebook page is a clearinghouse for our events and appeals particularly to seniors. Its companion, the Detroit Jewish History page, which JHSM's current president moderates, has nearly 8,000 active members who are interested in reminiscing and capturing family history. It is a great resource for crowdsourcing information. Our YouTube channel, which hosts our Zoom programs from the last two years, boasts about 7,500 views. The most popular programs are split evenly between professional and history-enthusiast presenters. We are also a founding partner of *Nu?Detroit*, an online site for news and commentary about Jewish Detroit that attracts a diverse range of young and middle-aged adults.[16]

This outreach has helped us think more broadly about the stories we tell. But it has also encouraged us to practice history as a form of activism. The return of virulent anti-Semitism has intensified JHSM's mission—especially as it relates to three historical figures based in Michigan: Henry Ford, Charles Lindbergh, and Father Charles Coughlin. The return of their hate speech has moved JHSM to intervene in public discourse, partner with other social justice organizations, and create public lectures and exhibits to help educate. Our current vision statement ("Illuminating the past for a brighter future"), adopted in 2020, is meant to capture the importance of history-focused activism, within and beyond the Jewish community.

The 1959 founders' other two organizational aims concerned collecting and caring for historical materials. As a volunteer-run organization without many resources, JHSM collected modestly through its first several decades. But in 1983 it received thirteen filing cabinets of materials from the retiring founding editor of the *Detroit Jewish News*. Because JHSM was not in a position to store, maintain, or provide regular access to this sizeable collection, a campaign was launched to create a permanent home for it elsewhere. This was an unusual decision for a historical society to make, but one with the community's best interest in mind. Initially, the papers were deposited at the Burton Historical Collection at the Detroit Public Library. Ultimately, they formed the basis of the Leonard N. Simons Jewish Community Archives, established in 1991 and today housed at the Jewish Federation of Metro Detroit and its offsite storage at the Walter Reuther Library at Wayne State University. Although the Simons Archives are separate from JHSM, the organizations enjoy a close working relationship.[17]

In the intervening years, it was crucial for the organization to distinguish its functions and audience from those of an archive. Consequently, the break also initiated JHSM's pivot to serving a primarily general audience with history-enthusiast offerings, whether tours, site visits, or opportunities for the public to share and document family stories. For many years, that pivot worked. But now that JHSM continues to professionalize, with trained historians on staff conducting research and giving presentations, the challenges of having such limited collections have come to the fore. The community's history-keeping organization is now separate from the historical record it was created to preserve and protect. The separation also restricts the functions JHSM can fulfill. Programming and publications are impactful activities that will continue to be foundational. But it is difficult to sustain a historical society that provides so few services that are also so difficult to fundraise for. In short, JHSM has little to "sell."

To remedy this, at present there is a move afoot to expand JHSM's functions. Certainly, there are many synagogues across Michigan that hold their own collections separate from Federation's archival collections. And Metro Detroit is home to the excellent Zekelman Holocaust Center. But surprisingly, there are no museums devoted to Michigan's Jewish history. Of course, many Jewish historical societies become museums because they inherit and inhabit historic synagogue buildings. JHSM has not had that good fortune, nor are there any surviving nineteenth-century synagogue structures in Metro Detroit.[18]

We have considered establishing a museum for at least forty years, as an alternative means of fulfilling the third and fourth organizational purposes outlined in 1959. But in the last three years, we have made more progress than in the previous sixty. Unexpectedly, the recent momentum for a museum began with our current logo. Every ten years, in celebration of another decade of mission-driven work, JHSM updates its identifying marks. Most versions have involved a rendering of Michigan's two peninsulas and a Magen David. For the sixtieth anniversary in 2019, we made a bold change. Inspired by the colorful and intricate roundel of a 1924 stained-glass window in our collections, our new, eye-catching logo is a star encircled in shards of ecru and blue. To make the organization feel as fresh and timeless as the new emblem, that same year we transitioned to being known by our acronym.[19]

Prompted by casting about for something unique among JHSM's modest object collections, the new logo has encouraged us to take seriously our museum idea. Because no local organizations collect Jewish objects beyond Judaica, there is no obvious or easy home for them. In recent years, stained glass from defunct synagogue buildings has migrated out of state, to be installed in new buildings. The repurposing is a blessing. Much of the stained glass currently in our collections was rescued from being dumped—a fate that has undoubtedly befallen many items of historic significance. But the stained-glass migration has catalyzed us to begin collecting objects in earnest—as a means of keeping those items connected to the communities to whom they are most meaningful.

In October 2020, JHSM formed an Exploratory Museum Task Force, which undertook six months of research into Jewish museums across North America and beyond. Leveraging the CORE committee's outreach strategies, this new advisory body studied close to fifty institutions, gathering exhibit, collections, program, attendance, and services data for each. It interviewed several dozen Jewish museum directors and curators for firsthand accounts of the challenges and opportunities of the field.

It joined two professional organizations: CAJM (Council of American Jewish Museums) and MMA (Michigan Museums Association). Because of COVID, it took virtual tours of a handful of Jewish museums—including the recently renovated ANU Museum of the Jewish People in Tel Aviv—and it analyzed the 2018 Detroit Jewish Population Study to understand the community's wants and needs. Encouragingly, Metro Detroit's Jewish population is stable, with about 72,000 people, representing just over 2 percent of the total population. It is also deeply supportive of Jewish cultural and educational institutions. Remarkably, despite its modest size, it has the highest per capita giving of forty-three comparison communities.[20]

On the strength of this heartening data, in February 2021 JHSM's board greenlit the task force to interview feasibility-study firms and return with a recommendation. After receiving proposals and presentations from five separate companies, the task force unanimously endorsed Gallagher & Associates, which has worked with numerous Jewish museums, including the Weitzman National Museum of American Jewish History, U.S. Holocaust Memorial Museum, ANU, Maltz Museum of Jewish Heritage, and Illinois Holocaust Museum. With the board's approval, we hired G&A in fall 2021. To date, we have finished the listening-session phase of the study. Feedback in hand, we are now creating an exhibit, to open at the Detroit Historical Museum in April 2024, to test the museum waters.[21]

JHSM's museum of Jewish Michigan is probably the better part of a decade away from opening, but already we are thinking deeply about how to construct the museum's narrative to reach several discrete audiences: Jewish adults and young Jewish families (the core of Jewish museums), students (Jewish and non), tourists (Jewish and non), and the interested general public. Working with these varied audiences in mind will be a tricky balancing act. How do we convey the depth, breadth, and diversity of Michigan's Jewry in ways that appeal and relate to all? How do we connect the museum to outstate communities, including Upper Peninsula residents who live ten or more hours away from Detroit? How do we frame achievements without resorting to a hall of fame? How do we square stories of acculturation, integration, or adaptability with those of distinctiveness and resilience? How do we highlight Jewish identity and Jewish values in ways that transcend the various constituencies within our audience? As Edward Rothstein has cautioned, "As faithful as Jewish museums might be to the promise of America, they tend to turn a peculiarly blind eye to the promise, and the substance, of Jewish identity itself."[22]

As a Jewish organization, JHSM has striven to be welcoming and accommodating to all people who identify as Jewish. We are *shomer Shabbos*, refraining from all organizational activities during Shabbat. We observe *yom tov* holidays. Event foods are vegetarian, with *glatt* kosher options. We avoid locations and practices that would exclude the Orthodox. These policies will be revisited as we inch closer to a museum. Will it be open during Shabbat and Jewish holidays? Will it have a kosher kitchen? What if the museum is housed in a former synagogue building that is also occupied by a Black church? We understand the dilemmas that these decisions will invite, particularly as we begin to be more serious about courting non-Jewish audiences.

In sum, after more than sixty years, JHSM finds itself poised to take its biggest, boldest leap yet. Drawing on our ongoing strengths in publications and programs, we turn to collecting material objects that capture the community's stories and laying plans to display them at a museum of our own making. Our hopes for this undertaking are lofty: to protect and preserve Jewish Michigan's material culture, to offer engaging and relevant histories for today's diverse audiences, to partner with high-profile organizations within and beyond the Jewish community, and to hold on to our core while also stretching our reach. We feel well prepared for this opportunity. With the labors of so many over so many decades to get JHSM to this point, as we like to say, our star is rising.

1. JHSM Articles of Incorporation (July 27, 1959); Allen A. Warsen, "Founding Our Society," *Michigan Jewish History* 1, no. 1 (March 1960): 1.
2. For more on Jewish migration in Detroit, see Lila Corwin Berman, *Metropolitan Jews: Politics, Race, and Religion in Postwar Detroit* (Chicago: University of Chicago Press, 2015).
3. See "Virtual Jewish World: United States," Virtual Jewish Library, which makes use

of JHSM sources: https://www.jewishvirtuallibrary.org/michigan-jewish-history.

4. Jewish Federation of Metro Detroit, "Community Briefing: 2018 Jewish Population Study Snapshot," https://jewishdetroit.org/community-briefing-2018-jewish-population-study-snapshot/.
5. Allen A. Warsen, *Autobiographical Episodes* (Oak Park, MI: n.p., 1971), 27. Richard Leland conversation with Catherine Cangany, December 2018.
6. "Greetings by Jacob R. Marcus," *Michigan Jewish History* 1, no. 1 (March 1960): 3.
7. Warsen, "Founding Our Society," 2.
8. In 2009, JHSM's "Settlers to Citizens" student bus tour—modeled on the organization's public bus tours—won the Outstanding Educational Program award from the Historical Society of Michigan. As one example of JHSM's partnerships with the Black community, see the 2017 "Defending Freedom" tour summary in the 2018 *JHSM Bulletin*, 10–12, available at www.jhsmichigan.org/publications/past-issues/.
9. Edie Resnick, "The Jewish Historical Society of Michigan Is Celebrating," *Michigan Jewish History* 49 (Fall 2009): 4–15.
10. Erin Einhorn's presentation can be found at https://youtu.be/-8iZbRKHdxg. Material about the Jewish developer who tried and failed to build a second segregation wall begins at 26:36.
11. Resnick, "The Jewish Historical Society Is Celebrating," 5. Judith Levin Cantor and Jeannie Weiner, "In the Beginning: The History of JHSM, Celebrating 60 Years," *Michigan Jewish History* 59/60 (2020): 76.
12. For its reconceptualization, *Michigan Jewish History* won the 2020 Outstanding Published Periodical Award from the Historical Society of Michigan. Our colorful annual report, *JHSM Bulletin*, won the award in 2021: https://hsmichigan.org/programs/awards/state-history-awards/. The award-winning issue can be found at https://www.michjewishhistory.org/assets/docs/Journals/2021%20Bulletin.pdf.
13. Resnick, "The Jewish Historical Society of Michigan Is Celebrating," 11.
14. Steven Watts, *The People's Tycoon: Henry Ford and the American Century* (New York: Vintage, 2005).
15. More about "The Henry Ford . . . THROUGH A JEWISH LENS" can be found here: https://myjewishdetroit.org/2018/11/01/the-henry-ford-through-a-jewish-lens/. The "expert set" is housed at https://www.thehenryford.org/collections-and-research/digital-collections/expert-sets/101799/.

16. JHSM's Facebook page: https://www.facebook.com/jewishhistoricalmichigan/. Detroit Jewish History Facebook page: https://www.facebook.com/groups/detroitjh/. Our YouTube channel is https://www.youtube.com/channel/UC1fUR9f8-fBRSdwGMf7d2Vw. *Nu?Detroit* can be found at: https://www.nu-detroit.com/.
17. Resnick, "The Jewish Historical Society of Michigan Is Celebrating," 10–11.
18. The Lillian and Albert Small Capital Jewish Museum in Washington, DC, began as the Jewish Historical Society of Greater Washington, before rescuing the Adas Israel synagogue and moving it three blocks to its current location: https://capitaljewishmuseum.org/about-us/. The Jewish Historical Society of Maryland, established in 1960, became the Jewish Museum of Maryland after acquiring and restoring the Lloyd Street Synagogue: https://www.loc.gov/rr/main/religion/jhs.html. There are a few nineteenth-century synagogue buildings still in existence outside of Metro Detroit, including Congregation Beth-El (now Beth Shalom) in Traverse City (1885): https://beth-shalom-tc.org/ and Temple Beth-El in Alpena (1889): https://templebethelalpena.org/history/.
19. For a history, including images, of JHSM's logos, see *JHSM Bulletin* 5 (2019): 5.
20. Summary and complete versions of the 2018 Detroit Jewish Population Study, conducted by the Jewish Federation of Metro Detroit, are accessible at: https://jewishdetroit.org/community-briefing-2018-jewish-population-study-snapshot/.
21. For a list of Gallagher & Associates' Jewish museum clients, see https://www.gallagherdesign.com/projects/.
22. Edward Rothstein, "The Problem with Jewish Museums," *Mosaic* (February 2016): https://mosaicmagazine.com/essay/history-ideas/2016/02/the-problem-with-jewish-museums/.

6

Rocky Mountain Jewish Historical Society and Beck Archives

A Hybrid Approach to Publicizing and Preserving Regional Jewish History

JEANNE E. ABRAMS

From their inception in 1976, the Rocky Mountain Jewish Historical Society (RMJHS) and Beck Archives of Rocky Mountain Jewish History, part of the Center for Judaic Studies and University Libraries at the University of Denver, have worked in tandem to publicize and preserve the vital Jewish history of the Rocky Mountain region, with an emphasis on Colorado. While the RMJHS and Beck Archives are not unique, they are unusual in that from the beginning, they were connected closely to a university and within a relatively short time became fully integrated into an academic institution. Thus, academics have always played a central role in their development, and programming and collecting policies have always been informed by input from scholars as well as Jewish community lay leaders.

At the same time, RMJHS and the Beck Archives are highly appreciated in both the Jewish *and* general Colorado community and are widely viewed as the "go to" address for research questions as well as *the* respected repository in which to deposit regional Jewish historical collections and artifacts. Although programming has been aimed primarily at a Jewish audience, many events, including exhibits, lectures, and related activities have attracted people from a variety of religious and ethnic groups. Moreover, the robust, rich archival collections held in the Beck Archives have served as valuable resources for researchers of all backgrounds and age cohorts from throughout the United States and even from across the world.

In 1975, Peryle Hayutin Beck approached the dynamic director of the University of Denver's Center for Judaic Studies, Rabbi Dr. Stanley M. Wagner, with the goal of founding some type of Jewish cultural organization to memorialize her late husband, Ira M. Beck, a leading local businessman who had a great interest in Jewish culture. After examining various possibilities, they agreed that the Jewish history of the region had received scant attention, leaving a void. With the assistance of prominent Jewish Denver lay leaders—including Beck; Arlen Ambrose, an attorney who served as the organization's first president; Faye Schayer, a businesswoman and Jewish community leader; and historian Marjorie Hornbein—as well as a host of others, many of whom had long established family roots in the area, the Rocky Mountain Jewish Historical Society was born.[1]

Wagner called upon the expertise of Dr. John Livingston, a Jewish professor of American history at the University of Denver. Livingston soon convinced Wagner, Mrs. Beck, and the fledgling board that, without an archive to collect historical materials to help document the story of Jews in the region, RMJHS would have only superficial influence. Connecting a Jewish historical society with a historical repository *and* a university poised the sister institutions to achieve a major impact, not only on an educated lay audience but also on scholars, students, genealogists, and researchers from all walks of life, including journalists and popular writers. For well over four decades, RMJHS and the Beck Archives have served as a rich resource for local community programming, lectures, and exhibits, as well as historical scholarship. The two entities work together as intertwined complementary organizations. The Beck Archives serve as the infrastructure to preserve regional Jewish history, while RMJHS is the front-facing organization, which helps to educate the public and build financial support and encourage individuals to share significant collections through donation of personal, organizational, and business records to the Beck Archives. From the onset, the goal has been to build the scope of its collections to reflect the experiences of Jews from all social and economic strata, from everyday people and grassroots organizations to political, economic, social, and religious leaders and influential institutions. Today, the Beck Archives host well over a million documents that reflect the contours of Jewish life in Colorado over a span of more than 160 years.

Soon after the founding of RMJHS and the Beck Archives, its first director Belle Marcus was hired. Well known in Denver's Jewish community, Marcus was a former educator with considerable passion and enthusiasm for local Jewish history. She inspired her board of lay leaders, mounted engaging programs, and worked with the board to encourage Jewish community leaders to donate historical family and organizational records and documents to the Beck Archives. The University of Denver (DU) provided a modest area in the stacks of the former library in the Mary Reed Building that offered at least a minimally acceptable environment for archival materials, and Marcus was given a small office at DU's Center for Judaic Studies (CJS) with Wagner as her supervisor. From the beginning, DU provided space and other infrastructure at no cost, as well as administrative and professional guidance.

Initially, RMJHS was given a modest budget by the CJS director that covered the salary of the director and programming and operating expenses. After Marcus retired and the CJS became somewhat financially challenged, RMJHS was asked to raise a portion of its budget, until eventually it was required to be self-sustaining. As part of the University of Denver, RMJHS operates under all the university's financial and budgeting rules and procedures. Although RMJHS has separate operating account funds, all expenditures must conform to DU policies and be approved before payments are issued. Currently, other than the salary of the director of RMJHS and Beck Archives, which is underwritten by DU as a faculty position, staff positions (in 2021 one full-time Beck reference archivist and a half-time Beck processing assistant) are dependent on soft money raised by the director. A modest contribution is also transferred to the Center for Judaic Studies each year to help offset operating costs, including supplies and budgeting and programming assistance from CJS staff.

In 1982, Marcus retired as director of RMJHS to move with her husband to Florida. A search for her replacement was undertaken, and Belle recalled a PhD student at the University of Colorado, Jeanne Abrams, who had visited the Beck Archives to conduct research on her doctoral dissertation on the history of the Denver Jewish Consumptives' Relief Society tuberculosis sanatorium. She invited Abrams to apply for the position. All the other candidates for the job were community laypeople, some of them prominent in local Jewish society. However, Professor Livingston convinced Dr. Wagner and the board that if they really wanted to make RMJHS and the Beck Archives a nationally respected institution, they needed to hire an academic. Abrams was offered the position in 1982, and she received her PhD in American history with a specialization in archival management the following year.

From the beginning, with the mentorship of Livingston and the support of the RMJHS board, Dr. Abrams consciously adopted a programmatic approach that would appeal to an educated lay audience but also incorporate the highest academic standards. For many years, Livingston served as the editor of the society's mini journal, *The Rocky Mountain Jewish Historical Notes*. He edited the publication with academic rigor, and contributors included respected trained historians (such as the late William Toll and cultural anthropologist Barbara Kirshenblatt-Gimblett), other academics, and talented amateur historians. Livingston, who was always exceptionally generous with his time and knowledge, sensitively and professionally worked with history buffs to polish their manuscripts so that the end product met his exacting expectations. He realized that local history vignettes were very attractive to the publication's diverse audience and that, moreover, laypeople were to be respected for their ability to add their stories to the complex tapestry of the American Jewish experience.

Livingston was honored with the first RMJHS Heritage Award in 1995 for his many contributions over nearly two decades to the society and the preservation of Rocky Mountain Jewish history. After Livingston's death, the publication of *Notes* continued for several years under the editorship of Abrams, but financial constraints and staff limitations resulted in the decision to cease the mini journal in 2008. However, all past issues have been digitized, and they continue to serve as a rich resource for historians, students, and community members. Articles continue to be cited in historical scholarship to this day.

Public lectures, including the Livingston Annual Memorial Program in American Jewish History initiated after John Livingston's passing in 2000, have featured Drs. Deborah Dash Moore, Alan Kraut, Jonathan Sarna, and Stephen Whitfield, among other prominent scholars. Engaging presentations are geared to attract a wide audience. For example, well over two hundred attendees came to hear Professor Whitfield speak on the Jewish influence on Broadway and Tin Pan Alley, which was delivered with verve as well as high-level scholarship. In 2011, RMJHS sponsored a very well-attended talk and musical performance by Dr. Michael Moloney, a professor of musicology at NYU, titled, "If It Wasn't for the Irish and the Jews," which also appealed both to laypeople and to academics.

The society also sponsored annual meetings featuring important programs on Jewish regional topics, including two very well-received talks by Dr. Stanley Hordes on Crypto-Jews in the Southwest, which focused on his research in New Mexico and Colorado. Perhaps more noteworthy, RMJHS twice hosted the national scholars' conferences sponsored by the Academic Council of the American Jewish Historical Society and its Academic Council. The first of the two, in 1989, shed light on the Jewish experience in the American West and resulted in the publication of *Jews of the American West*, edited by Livingston and fellow American Jewish history scholar Moses Rischin and published in 1991 by Wayne University Press.[2] A second Biennial Scholar's Conference in 2000 overlapped with the RMJHS Annual Heritage Dinner event, focusing on Colorado Jews in the media. Legendary television journalist Marvin Kalb served as the banquet's keynote speaker. Local Denver laypeople were invited to all sessions of the conference.

In 2008, another milestone occurred when RMJHS hosted the acclaimed American Jewish Historical Society exhibit "From Haven to Home: Three Hundred and Fifty Years of the American Jewish Community," which was launched to celebrate the 350th anniversary of Jewish settlement in America. The travelling exhibit included fifteen huge moveable panels, each over eleven feet high. RMJHS was able to secure this exhibit, which normally cost $50,000 to rent, at no charge if Abrams and the RMJHS board could "make it happen" with only four weeks' notice, as a previously scheduled venue for the exhibit had fallen through. Although it was an intense month, the affair was successfully accomplished. The impressive exhibit opened on January 11, 2008, with a VIP kickoff reception of over 125 people in the lobby of the main branch of the Denver Public Library (DPL). The partnership with DPL, the American Jewish Historical Society (AJHS), and the Denver Mizel Museum of Judaica was a very satisfying and productive one. Thousands of people viewed the exhibit, which was held over for an extra month because of popular demand. RMJHS was especially pleased to be able to mount a local Colorado Jewish history component, with all photographs, memorabilia, and objects coming from the Beck Archives—a wonderful opportunity to publicize the rich collection to a wider audience beyond the Jewish community. RMJHS volunteers were trained as docents. Several school and adult groups toured the exhibit, guided by the docents as well as the RMJHS director.

The exhibit was a high-profile event and received outstanding feedback and broad publicity for the Beck collections specifically and the University of Denver as a whole, which certainly helped to fulfill the DU chancellor's charge relating to the "public good." In 2013, the Beck Archives partnered again with the AJHS to contract an agreement for the Beck Archives to store and travel the exhibit when appropriate. To launch the joint project, "Haven to Home" was shown for a six-week run at DU's University Libraries, with panels distributed over three floors. The exhibit drew a robust audience, including DU students, faculty, and the general public.

In 2009 and again in 2011, RMJHS participated in a joint partnership with the Denver Public Library and other local historical societies and archives to help carry out two multimillion-dollar grants from the federally funded independent Institute of Museum and Library Services (IMLS):

"Creating Communities" and "Creating Your Community." These key initiatives resulted in information and materials relating to the Colorado Jewish community being incorporated into a DPL website and allowed for wider local programming focusing on an audience that included a variety of religious and ethnic groups.

In 2015, a generous grant from the Rose Community Foundation of Denver (RCF) allowed RMJHS to circulate the "Haven to Home" exhibit to local Jewish organizations over the course of a year at a modest rental fee. Additionally, due to lack of space in New York City and the expense of travelling the huge exhibit, RMJHS partnered with AJHS to store the exhibit at a DU offsite facility and to create a smaller, easier-to-ship version to enable it to travel around the US more efficiently.

Other innovative programming included partnerships with various Denver cultural and philanthropic organizations. In 2009, RMJHS received a $50,000 grant from RCF to organize and sponsor programs to celebrate the 150th anniversary of Denver's Jewish community, which also coincided with Denver's 150th anniversary. Those funds helped support several public lectures of high academic quality, including a talk by cultural historian Dr. Jenna Weissman Joselit on Jewish foodways. It also featured a showing of a one-woman play on Golda Meir, a bus tour of local Jewish sites for twenty–thirty somethings, a family tree history program for children cosponsored with the Colorado Historical Society, a genealogy workshop by leading Jewish genealogist Arthur Kurtzweil, and the production of the RMJHS dinner video *Blazing the Trail: Denver's Early Jewish Pioneers*. Most crucially, the grant helped support the creation of a state-of-the-art exhibit of the same name, which was produced in cooperation with the Mizel Museum of Judaica and mounted at the Singer Gallery at the Denver Jewish Community Center for a six-week run. The 150th anniversary programming was aimed at telling the story of the founding and development of Denver's Jewish community within the larger context of the state and region.

While under Belle Marcus, the Beck Archives had an informal affiliation with DU's Penrose Library Special Collections. Abrams worked assiduously to make that a clearer and more formal connection. In 1997,

Abrams joined the University Libraries (then Penrose Library) faculty as an assistant professor and was promoted to associate professor in 2002. Following the publication of her book, *Jewish Women Pioneering the Frontier West: A History in the American West*,[3] and a host of articles in academic journals and popular media, Abrams was promoted to full professor in 2006. In 2015, after numerous other notable publications, including *Revolutionary Medicine: The Founding Fathers and Mothers in Sickness and in Health*,[4] she was named the University of Denver Lecturer, the highest award given each year to the faculty member who has demonstrated "superlative research and scholarship." Abrams holds a joint appointment between the Center for Judaic Studies and the University Libraries, where her annual review is conducted.

Working with the dean and administration of the University Libraries, in 1997 the Beck Archives were incorporated into Special Collections and the Beck collections moved to the ultramodern compact shelving in the main library building. Abrams has continued to consciously build the Beck Archives by bringing in such significant collections as the records of two major American and Colorado tuberculosis institutions, the Jewish Consumptives' Relief Society (JCRS) and the National Jewish Hospital for Consumptives (NJH), both of which have acquired national reputations and are considered among the best of their kind in the United States. The two health-related collections have served as the focus of several significant grants, including one from The Mellon Foundation in 2019–2020 for an innovative transcribing project. The Beck Archives have continued to grow both in size and importance and today comprise over 350 separate, discrete collections.

For the last several years, the Special Collections department in the DU University Libraries, where the Beck Archives reside, has made a concerted effort to encourage faculty across the disciplines to incorporate the use of primary sources into their teaching curricula. Similar programs have emerged in other institutions and have become an especially strong focus within the archives community. As an early adopter, the DU Libraries developed a teaching model for first-year seminars and upper division undergraduate courses stressing the value of primary sources in research.[5] Between 2015 and 2019 alone, Abrams, the Beck Archives curator, taught forty-eight classes with a total of 900 students featuring primary sources from a variety of Beck collections. Departments participating in the program included history, sociology, writing, emergent digital practices, languages and literatures, English, and geography. The program, titled Unmediated Archives: Creating an Immersive Experience for Undergraduate Students across the Disciplines, was the recipient of the 2018 Primary Source Award for Teaching from the Council of Research Libraries. The award was presented to Abrams and three of her library faculty colleagues who worked as a team with faculty in various disciplines. The project has enhanced the importance of the Beck Collections in the library, the university, and across the country.

The Beck Archives have thus been used frequently by undergraduates at the University of Denver for many years. One innovative example is a 2019 grant from the Council of Independent Colleges, which allowed the Beck curator and several DU professors to mentor a cohort of eight college juniors and seniors. The students created outstanding projects that utilized the JCRS collection to offer real-life practical recommendations for advancing health care initiatives aimed at the underserved, using JCRS as a model.

Another Beck collection that has been incorporated into the syllabi of DU classes from sociology to history is the Henry Lowenstein Papers. Lowenstein escaped the horrors of Nazi Germany through the Kindertransport program in England, but his parents and sister remained behind and suffered severe deprivation in Berlin. Fortunately, all the Lowenstein family survived the Holocaust, and Lowenstein's mother Maria was able to retain and collect rare documents from their time in Germany and bring them to America after World War II. These included Henry's Jewish boy scout card and Nazi directives aimed at Jewish citizens. These evocative materials were part of a student exhibit for a sociology of immigration class. Documents of Maria Lowenstein, an accomplished artist who often hosted cultural salons in Berlin, were used as the centerpiece for a history class on Europe between the wars. The JCRS and NJH collections also served for several years as the basis for creative assignments for a history of medicine class offered in the DU history department.

Augmenting the work of the Beck Archives at DU, innovative programming has continued to characterize the work of RMJHS. In 2019, the society created "A Legacy of Healing: Colorado Jewish Leadership in Health Care," the inaugural exhibit in the new Ballantine Gallery at History Colorado, a leading state cultural institution. Abrams served as the exhibit curator. Utilizing vivid primary source materials from the Beck Archives, the exhibit illuminated the pioneering impact Jews made in providing health care in the state, for not only the Jewish population but also the general community and especially the impoverished. Region visibly played a central role in health care, and by the 1880s Colorado had earned an international reputation as "The World's Sanatorium." Thus, the subject of health seekers and health care was especially significant in the Rocky Mountain area. Before COVID-19 forced the exhibit to close early, it drew nearly 6,000 diverse visitors, and the gala opening reception attracted over 200 attendees from a variety of religious and ethnic groups.

The percentage of the RMJHS/Beck budget that needed to be raised by the society increased annually following Abrams's hiring in 1982. In 1992 the entire budget, including the director's salary, fell upon RMJHS and its director. Although this was a challenging transition, with the support of the university, the RMJHS board, and generous donors, the goal was fulfilled, and the organizations have operated in the black with a fund surplus every year. This feat was accomplished in a variety of ways. When Dr. Abrams was appointed to the DU faculty, part and then all of her salary was covered by the DU administration. Funds for operating costs, including staff and programming, came from a combination of sources, including membership in different categories, starting with $30 a year for a simple membership and rising to the $1,000 Heritage Patron level.

In addition, several endowments were initiated with the generous support of leading donors, including the Beck Endowment, Milton Morris Endowment, Marjorie Hornbein Endowment, and E. James and Eleanor Judd Endowment. Quarterly interest from the combined endowments generates funding for staffing, operations, and programming. Additional grants from foundations for specific programs and events, along with generous contributions from private supporters, have ensured the financial stability of the society and allowed for the growth of the Beck Archives as well.

One of the primary sources of public support for RMJHS comes through the Annual Heritage Award Dinner, which was initiated in 1995. For the last twenty years, Dr. Abrams has written and directed a documentary film produced by Denver's Starwest Productions highlighting a particular aspect of Colorado Jewish history. The films draw heavily on the collections in the Beck Archives, incorporating engaging photographs, documents, memorabilia, and oral history interviews. Each film connects to the dinner theme, such as early Jewish women, politicians, entrepreneurs, farmers, or artists, and the lives of the dinner honorees. One particularly popular film was *At Home on the Range: Colorado Jewish Cowboys and Cattle Raisers*, which especially resonated because of its Western theme. Although the films aim to be celebratory, as they showcase contributions of particular Jewish groups to the growth of Colorado, the research is conducted meticulously and the subject is placed in the context of the wider American Jewish experience, often contrasting or comparing Jewish life in the West with that of other regions of the country. Controversial subjects are handled sensitively but honestly. For example, the story of Otto Mears, a Russian Jewish immigrant who helped construct the roads of Colorado's western slope, and who has been celebrated as "The Pathfinder," also negotiated with local Indian tribes to encourage them to sell land to the US government for very modest sums. Both aspects of Mears's life are examined. These films have successfully engaged the dinner audiences of roughly 250 annually. In addition to generating financial support, they attract interest in the work of the society and the preservation of primary sources, often prompting donations of historical documents and material objects.

Several theater parties were also held over the years, including plays focusing on other regions of the country with fraught subjects: *Driving Miss Daisy*, about the relationship between a Southern Jewish woman and her Black driver, and *The Whipping Man*, the story of a Jewish Confederate Civil War soldier who comes home to his ruined plantation to find two of the family's former enslaved people in residence. Each play was followed by a talkback with the play's producers, actors, and a scholar to help examine and illuminate the sensitive, often controversial issues addressed.

The RMJHS director and board members have worked in tandem effectively and in a positive, mutually supportive relationship for four decades. Despite several initiatives to draw in people in their twenties, thirties, and forties, the main cohort remains those over fifty, particularly seniors. As is the case with many cultural institutions, attracting and maintaining support from younger people continues to be a challenge, although there are currently three RMJHS board members in their forties. Preparing for the future and Abrams's retirement down the road, Abrams initiated an RMJHS Directorship Endowment in 2017 in consort with CJS and DU administrators and the RMJHS board, led by longtime president Mark Boscoe. A local attorney with deep Jewish roots in the Denver community, Boscoe has ably served to enlarge the footprint of RMJHS and the Beck Archives and has been a tireless booster and financial supporter. Directorship Endowment, intended to ensure the sustainability of both the society and archives, achieved its ambitious funding goal in September 2021. When Abrams retires, her position will be divided into two full-time positions as the skill sets Abrams has called on are today unlikely to be found in one person. The Beck Archives curator will be fully funded as a faculty position through the University Libraries. The RMJHS director's position will be underwritten by yearly releases from the RMJHS Directorship Endowment. The person who fills that position will be tasked with teaching several college courses related to the broad American Jewish experience, promoting and utilizing the Beck Archives, and undertaking robust program and fundraising initiatives to help fulfill the combined mission of preserving and publicizing Rocky Mountain Jewish history and culture. The Beck curator and the RMJHS director will be strongly encouraged to work cooperatively to achieve these goals.

Local and regional Jewish historical societies and connected archives have often been an underappreciated source of valuable contributions to the development of the complex story of American Jewish history. Primary sources are the lifeblood of historical research and scholarship. Although academics have sometimes been dismissive of or patronizing about local

Jewish historical societies, claiming that they merely promote filiopietism or that they tend to be overly nostalgic, the supporters of those historical organizations have often been at the forefront of initiatives for collecting and sharing historical records from both individuals and organizations. These have included iconic photographs, documents, and material objects that help illuminate the complex and varied American Jewish experience locally, regionally, and nationally.

Although the intertwined relationship between the Rocky Mountain Jewish Historical Society and Beck Archives at the University of Denver may be somewhat unusual, Jewish historical societies throughout the United States often have ties with local repositories, either specifically Jewish in nature or more broadly inclusive and varied. Not only do historical societies help to facilitate the preservation of primary sources of American Jewish history but their members are frequently the leading financial supporters of those repositories. They also help underwrite programming that brings the stories of American Jews to a wider audience and shed light on the life experiences of Americans from diverse ethnic and religious backgrounds.

At times, especially in the past, some local history "boosters" have exhibited a purely celebratory outlook and have focused on the contributions of their ancestors or their Jewish co-religionists, but many others have demonstrated a genuine appreciation for the ever-changing contours of American Jewish history. They understand that there were both dark chapters and bright ones in that historical record and that all aspects need to be examined with integrity. Many are also very proud of their regional American roots and remind us that Americans, including Jews, often exhibit a special interest in and allegiance to their geographical surroundings. The study of regional history provides nuance and added value to the story of the larger American Jewish landscape. In an oral history interview conducted many years ago, Jack Weil, a prominent Denver Jewish businessman who founded and ran the highly successful Rockmount Ranch Wear manufacturing company and store for over six decades until his death at the age of 107, declared, "The West is not a place, it's a state of mind." Whether that is a true reflection of reality or only an idealized aspiration, countless western citizens, including Jews, have operated on the belief that regionalism counts and that the area has afforded them unprecedented opportunity.

Finally, although early Jewish historical societies may have overemphasized the contributions that Jews made in their local areas to bolster the image of Jews in the wider community and to portray their co-religionists as a valuable ethnoreligious group in an effort to combat anti-Semitism, these groups and their aims have evolved. Today, many Jewish historical societies in all regions of the country have become quite sophisticated in their governance and mission. They have hired trained historians, archivists, and experts in the field of public history to serve as organization administrators. Instead of belittling historical societies as amateur institutions, it might prove far more valuable for the academic community to form alliances and build partnerships with Jewish historical societies throughout the US to benefit both parties and increase interest in their common goal of making the study of American history more professional and yet still accessible to a wider audience.

1. Factual information about the founding, programming, and financial initiatives undertaken by the RMJHS and Beck Archives were extracted from the Minutes, 1977–2021, RMJHS Collection, on deposit in the Beck Archives of Rocky Mountain Jewish History, Special Collections, University of Denver Libraries.
2. Moses Rischin and John C. Livingston, eds., *Jews of the American West* (Detroit: Wayne State University Press, 1991).
3. Jeanne E. Abrams, *Jewish Women Pioneering the Frontier West: A History in the American West* (New York: NYU Press, 2006).
4. Jeanne E. Abrams, *Revolutionary Medicine: The Founding Fathers and Mothers in Sickness and in Health* (New York: NYU Press, 2013).
5. Patricia Garcia, "Accessing Archives: Teaching with Primary Sources in K–12 Classrooms," *The American Archivist* 80, no. 1 (2017): 189–212; Amanda Norman and Amie Oliver, "Cultivating Class Projects in the Archives," *Archival Outlook* (May/June 2014): 10–11, 25; Sonia Yaco, Caroline Brown, and Lee Konrad, "Linking Special Collections to Classrooms: A Curriculum-to-Collection Crosswalk," *The American Archivist* 79, no. 2 (2014): 417–77.

7

Judaism in the Desert

Arizona Jewish Historical Society

LAWRENCE BELL*

The Arizona Jewish Historical Society (AZJHS) was founded in 1981 by a group of longstanding Jewish residents of the state. At the time, the roughly thirty signatories to the charter were concerned that the stories of Arizona's Jewish pioneers were at risk of being forgotten. Their primary aims were to record oral histories of older Jewish residents and to collect any materials they could about the early Jewish presence and contributions in Arizona, particularly in Phoenix. The all-volunteer team of oral history collectors received some training from professionals before setting out on this important work. Thus began a Jewish community archive that now holds over 300 oral and video histories of local residents and more than 50,000 photographs, artifacts, and documents (minute books, newsletters, synagogue records, etc.).

The original iteration of AZJHS, led primarily by founding president Jerry Lewkowitz (b. 1929) and volunteer executive director Pearl Newmark (1916–2014), former publisher of the *Phoenix Jewish News*, ran occasional exhibits and had fundraising galas but was mainly focused on documentation. This effort crystallized even further under the executive directorship

* Transcribed and edited from a Zoom interview with Jonathan L. Friedmann and Joel Gereboff on March 21, 2022.

of Beryl Morton (1929–2002), who joined the society as its curator and archivist in the late 1980s. A disciple of Sylvia Plotkin (1924–1996), founder of the Sylvia Plotkin Judaica Museum (est. 1967) and wife of influential Phoenix rabbi Albert Plotkin (1920–2010), who served Temple Beth Israel for over fifty years as rabbi and rabbi emeritus, Morton led the organization of a large community archive at the AZJHS. She also launched the society's website and helped develop Shema Arizona, an online collaboration with Arizona State University Libraries containing photos, oral histories, graphics, sound excerpts, and music from Arizona Jewry. Morton worked closely with community leader Risa Mallin, who succeeded her as executive director when Morton succumbed to cancer in 2002.

AZJHS's initial phase as a primarily archival and oral history association culminated in 2001–2002 with the purchase of the historic Temple Beth Israel building, the first Jewish house of worship constructed in the Phoenix area. Built in 1921 in downtown Phoenix, the building had since been a religious and social hub for the city's Chinese American community (1951–1981) and then a Spanish-speaking Baptist church, Iglesia Bautista Central (1981–2002). At the same time that AZJHS was raising $540,000 to buy the property, a larger capital campaign was underway to relocate the local Jewish Community Center from Phoenix to a campus in North Scottsdale that also includes the Jewish Federation, Bureau of Jewish Education, and other community agencies. This adversely impacted the ability of AZJHS to raise funds for its own capital campaign and led several members of the board to leave the organization over objections to the purchase of the historic temple.

AZJHS completed the purchase of the building in 2002, renaming it the Cutler-Plotkin Jewish Heritage Center in honor of Rabbi Albert Plotkin and in memory of James and Bettie Cutler, community leaders and philanthropists who were killed in a tragic car accident in 1980. For the next few years, the building remained in a dilapidated state, with offices and archives still housed offsite as the organization struggled to raise funds for the restoration of the facility. In 2004–2005, an early effort to transform the site into a Holocaust museum failed, and Mallin retired as executive director. I was hired to replace her.

At the time, I was a newly minted PhD struggling to find employment in a tight academic job market. I was born into a Phoenix family with deep involvement in Jewish communal life. My grandmother, Lee Kazan, ran the senior program at the local JCC for many years, and family members were active with Temple Beth Israel and other local Jewish organizations. I was the first full-time executive director of AZJHS and the first with an academic background. I did my undergraduate studies at Arizona State University (ASU) and earned a PhD in history from The Ohio State University with a dissertation on the Jews of Argentina during the presidency of Juan Domingo Perón (1946–1955). This research provided much insight into how a Jewish community works and helped me to understand the competing political, social, and economic dynamics of our Jewish community in Phoenix. As a former academic, I see the mission of AZJHS (and perhaps all Jewish history associations) as distinct from that of the academy. We are not primarily interested in "problematizing" the Jewish experience but rather in cultivating Jewish identity and presenting a positive image of Jews to those outside our community. There is plenty of self-critique and infighting to go around. I want people to feel good about being Jewish. Our mission is cultural and educational rather than political.

This does not mean there is antagonism between us and academia. On the contrary, scholars make regular use of our archival material, and we collaborate with ASU's Jewish studies program. However, academic goals are not always aligned with Jewish communal goals. In my view, Judaism is a lived experience, not something that can simply be studied or, worse yet, critiqued, according to the latest intellectual trends. Indeed, one of the ways we can help the academy is by presenting and disseminating scholarly research—which is often too dense and detailed for public consumption—in accessible and entertaining ways.

Organizations like ours are also perfect places for student interns from different programs, such as religious studies, Jewish studies, history, hospitality and tourism, architecture, film, visual arts, and technology. These broad skill sets are essential for public history, and public history is, I believe, essential for cultivating pride and love of one's neighbor. In public history, we create the narrative and make it available to the public in a very accessible way.

Since I began with AZJHS, I have found different ways to imbue our historic building with this vibrant, living energy. Early on, this meant securing funds ($3.5 million) to restore the site into an attractive and fully functional venue, which was completed on January 1, 2010. Money for the restoration came from a mixture of both Jewish and non-Jewish donors committed to Phoenix and its history, along with significant gifts from local philanthropic foundations and charitable trusts.

Unlike some other societies, AZJHS did not receive support from our local Jewish Federation during this period. This had certain benefits: we were not beholden to the Federation (or any other institution), and we have remained an autonomous, flexible, creative organization. This is part of our "local flavor." Arizonans tend to be independent, self-directed, and contrarian (e.g., our refusal to adopt daylight saving time). This independent spirit goes well beyond the content of our projects and programs.

Although our archive and oral history projects were the foundation of the society, in many ways we have moved beyond them as we have grown. Archiving is still ongoing, with work currently being done to digitize and make the collection available online (about 5 to 10 percent is digitized at the time of this writing). Our archive has benefited especially from the help of a volunteer, Martin Richelsoph, a retired records manager for the state of Arizona who has served as our archivist for the past fifteen years. But an impressive archive is not enough to bring large numbers of people to our center. Over the years, we have experimented with different programs and attractions. A state-of-the-art audiovisual system was installed in 2010, and we have been showing a monthly film series ever since. We are careful not to compete with the Greater Phoenix Jewish Film Festival but instead to show only documentaries about Jewish history and culture. Other ongoing activities include a monthly book club, a Jewish genealogy group, a summer music series, and more recently a monthly series of Holocaust education seminars.

Exhibits are also shown at the building, typically running for three to six months. Recent examples include the centennial exhibit celebrating the site itself (1921–2021), and "Mid-Century Jewish Life in Phoenix," a look at Jewish life in the region from 1945 to 1975. Another exhibit of note, "Judaism in the Desert," had storytelling panels for participating congregations and showcased local Jewish diversity. An exhibit on wedding attire spanning 100 years concluded with two men's suits from a couple who was married at our Jewish Heritage Center in 2014, a year before same-sex marriage was legalized. A *tikkun olam* series exploring how art and artists can heal the world began with local Jewish artist Beth Ames Swartz and continued with non-Jewish artists who addressed pressing topics such as homelessness and the environmental crisis. Through the latter exhibit, musical performances, the film series, and other initiatives, we have developed an arts and culture profile in downtown Phoenix, where there are relatively few historic buildings and very little Jewish presence.

Attendance for our programs is almost always free. Donations are requested but not required. Our goal is to increase public participation by removing as many barriers as possible, including cost. People who attend our events very often do donate and join as members. Annual membership for AZJHS is $50 and up for a couple (with various higher levels available), although that may change as the "husband-wife" model on which it was based becomes less relevant. We have roughly 700 family unit members.

Even more significant for bringing life to the building has been opening the Cutler-Plotkin Jewish Heritage Center to weddings, memorials, *b'nai mitzvahs*, corporate receptions, fundraisers, community organization meetings, and Jewish religious services for congregations ranging from Chabad to Humanistic. I am often asked, "Where do I go to shul?" My reply: "Whoever's having a service here, that's where I go."

Along these lines, the first professional we hired after me was an events coordinator (we now have a professional staff of four full-time employees and eight part-time employees and interns). We quickly became a well-known events center and popular "niche venue" in the Phoenix area. By accident, we made the right choice to not install a kitchen. This enabled us to provide a neutral eating space open to all types of people and their catering desires. We have also had success hosting a jazz series and other programs not necessarily directed toward Jewish audiences. The more we diversify and get away from the Arizona Jewish story, the more Jewish transplants and non-Jews are attracted to our offerings.

When it comes to Jewish programming, we strive to be apolitical. This sometimes means avoiding certain speakers or topics that might alienate one side of the political aisle or the other. Arizona—and its Jewish community—is a mixture of red and blue, a reality that informs and is reflected in our activities. Our purpose is to educate, not to inculcate. We seek to provide accurate information to the public in a fun and entertaining way. For instance, while we do not shy away from discussing Israel, we do so in ways focusing more on Israel's accomplishments rather than its flaws. In 2018, we presented a solo photography exhibit of Joel Zolondek, a contributor to the local *Jewish News*, titled "Israel at 70: The Diverse Faces of Israel," featuring images he captured during six visits to Israel since 1978. We are not afraid to encourage discussion of Israel's political policies as well, but our role as an organization is not to be anti-Zionist or unceasingly critical of Israel. Many other voices in our Jewish community and beyond are better suited to that function.

We are also very active in promoting positive relations with members of other cultural and faith communities in Phoenix. Over the past decade, we have partnered with the regional consul generals of the Republics of Poland and Mexico, with our neighboring Irish Cultural Center, with the Arizona Interfaith Movement, and with members of our local Chinese American community, who have a shared history in our building. We have also created a very positive relationship with the Pilgrim Rest Baptist Church, one of Phoenix's largest African American Christian churches, aimed at promoting positive relations with our African American brothers and sisters—relations which unfortunately have frayed since the civil rights alliance of the 1960s. We do not try to brush our dirt under the rug; rather, we strive to add more positivity to the discussion. Unfortunately, many Jews, myself included, grew up in an environment in which being Jewish was often considered a bad thing. One of my deepest goals with the AZJHS is to promote more Jewish self-appreciation, self-love, and self-respect. As a result, we tend to present the positive aspects of our historical experience in contrast to the negative narratives often found in popular stereotypes about Jews, Judaism, and, more recently, Zionism.

Like every Jewish community and historical society, we have difficulty connecting with younger generations. When my board tells me, "We have to get more young people involved," I say: "Young people get into history when they get older, so the good news is that they're making new old people every day." Yet, while this truism specifically applies to AZJHS membership, we have found opportunities for multigenerational and multiethnic engagement around the Holocaust. About five years ago, we hosted a successful exhibit featuring Robert Sutz, a local artist who has created a series of life masks, portraits, and paintings of the Holocaust and survivors of the Holocaust. In 2018, this led us to launch a formal capital campaign to create a Holocaust education center on our campus, and we are now seeking to raise $15 million for a 17,000-square-foot addition to our site.

Our project will focus primarily on the personal narratives of Holocaust survivors, using their experiences as a window into the larger topic. We feel strongly that the Holocaust should not become a stone around the necks of young people. Instead, Holocaust education, as we envision it, should highlight the inspiration that exists in survivors' stories—looking at the ways they were able to persevere and the lessons they can teach from their experiences.

The main exhibit will create an emotional arc in four stages, perhaps even moving through a physical descent and ascent: (1) present-day intolerance—wars, racism, authoritarianism, etc.; (2) descent—information on the Holocaust; (3) storytelling—interactive holograms of local survivors; (4) ascent—a call to action, pledge, or commitment to doing something to make the world a better and kinder place. The museum will mainly serve area schools and families. Engaging young people has already begun with our monthly seminars with survivors, as well as victims of other atrocities. We also recently created a Holocaust education TikTok contest for local students, coordinated directly with classroom teachers. In addition to encouraging students to speak out against injustice, we also help them listen and understand viewpoints that may be different than their own.

In many ways, the Holocaust can and often does create a negative perception of Jews centered on the theme of oppression. Yet, there is also a pressing need for this kind of project now, given the increasing breakdown of America's democratic traditions and the radicalization of both right-wing and left-wing politics occurring in this country. The experience of the Holocaust shows us where such a breakdown can lead. Memory and cautionary lessons need to be kept alive, and who better to curate this memory than a Jewish historical society? I firmly believe that Jewish communities should be the custodians of our own history, not just in the religious sense but in a scientific sense as well. This applies to keeping our own artifacts, telling our own stories, and determining our own identities and destinies.

AZJHS began as a weed. It was not planted in the Jewish community garden. Nobody wanted to kill it, but nobody watered it either. We learned to find our own water in the Arizona desert, and we grew. Now, we are a fixture of Arizona's Jewish community and increasingly among our local arts and culture community as a whole. We are among the groups that other organizations approach when they want to do something or if they want a partner. We are leaders in promoting a positive vision of Jewish identity through preservation, education, culture, and outreach.

Appendix

Local and Regional Jewish Historical Societies

Organizations in this appendix are ordered according to their date of formation.

Rhode Island Jewish Historical Association
Founded: 1951
Publishes: *Rhode Island Jewish Historical Notes* (1954–)
Website: www.rijha.org
Mission: To procure, collect, and preserve books, records, pamphlets, letters, manuscripts, prints, photographs, paintings, and any other historical material relating to the history of the Jews of Rhode Island; to encourage and promote the study of such history by lectures and otherwise; and to publish and diffuse information as to such history.

Southern California Jewish Historical Society
Founded: 1952
Published: *Western States Jewish History Quarterly* (1968–1983)
Mission: The Southern California Jewish Historical Society was founded in 1952 to stimulate interest in local, regional, and national Jewish history and to preserve records, artifacts, and other historical data.

Southern Jewish Historical Society
Founded: 1957 (went moribund); relaunched 1977
Publishes: *The Journal of the Southern Jewish Historical Society* (1958–1963); *Southern Jewish History* (1998–); *The Rambler* [newsletter] (1996–)
Website: https://www.jewishsouth.org/
Mission: Since 1977, the Southern Jewish Historical Society (SJHS) has worked to foster scholarship about the experience of southern Jews. With

an annual conference, academic journal, and active grants and awards programs, the society has helped to move southern Jewish history from the margins of the American Jewish narrative into the mainstream. The SJHS has been in the forefront of the study of the Jewish South for over forty years.

Jewish Historical Society of Michigan
Founded: 1959
Publishes: *Michigan Jewish History* (1960–); *Michigan Jewish History Bulletin* (2015–)
Website: https://www.michjewishhistory.org/
Mission: Founded in 1959, Jewish Historical Society of Michigan, a nonprofit educational organization, interprets and highlights the history of Jewish Michigan. Through the past, we understand our present and actively shape our future.
Main purposes:

1. To promote the study and research of Michigan Jewish history by encouraging all efforts to create a wider interest on the part of Michigan Jews in the growth and development of their many respective communities.
2. To foster the collection, preservation, and publication of materials on the history of the Jews of Michigan, to which purpose the society publishes *Michigan Jewish History*, a semiannual journal, and has established the Burton Historical Collection of the Detroit Public Library as a permanent archive-depository for Michigan Jewish historical source material.
3. To encourage all projects, celebrations, and other activities which tend to spread authentic information concerning Michigan Jewish history, such as the erection by the society, in conjunction with the Michigan Historical Commission, of the historical market commemorating Michigan's first Jewish settler at the restored Fort Michilimackinac.
4. To cooperate with national Jewish historical societies as well as with other state and regional Jewish historical groups.

Jewish Historical Society of Greater Washington
Founded: 1960; now part of the Lillian and Albert Small Capital Jewish Museum
Published: *The Record* (1966–2012)
Website: https://capitaljewishmuseum.org/
Mission: The Jewish Historical Society of Greater Washington and its Lillian and Albert Small Jewish Museum preserves, chronicles, and presents the story of the local Jewish community through archival collections, exhibitions, educational programs, publications, and the restoration and preservation of the oldest synagogue building in the nation's capital.
Main purposes:

1. To bring together people interested in American Jewish history and in the history of the Jews of this area.
2. To collect, catalog, and preserve manuscripts, printed materials, works of art, memorabilia, and other objects relating to the Jews of this area and to establish suitable facilities for preserving and storing the materials acquired by the society.
3. To encourage research, promote publications, and arrange exhibits and lectures relating to the history and achievements of the Jews in the area.
4. To engage in any other activities which may further the above purposes.
5. The society shall have as its objective the gathering, preservation, interpretation, and preservation of historical materials dealing with the Jewish presence in the Greater Washington area, and for those purposes shall establish and maintain a museum open to the public.

Jewish Historical Society of Maryland
Founded: 1960
Published: *Generations* (1978–2012); *Historical Happenings* [newsletter] (1985–1996); *Museum Matters* [newsletter]
Website: http://jewishmuseummd.org/tag/maryland-historical-society/
Mission: We connect people to Jewish experiences and Maryland's Jewish

community to its roots. We inspire everyone to explore history, take action, and imagine a better future. The society is now part of the Jewish Museum of Maryland.

Indiana Jewish Historical Society
Founded: 1968 (first board meeting in 1972)
Publishes: *Indiana Jewish History* (1973–); *Historical News* [newsletter]
Website: http://www.ijhs.org/
Mission: Founded in Fort Wayne, the Indiana Jewish Historical Society is now headquartered in Indianapolis. The society aims to collect, preserve, publish, and share material involving two hundred years of Jewish life in Indiana. Another goal of the Indiana Jewish Historical Society is to provide data not always available to historians, scholars, and authors, thus helping to provide an awareness of the role played by Jews and Jewish communities in the creation of the religious climate of Indiana. The IJHS founders ensured that the Jewish experience throughout the state would be preserved and conveyed.

Jewish Historical Society of Greater St. Louis
Founded: 1968 (inactive)

Dallas Jewish Historical Society
Founded: 1971
Website: https://djhs.org/
Mission: It is the mission of the Dallas Jewish Historical Society to preserve and protect collection of written, visual, and audible materials that document the history of the Dallas Jewish community, to make these materials available to the public and researchers, and to keep the past as a living legacy to our community.

Jewish Historical Society of Greater Hartford
Founded: 1971
Publishes: *Greater Hartford Heritage* [newsletter]; *Connecticut Jewish History* (three volumes)

Website: https://jhsgh.org/
Mission: Telling our stories, preserving our history. The Jewish Historical Society of Greater Hartford collects, preserves, and shares the history of the Jewish community of the region by telling stories of Jewish life, culture, and contributions to our part of Connecticut. We are committed to reaching our different audiences through exhibitions, publications, education, and other community outreach programs.

Jewish Historical Society of New York
Founded: 1973 (inactive)
Founded after the American Jewish Historical Society moved to Boston.

Jewish Historical Society of Annapolis
Founded: 1975 (inactive)

Jewish Historical Society of Delaware
Founded: 1975
Publishes: Newsletter
Website: https://jhsdelaware.org/
Mission: The Jewish Historical Society of Delaware was founded in 1974 and incorporated in 1975 for the purpose of acquiring, preserving, and publishing materials pertinent to the history of Jewish settlement and life in the state of Delaware. Our collection contains priceless organizational records, family papers, memoirs, and photographs. The society publishes a newsletter, creates exhibits and displays, produces educational materials, and serves as a resource center for genealogists, researchers, organizations, and other interested persons.

Jewish Historical Society of Greater New Haven
Founded: 1976
Website: https://jewishnewhaven.org/about-us/jewish-new-haven/jewish-historical-society-of-greater-new-haven-1519338404
Mission: The Jewish Historical Society of Greater New Haven, founded in 1976, is a nonprofit organization dedicated to collecting and preserving

historical documents, photographs, artifacts, and memorabilia of the Jewish community of the greater New Haven region, and to reaching a broad and diverse audience through publications, exhibitions, seminars, and educational programs.

Jewish Historical Society of Oregon
Founded: 1976; merged in 1989 to become Oregon Jewish Museum and Center for Holocaust Education
Published: *The Scribe* (five issues)
Website: https://www.ojmche.org/
Mission: The Oregon Jewish Museum and Center for Holocaust Education (OJMCHE) explores the legacy of the Jewish experience in Oregon, teaches the universal lessons of the Holocaust, and provides opportunities for intercultural conversation. OJMCHE challenges our visitors to resist indifference and discrimination and to envision a just and inclusive world.

Jewish Historical Society of Trenton
Founded: 1976 (inactive)

Rocky Mountain Jewish Historical Society
Founded: 1976
Published: *Rocky Mountain Jewish Historical Notes* (1977–2008)
Website: https://www.du.edu/ahss/cjs/rmjhs/index.html
Mission: The Rocky Mountain Jewish Historical Society is one of the premier local Jewish historical societies in the United States. It is the largest and most exhaustive historical society of its kind in the region. With its Ira M. and Peryle Hayutin Beck Memorial Archives, the historical society preserves the fascinating history of Jews in the West and serves the needs of scholars and other individuals interested in historical research. The purpose of the society is to sponsor, promote, and foster any historical activity that will lead to a greater appreciation and comprehension of the Jewish experience in the Rocky Mountain region. The Rocky Mountain Jewish Historical Society offers robust resources for researchers, historians,

scholars, archivists, and community members who are interested in studying and preserving Jewish History in the Rocky Mountain region.

Chicago Jewish Historical Society
Founded: 1977
Publishes: *Chicago Jewish History* (1977–)
Website: http://chicagojewishhistory.org/
Mission: The society's purpose is to discover, preserve, and share information about the Jewish experience in the Chicago area. To this end the society gathers and maintains appropriate written, spoken, and photographic records; publishes historical overviews; sponsors topical and timely lectures; offers tours of Jewish historical sites; and provides a community forum for all interested groups and individuals.

Jewish Historical Society of Central New Jersey
Founded: 1977
Publishes: Newsletter
Website: https://www.jewishgen.org/jhscj/
Mission: The mission of the Jewish Historical Society of Central Jersey is to promote, research, and publish all facets of Central New Jersey's Jewish experience. We maintain an archival collection which is available to researchers. We promote educational programs and exhibits for both the Jewish and general communities. We hope to foster pride in our heritage to all our Jewish constituents, whether they are old-time residents or recent arrivals.

Jewish Historical Society of the North Shore (Swampscott, Massachusetts; now Jewish Heritage Center of the North Shore)
Founded: 1977
Website: http://jhcns.org/History.html
Mission: The North Shore Jewish Historical Society was conceived as a nonprofit volunteer organization with the following purposes:

1. To promote increased public awareness of Jewish history and accomplishments around the North Shore.

2. To encourage scholarly study and collect and preserve primary evidence of this history.
3. To sponsor meetings, publications, and other forms of information about Jewish life along the North Shore.

Jewish Historical Society of North Jersey
Founded: 1979
Website: https://jhsnj.wordpress.com/
Mission: The mission of the Jewish Historical Society of North Jersey is to collect, preserve, and make available the documentary heritage of Jewish life and culture in Passaic, Bergen, and Hudson Counties.

Jewish Historical Society of Staten Island
Founded: 1979
Website: http://www.jewishhistoricalsocietysi.org/
Mission: The Jewish Historical Society of Staten Island sees as its mission to preserve the unique history of the Jewish Community of Staten Island, to make people aware of that history and of the contribution of the Jewish community to the entire Staten Island community as well as promoting knowledge and awareness of the length and breadth of Jewish history. Staten Island, like all communities, is constantly changing. The story of past generations of the Island's Jewish community will be irretrievably lost unless we make a concerted effort to preserve it. At present, when memories of the period of mass immigration and the life in the "old country" which preceded it are fast fading many people are looking to the history of the Jewish communities in which they are living for a sense of rootedness and continuity, this work is all the more important.

El Paso Jewish Historical Society
Founded: 1980 (inactive)
Published: *El Paso Jewish Historical Review* (1982–1987)

Jewish Historical Society of San Diego
Founded: 1980

Website: https://jhssandiego.pastperfectonline.com/
Mission: Founded in 1980, the Jewish Historical Society of San Diego is a nonprofit corporation whose mission is to collect, preserve, and disseminate information about San Diego's Jewish past. In 1999, the Jewish Historical Society of San Diego, under the leadership of Stanley and Laurel Schwartz, partnered with the Jewish Studies Program at San Diego State University, formerly the Lipinsky Institute for Judaic Studies, directed by Dr. Lawrence Baron. Together they established the Jewish Historical Society of San Diego Archives.

Texas Jewish Historical Society
Founded: 1980
Publishes: *Texas Jewish Historical Society News Magazine* (1980–)
Website: https://txjhs.org/
Mission: The Texas Jewish Historical Society has sponsored and encouraged research, publications, and projects on Texas Jewish history, providing a forum for scholars, students, journalists, and genealogists.

Arizona Jewish Historical Society
Founded: 1981
Website: https://www.azjhs.org/azjhs
Mission: The Arizona Jewish Historical Society was founded in 1981 to preserve the rich history of Jews in Arizona. To that end, the society houses a large archival collection, including more than 50,000 documents, photographs, artifacts, and other memorabilia, as well as hundreds of oral and video history interviews. These materials are available to the public for research and educational purposes.

Columbus Jewish Historical Society
Founded: 1981
Website: http://columbusjewishhistory.org/
Mission: The mission of the Columbus Jewish Historical Society is to collect, preserve, and publish materials on the history of the Jewish people of Columbus and central Ohio; to encourage projects, celebrations, and

activities which spread authentic information concerning Columbus and central Ohio Jewish history; to create a society concerned with the past, present, and future; and to enlighten the membership of the society, the Jewish community, and the general public on the achievements of our people and the growth of Jewish community life from the days of the early settlers.

Washington State Jewish Historical Society
Founded: 1981 (preceded by the Seattle Jewish Archives Project, 1968)
Publishes: *Nizkor–Let Us Remember* [newsletter] (1981–)
Website: https://www.wsjhs.org/welcome.html
Mission: The mission of the Washington State Jewish Historical Society is to promote interest in and knowledge of the life, history, and culture of the Jewish people and communities of Washington State. We are dedicated to discovering, preserving, and disseminating this history through publications, exhibits, displays, speakers, and tours.

Nebraska Jewish Historical Society
Founded: 1982
Publishes: *L'Dor V'Dor* [newsletter] (1983–); a journal for some years, latest in 2017 (vol. 15)
Website: https://nebraskajhs.com/
Mission: The mission of the Nebraska Jewish Historical Society (NJHS) is to preserve the histories of the Jewish families who settled in Nebraska and Council Bluffs, Iowa. The NJHS will promote the acquisition, cataloging, and use of the collected materials which depict this history by:

1. Providing community programs and exhibits in varied media formats.
2. Publications to members and professionals.
3. Fostering research promoting museum projects and related educational / cultural activities.

Jewish Historical Society of Fairfield County (Connecticut)
Founded: 1983
Website: http://www.jhsfc-ct.org/index.html
Mission: The Jewish Historical Society of Fairfield County strives to build intergenerational community through sharing and preserving Jewish history, heritage, and culture. We tell the story of the human experience through Jewish eyes. The organization's name changed several times, starting as the Jewish Historical Society of Stamford.

Western States Jewish History Association
Founded: 1983
Publishes: *Western States Jewish History* (1983–2018) (formerly *Western States Jewish Historical Quarterly* 1968–1983); relaunched in 2020
Website: http://www.jmaw.org/
Mission: Western States Jewish History began as an offshoot of the Southern California Jewish Historical Society. The association is dedicated to the discovery, collection, and dissemination of items and information pertaining to Jews of the region. The online Jewish Museum of the American West, launched in 2013, features hundreds of exhibits on the region's early Jewish pioneers. The association's archives are divided and housed at the Charles E. Young Library of UCLA, Huntington Library, Autry Museum of the American West, and American Jewish University.

Jewish Historical Society of the Upper Midwest
Founded: 1984
Publishes: *Upper Midwest Jewish History* (1998–2020); *Generations* [newsletter]
Website: http://www.jhsum.org/
Mission: The purpose of the society is to promote the vitality and continuity of Jewish culture in the Upper Midwest through preservation, interpretation, and education.

New Mexico Jewish Historical Society
Founded: 1985

Publishes: *Legacy* [newsletter] (1985–)
Website: https://nmjhs.org/
Mission: Established in 1985, the New Mexico Jewish Historical Society's mission is to tell and share the stories of the many Jewish groups that came and stayed and helped shape New Mexico into the unique place that it is in the American Southwest. The society sponsors ongoing research, presents lectures, holds conferences, shows films, maintains archives, sells publications about the history of pioneer Jewish families, and publishes an award-winning newsletter, *Legacy.*

Jewish Historical Society of Memphis and the Mid-South
Founded: 1986
Publishes: *Southern Jewish Heritage* [newsletter] (1987–)
Website: http://www.jhsmem.org/
Mission: Through our programs, newsletter, and projects, we offer connection, understanding, and pride in the achievements of the generations of Jews that preceded our own. It is our mission to preserve and share this valuable history for the generations of the future.

Jewish Historical Society of New Jersey (MetroWest)
Founded: 1990
Website: https://www.jhs-nj.org/
Mission: The mission of the Jewish Historical Society of New Jersey, founded in 1990 by Saul Schwarz and Ruth and Jerome Fien, is to serve as the archival repository of the Jewish community of Greater MetroWest, encompassing Essex, Morris, Sussex, Union, and portions of Somerset counties of New Jersey. We adhere to our mission by collecting, preserving, maintaining, and making available to the public the records of administrative, legal, fiscal, or historical value, historical artifacts, books, oral history, and manuscript collections. The society serves the Jewish and general communities as a research center, exhibit center, producer of public forums, and publisher of books and papers on topics of historical Jewish interest.

Jewish Historical Society of South Carolina
Founded: 1994
Publishes: Magazine/Newsletter
Website: http://jhssc.org/about/history/
Mission: In April 1994, Jewish Historical Society of South Carolina was formally inaugurated for the express purpose of encouraging the collection, study, and interpretation of South Carolina Jewish history and to increase awareness of that heritage among Jews and non-Jews.

Iowa Jewish Historical Society
Founded: 1996
Website: https://www.jewishdesmoines.org/our-pillars/iowa-jewish-historical-society/
Mission: The Iowa Jewish Historical Society is an educational institution. Our mission is to inspire people from every background to connect with and preserve Iowa's Jewish history and culture.

Milwaukee Jewish Historical Society
Founded: 1997
Website: https://jewishmuseummilwaukee.org/
Mission: The Jewish Museum Milwaukee is dedicated to cultivating awareness of the past and preserving our Jewish heritage for future generations. MJHS was initially started by the Jewish Federation Women's Division Roots/Archives in 1980s. As of 2008, the organization is part of the Jewish Museum Milwaukee.

Jewish Heritage Foundation of North Carolina
Founded: 1999
Website: https://jewishnc.org/
Mission: The Jewish Heritage Foundation of North Carolina is the only statewide independent organization dedicated to collecting, preserving, and presenting the history of the Jewish people of our state. To serve our mission we honor our history, celebrate our culture, and connect our communities.

Orange County Jewish Historical Society (California)
Founded: 1999
Website: https://jewishorangecounty.org/about/who-we-are/historical-society
Mission: The mission of the Orange County Jewish Historical Society is to discover, preserve, and promote public awareness of the history and contributions of the Jewish community in Orange County.

Jewish Historical Society of Western Massachusetts
Founded: 2008
Website: http://jhswm.org/
Mission: The Jewish Historical Society of Western Massachusetts is a nonprofit organization whose goals are educational and cultural. The society provides a resource facility for research on Jewish life and activities in Western Massachusetts.

Jewish Historical Society of Southwest Florida
Founded: 2010
Website: https://www.jhsswf.org/
Mission: We are the next generation of the Southwest Florida's Jewish Pioneers. It is up to us to keep their stories preserved, so that the future generations will know what the Jews have contributed to Southwest Florida's development, economy, and culture since the nineteenth century.

Southern Nevada Jewish Heritage Project (UNLV Libraries)
Founded: 2014
Website: https://digital.library.unlv.edu/jewishheritage
Mission: The Southern Nevada Jewish Heritage Project at the UNLV University Libraries is a multiyear initiative to collect, preserve, and provide access to primary sources documenting the history of the Jewish community of Southern Nevada. The project's goals are to conduct oral histories that capture firsthand testimony about Jewish life in Las Vegas; to seek personal and organizational archives about the community and ensure their preservation; to provide online access to selected historical

resources that support research, teaching, and learning; and to engage the Jewish and Las Vegas communities in appreciation of this rich history.

Wyner Family Jewish Heritage Center (New England)
Founded: 2015
Website: https://www.jewishboston.com/organization/wyner-family-jewish-heritage-center/
Mission: The Wyner Family Jewish Heritage Center at the New England Historic Genealogical Society is a destination for exploring and preserving the histories of Jewish families and institutions of Jewish families and institutions in New England and beyond. The center engages historians, genealogists, partner organizations, and the general public in the study of Jewish history, culture, and legacies through its extensive archival collections, educational programs, exhibits, and public events. The archive was formerly the New England Archive of the American Jewish Historical Society.

Jewish Historical Society of South Florida
Founded: no year available (inactive)

Peninsula Jewish Historical Society (Virginia)
Founded: no year available
Website: https://ujcvp.org/peninsula-jewish-historical-society/

Works Cited

Abrams, Jeanne E. *Jewish Women Pioneering the Frontier West: A History in the American West*. New York: NYU Press, 2006.

———. *Revolutionary Medicine: The Founding Fathers and Mothers in Sickness and in Health*. New York: NYU Press, 2013.

Abrams, Nan. "The Greenwalds of Humboldt County: The Emerald Opiate Ring and the Case of the Chinese Certificates." Edited by Victoria Fisch. *Western States Jewish History* 43, no. 2 (2011): 101–15.

"Activities of the Society." *Southern California Quarterly* 43, no. 3 (1961): 358–59.

Agresti, Olivia Rossetti. *David Lubin: A Study in Practical Idealism*. New York: Little, Brown, and Co., 1922.

Appel, John J. *Immigrant Historical Societies in the United States, 1880–1950.* New York: Arno, 1980.

Aptroot, Marion. *Yiddish Language Structures*. Berlin: De Gruyter, 2013.

Aron, Stephen. "Jewish Los Angeles in the Making: The Early Pioneer Merchants and Bankers." *Western States Jewish History* 38, nos. 3–4 (2006): 1–2.

Bachrach, Deborah Y. "Christian Science and Jews in Minnesota: Background for Early Concerns." *Western States Jewish History* 50, no. 2 (2018): 33–50.

Baker, Zachary M. "Local Jewish History and Genealogy: The Rhode Island Experience." *Toledot: The Journal of Jewish Genealogy* 2, no. 2 (Fall 1978): 14–15.

Baron, Salo. "American Jewish History: Problems and Methods." *Publications of the American Jewish Historical Society* 39, no. 3 (1950): 207–66.

———. "Communal Responsibility for Jewish Social Research." *Jewish Social Studies* 17, no. 2 (1955): 22–45.

———. "Conference Theme." *Publications of the American Jewish Historical Society* 46, no. 3 (1957): 137–40.

———. "Opening Statement." *Jewish Social Studies* 17, no. 3 (1955): 176.

———. "Reply to Professor Abraham Karp's Address." *American Jewish History* 71, no. 4 (1982): 497–500.

———. *Steeled by Adversity: Essays and Addresses in American Jewish Life*, edited by Jeanette M. Baron. Philadelphia: Jewish Publication Society, 1971.

Barry, Jay. *Gentlemen Under the Elms*. Providence, RI: Brown Alumni Monthly, 1982.

———. "Israel J. Kapstein of Brown." *Rhode Island Jewish Historical Notes* 14, no. 2 (2004): 281–303.

Bastian, Jeannette A., and Ben Alexander. "Introduction, Communities and Archives—A Symbolic Relationship." In *Community Archives: The Shaping of Memory*, edited by Ben Alexander and Jeannette Allison Bastian, xxi–xxiv. London: Facet, 2009.

Bauman, Mark K., ed. *Dixie Diaspora: An Anthology of Southern Jewish History*. Tuscaloosa: University of Alabama Press, 2006.

———. "Editor's Note on History and Memory." *Southern Jewish History* 10 (2007): 23–24.

———. "From the Editor." *Southern Jewish History* 1 (1998): v–vi.

———. *A New Vision of Southern Jewish History*. Tuscaloosa: University of Alabama Press, 2019.

———. "Regionalism." In *Oxford Handbook of American Jewish History*, edited by Michael Cohen and Shari Rabin. New York: Oxford University Press, forthcoming.

———. "Revisiting History." *Southern Jewish History* 10 (2007): 25–26.

———. *The Southerner as American: Jewish Style*. Cincinnati, OH: American Jewish Archives, 1996.

Bauman, Mark K., and Berkley Kalin, eds. *The Quiet Voices: Southern Rabbis and Black Civil Rights from 1880s to the 1990s*. Tuscaloosa: University of Alabama Press, 1997.

Berger, Natalia. *The Jewish Museum, History and Memory, Identity and Art from Vienna to Bezalel National Museum, Jerusalem*. Leiden: Brill, 2017.

Berger, Paul. "America's Oldest Synagogue Wrestles with Court Battle and Its Own Decline." *Rhode Island Jewish Historical Notes* 17, no. 1 (2015): 160–67.

Berman, Hy, and Jay Weiner. *Professor Berman: The Last Lecture of Minnesota's Greatest Public Historian*. Minneapolis: University of Minnesota Press, 2019.

Berman, Lila Corwin. *Metropolitan Jews: Politics, Race, and Religion in Postwar Detroit*. Chicago: University of Chicago Press, 2015.

Bernstein, Charles B. "The History of the Chicago Jewish Historical Society: Its First Year, January 1977–January 1978." *Chicago Jewish Historical Society* (1978).

Bernstein, David. "The American Jewish Tercentenary." *American Jewish Yearbook* 57 (1956): 101–18.

Biale, David. "Louis Finkelstein, Mordecai Kaplan, and American 'Jewish Contributions to Civilizations.'" In *The Jewish Contribution to Civilization: Reassessing an Idea*, edited by Jeremy Cohen and Richard Cohen, 185–97. Oxford: Littman Library of Jewish Civilization, 2008.

Bisno, Julius. "Southern California Jewish Historical Society." *Publications of the American Jewish Historical Society* 42, no. 4 (1953): 420–23.

———. "The Third Annual Meeting of the Southern California Jewish Historical Society." *Publications of the American Jewish Historical Society* 46, no. 2 (1956): 120–21.

Bloch, Joshua. "American Jewish Historiography: A Survey of Some of the Literature on the History of the Jews in America." *Jewish Quarterly Review* 45, no. 4 (1955): 434–50.

Blumberg, Herman J., and Benjamin Braude, eds. *"Open Thou Mine Eyes . . .": Essays on Aggadah and Judaica Presented to Rabbi William G. Braude on His Eightieth Birthday and Dedicated to His Memory*. Hoboken, NJ: KTAV Publishing, 1992.

Blumberg, Janice Rothschild. "The Distance Traveled: Reminiscences of Twenty-Five Years in SJHS." *Southern Jewish History* 10 (2007): 13–26.

Braude, William G. *Jewish Proselytizing in the First Five Centuries of the Common Era: The Age of the Tannaim and Amoraim*. Providence, RI: Brown University Pres, 1940.

———. *Pesikta Rabbati: A Translation from the Hebrew*, 2 vols. New Haven, CT: Yale University Press, 1968.

———. "Preface." *Rhode Island Jewish Historical Notes* 1, no. 1 (1954): 3.

———. "Recollections of a Septuagenarian" (Part 1). *Rhode Island Jewish Historical Notes* 8, no. 3 (1981): 345–72.

———. "Recollections of a Septuagenarian" (Part 2). *Rhode Island Jewish Historical Notes* 8, no. 4 (1982): 401–41.

Braude, William G., and Israel J. Kapstein. *Pesikta-de-Rab Kahana: R. Kahana's Compilation of Discourses for Sabbaths and Festal Days.* Philadelphia: Jewish Publication Society of America, 1975.

———. *Tanna Debe Eliyyahu: The Lore of the School of Elijah.* Philadelphia: Jewish Publication Society of America, 1981.

Broches, Samuel. *Jews in New England.* New York: Bloch, 1942.

Brodkin, Karen. *How Jews Became White Folks and What That Says about Race in America.* New Brunswick, NJ: Rutgers University Press, 1998.

Brodsky, Judith Kapstein. "Kappy and Stella." *Rhode Island Jewish Historical Notes* 14, no. 2 (2004): 304–21.

Burkhimer, Michael. *100 Essential Lincoln Books.* Nashville: Cumberland, 2003.

Butler, Jon. "Jacob Rader Marcus and the Revival of Early American History, 1930–60." *American Jewish Archives Journal* 50 (1998): 29–39.

Cahn, Louis F. "The Early Days of the Jewish Historical Society of Maryland." *Generations* 1, no. 1 (1978): 2–13.

California Inventory of Historic Resources. Sacramento: California Department of Parks and Recreation, 1976.

Cantor, Judith Levin. "Documenting the Past for Future Generations: Celebrating the 40th Anniversary of the Jewish Historical Society of Michigan." *Michigan Jewish History* 39 (1999): 27–33.

Cantor, Judith Levin, and Jeannie Weiner. "In the Beginning: The History of JHSM, Celebrating 60 Years." *Michigan Jewish History* 59/60 (2020): 76.

Carvalho, Solomon Nunes. *Incidents of Travel and Adventure in the Far West with Colonel Fremont's Last Expedition* [1856]. Lincoln: University of Nebraska Press, 2004.

Casson, Fiona. "The Small Politics of Everyday Life: Local History Society Archives and the Production of Public Histories." *Archives and Records* 38, no. 1 (2017): 45–60.

A Catalog of Historic Letters, Books and Documents from the Private Library of

Justin Turner, Exhibited at the State University of Iowa Library, May 1–May 27, 1954. Iowa City: University of Iowa, 1954.

Cauvin, Thomas. *Public History: A Textbook of Practice*. New York: Routledge, 2016.

———. "The Role of Public History: An International Perspective." *Historia Critica* 68 (2018): 3–26.

Celebrating 50 Years, 1960–2010: 50th Annual Meeting, Program and Commemorative Booklet. Jewish Historical Society of Greater Washington and Lillian and Albert Small Jewish Museum, November 14, 2010.

Chafe, William H. "One Hundred Years of History: Extraordinary Change, Persistent Challenges." In *The Organization of American Historians and the Writing and Teaching of American History*, edited by Richard S. Kerkendall, 59–62. New York: Oxford University Press, 2011.

Chandler, Robert J. "A Stereotype Emerges." *Western States Jewish History* 21, no. 4 (1989): 310–12.

Clar, Reva, and William M. Kramer. "Chinese-Jewish Relations in the Far West: 1850–1950, Part I." *Western States Jewish History* 21, no. 1 (1988): 12–35.

———. "Chinese-Jewish Relations of the Far West: 1850–1950, Part II." *Western States Jewish History* 21, no. 2 (1989): 132–53.

Clark, David. "Jewish Museums: From Jewish Icons to Jewish Narratives." *European Judaism* 36, no. 2 (2003): 4–17.

———. "Jewish Museums: Performing the Present through Narrating the Past." *Jewish Cultural Studies* 4 (2008): 271–92.

Cogan, Sara G. *The Jews of Los Angeles, 1849–1945: An Annotated Bibliography*. Berkeley: Western Jewish History Center, 1980.

———. *The Jews of San Francisco & the Greater Bay Area, 1849–1919: An Annotated Bibliography*. Berkeley: Western Jewish History Center, 1973.

———. *Pioneer Jews of the California Mother Lode, 1849–1880: An Annotated Bibliography*. Berkeley: Western Jewish History Center, 1968.

Community Outreach Program: Reuse Alternatives. Los Angeles: Breed Street Shul Project, 2003.

Constitution and By-Laws of the Hebrew Benevolent Society of Los Angeles, California. Los Angeles: Southern California Jewish Historical

Society, 1954.

Cox, Richard. "Foreword." In *Identity Palimpsests: Archiving Ethnicity in the U.S. and Canada*, edited by Dominique Daniel and Amalia Levi, ix–xiv. Sacramento: Litwin, 2014.

Crew, Spencer R. "Public History: Past and Present." In *The Organization of American Historical Writing and Teaching of American History*, edited by Richard S. Kerkendall, 301–5. New York: Oxford University Press, 2011.

D'Ancona, David A. "An Answer to Anti-Semitism: San Francisco, 1883." *Western States Jewish Historical Quarterly* 8, no. 1 (1975): 59–64.

Daniel, Dominque, and Amalia S. Levi. "Introduction: From Containing to Shaping to Performing Ethnicity in Archives." In *Identity Palimpsests: Archiving Ethnicity in the U.S. and Canada*, edited by Dominique Daniel and Amalia Levi, 1–11. Sacramento: Litwin, 2014.

Davis, Moshe. "Preface: 'And Seek the Peace of the City,' The Program of the American Jewish History Center." In *The History of the Jews of Milwaukee*, edited by Louis J. Swichkow and Lloyd P. Gartner, vi–xii. Philadelphia: Jewish Publication Society of American, 1963.

Davis, Moshe, and Isidore S. Meyer. "First Seminar: Local and Regional History; Proceedings of the Conference of Historians Convened by the American Jewish Historical Society on the Occasion of the 300th Anniversary of the Settlement of the Jews in the United States, Held at Peekskill, New York, Sept. 12th and 14th, 1954." *Publications of the American Jewish Historical Society* 46, no. 3 (1957): 177–93.

———. "Preface: The Writing of American Jewish History; Proceedings of the Conference of Historians Convened by the American Jewish Historical Society on the Occasion of the 300th Anniversary of the Settlement of the Jews in the United States, Held at Peekskill, New York, Sept. 12th and 14th, 1954." *Publications of the American Jewish Historical Society* 46, no. 3 (1957): 135–36.

de Packman, Ana Begue. "Marco Ross Newmark." *Southern California Quarterly* 41, no. 4 (1959): 292–96.

Decter, Avi. *Interpreting American Jewish History at Museums and Historic Sites.* Lanham, MD: Rowman and Littlefield, 2017.

———. "New Vistas on Jewish History and Culture." *Sh'ma* 31, no. 5

(2001): 1–2.

Deverell, William. "Organizational and Spiritual Leadership." *Western States Jewish History* 38, nos. 3–4 (2006): 206–7.

Dichtl, John R. "Epilogue: Moving History from Nice to Essential." In *An American Association for State and Local History Guide to Making Public History*, edited by Bob Beatty, 255–32. Lanham, MD: Rowman and Littlefield, 2017.

Diner, Hasia. "American Jewish History." In *Oxford Handbook of Jewish Studies*, edited by Martin Goodman, 470–90. New York: Oxford University Press, 2002.

———. "Looking Back on American Jewish History." In *American Jewry: Transcending the European Experience?*, edited by Christian Wiese and Cornelia Wilhelm, 352–65. London: Bloomsbury, 2017.

———. "Oscar Handlin: A Jewish American Historian." *Journal of American Ethnic History* 32, no. 3 (2013): 53–61.

———. "The Study of American Jewish History: In the Academy, in the Community." *Polish American Studies* 65, no. 1 (Spring 2008): 41–55.

———. *A Time for Gathering: The Second Migration, 1820–1880*. Baltimore, MD: Johns Hopkins University Press, 1992.

———. "Why American Historians Really Ignore American Jewish History." *American Jewish History* 95, no. 1 (2009): 33–41.

Diner, Hasia, and Tony Michels. "Considering American Jewish History." *OAH Newsletter* 35, no. 4 (2007): 9, 18.

Dinin, Samuel. "*The Jews of California* – Review." *The California Historical Society Quarterly* 41, no. 1 (1962): 162–63.

Dinnerstein, Leonard. *The Leo Frank Case*. New York: Columbia University Press, 1968.

Dinnerstein, Leonard, and Mary Dale Palsson, eds. *Jews in the South*. Baton Rouge: Louisiana State University Press, 1973.

A Display of Lincolniana from the Collection of Justin G. Turner. San Francisco: San Francisco Public Library, 1960.

Doyle, Debbie Ann. "The Future of Local Historical Societies." *Perspectives on History* 50, no. 9 (2012), https://www.historians.org/publications-and-directories/perspectives-on-history/december-2012/the-future-of-local-historical-societies.

Dubow, Sylvan M. "The Jewish Historical Society of Greater Washington: Its Archival Program." *American Archivist* 30, no. 4 (1967): 575–80.

Duker, Abraham G. "An Evaluation of Achievement in American Jewish Local Historical Writing." *Publications of the American Jewish Historical Society* 49, no. 4 (June 1960): 215–53.

Dworkin, Benjamin. "Southern California Jewish Historical Society Meeting of Officers and Governing Board." *Publications of the American Jewish Historical Society* 46, no. 2 (1956): 122–23.

Dykstra, Robert R. *The Cattle Towns*. New York: Alfred A. Knopf, 1968.

Early Americana: A Loan Exhibition of Original Manuscripts of the Period 1630–1800 from the Justin G. Turner Collection to Commemorate the 170th Anniversary of the Signing of the United States Constitution, Sept. 17, 1787; Sept. 16–Oct. 13, 1957. Los Angeles: California Museum of Science and Industry, 1957.

Eckman, Julius. "Jewish Lecturing to Christian Groups: An 1872 View." *Western States Jewish History* 17, no. 2 (1985): 156–59.

"Editorial Policy and Manuscript Guidelines." *The Record* 18 (1991): 71.

Egnal, Freda. "An Annotated Critical Bibliography of Materials Relating to the History of the Jews in Rhode Island, Located in Rhode Island Depositories (1678–1966)." *Rhode Island Jewish Historical Notes* 4 (1966): 305–6.

Einstandig, Max. "The Beginning of the Indiana Jewish Historical Society." *Indiana Jewish History* 29 (1993): 5–12.

Eisenberg, Ellen, Ava F. Kahn, and William Toll. *Jews of the Pacific Coast: Reinventing Community on America's Edge*. Seattle: University of Washington Press, 2009.

Engh, Michael E. "'Charity Knows Neither Race nor Creed': Jewish Philanthropy to Roman Catholic Projects in Los Angeles, 1856–1876." *Western States Jewish History* 21, no. 2 (1989): 154–65.

———. *Frontier Faiths: Church, Temple, and Synagogue in Los Angeles, 1846–1888*. Albuquerque: University of New Mexico Press, 1992.

Epstein, David W. "DUNIE'S—The Missing Delicatessen, Somewhere in the West." *Western States Jewish History* 30, no. 3 (1998): 256–61.

———. "One Special Memory of Rabbi William M. Kramer." *Western States Jewish History* 37, no. 1 (2004): 9.

———. "The Times, They Are a Changing." *Western States Jewish History* 49, no. 4 (2015): 3–4.

———. "To Rabbi William M. Kramer: A Promise Complete." *Western States Jewish History* 47, no. 1 (2014): 80.

———. *Why the Jews Were So Successful in the West . . . and How to Tell Their Stories*. Woodland Hills, CA: Isaac Nathan, 2007.

Epstein, David W., and Gladys Sturman. Letter to subscribers to *Western States Jewish History*, June 2016.

Evans, Eli N. *The Provincials: A Personal History of the Jews in the South*. New York: Free Press, 1973.

———. "Reflections on the Past and Future of the Southern Jewish Historical Society." *Southern Jewish History* 10 (2007): 89–101.

Fain, Norma Pratt. "Women Moving Forward: Dreamers, Builders, Leaders: A History of Jewish Women in Southern California." *Legacy: Journal of the Southern California Jewish Historical Society* 1, no. 3 (1989).

Feingold, Henry. "Review of *Jewish Life in Philadelphia*, Murray Friedman, *Philadelphia Jewish Life, 1940–85*, Murray Friedman, *The Jews of Washington, D.C.: A Communal History Anthology*, David Altshuler, *American Jewish History* 76, no. 4 (1987): 522–28.

Ferris, Marcie Cohen, and Mark I. Greenberg, eds. *Jewish Roots in Southern Soil*. Waltham, MA: Brandeis University Press, 2006.

Fischer, Leslie H., Jr. "Historical Societies As History: A Review Essay." *The Wisconsin Magazine of History* 81, no. 1 (1997): 55–58.

Fisher, George. "Religious Equality in California, 1862." *Western States Jewish History* 20, no. 1 (1987): 73–76.

Foster, Geraldine S. "In the Beginning: How Our Association Grew and Took Root." *Rhode Island Jewish Historical Notes* 61, no. 2 (2012): 387–91.

Friedmann, Jonathan L. *Jewish Gold Country*. Charleston, SC: Arcadia, 2020.

———. *Jewish Los Angeles*. Charleston, SC: Arcadia, 2020.

Friedmann, Jonathan L., and John F. Guest. *Songs of Sonderling: Commissioning Jewish Émigré Composers in Los Angeles, 1938–1945*. Lubbock: Texas Tech University Press, 2021.

"From the Librarian." *UCLA Librarian* 9, no. 4 (1955): 24.

Gabler, Neal. *An Empire of Their Own: How the Jews Invented Hollywood*. New York: Anchor, 1989.

Garcia, Patricia. "Accessing Archives: Teaching with Primary Sources in K–12 Classrooms." *The American Archivist* 80, no. 1 (2017): 189–212.

Gardner, James B., and Paula Hamilton. "The Past and Future of Public History: Developments and Challenges." In *Oxford Handbook of Public History*, edited by Paula Hamilton and James B. Gardner, 1–25. New York: Oxford University Press, 2017.

Gartner, Lloyd P. "Rudolf Glanz (1892–1978)." *American Jewish History* 69, no. 2 (1979): 270–73.

Geipel, John. *Mame Loshn: The Making of Yiddish*. London: Journeyman, 1982.

Gereboff, Joel. "Integrating Local Jewish Historical Societies and Public History." *Shofar: An Interdisciplinary Journal of Jewish Studies* 13, no. 3 (1995): 53–72.

Ginsberg, Louis. *Chapters of the Jews of Virginia, 1658–1900*. Petersburg, VA: privately published, 1969.

———. *History of the Jews of Petersburg, 1789–1950*. Petersburg, VA: privately published, 1954.

Glanz, Rudolf. "The 'Bayer' and the 'Pollack' in America." *Western States Jewish History* 45, no. 1 (2012): 73–94.

———. "From Fur Rush to Gold Rushes: Alaskan Jewry from the Late 19th to the Early 20th Centuries." *Western States Jewish Historical Quarterly* 7, no. 2 (1975): 95–107.

———. "Jews and Chinese in America." *Western States Jewish History* 38, no. 2 (2006): 112–32.

———. "The Jews in the Sandwich Islands." *Western States Jewish Historical Quarterly* 6, no. 3 (1974): 177–87.

———. *The Jews of California: From the Discovery of Gold until 1880*. New York: Waldon, 1960.

———. "Notes on the Early Jews of Arizona." *Western States Jewish Historical Quarterly* 5, no. 4 (1973): 243–56.

———. "Where the Jewish Press Was Distributed in Pre-Civil War America."

Western States Jewish Historical Quarterly 5, no. 1 (1972): 1–14.
Golden, Harry. *Our Southern Landsman*. New York: Putnam, 1974.
Goldowsky, Seebert J. *A Century and a Quarter of Spiritual Leadership: The Story of the Congregation of the Sons of Israel and David (Temple Beth-El) Providence, Rhode Island*. Providence, RI: Congregation of the Sons of Israel, 1989.
———. "The Genesis of an Amateur Historian, or Ruminations on How I Got That Way." *Rhode Island Jewish Historical Notes* 11, no. 1 (1991): 63–66.
———. "History of the Rhode Island Jewish Historical Association." *Rhode Island Jewish Historical Notes* 12, no. 3 (1997): 376–80.
———. "Local Jewish History—The Rhode Island Experience." *Rhode Island Jewish Historical Notes* 6, no. 4 (1974): 622–28.
Goldstein, Eric L. "Making History: An Interview with Saul Viener." *Southern Jewish History* 10 (2007): 39–88.
———. *The Price of Whiteness: Jews, Race, and American Identity*. Princeton, NJ: Princeton University Press, 2019.
Goodwin, George M. "The Brothers of Phi Epsilon Pi." *Rhode Island Jewish Historical Notes* 14, no. 1 (2003): 127–47.
———. "Class of 1896: Three Pawtucket Lads at Harvard." *Rhode Island Jewish Historical Notes* 16, no. 2 (2014): 621–65.
———. "The Design of a Modern Synagogue: Percival Goodman's Beth-El in Providence, Rhode Island." *American Jewish Archives Journal* 45, no. 1 (1993): 31–71.
———. "Wondrous *Rimonim*: Ownership, Holiness, Beauty, Rarity, and Value." *Rhode Island Jewish Historical Notes* 17, no. 1 (2015): 130–59.
———. "Woonsocket's B'nai Israel." *Rhode Island History* 58 (February 2000): 3–21.
Goodwin, George M., and Ellen Smith, eds. *The Jews of Rhode Island*. Waltham, MA: Brandeis University Press, 2004.
Goren, Arthur A. "A 'Golden Decade' for American Jews, 1944–55." In *A New Jewry? America Since the Second World War*, edited by Peter Medding, 3–20. New York: Oxford University Press, 1992.
Graham, Otis L., Jr. "Discovering Public History in an Unlikely Place,

UC Santa Barbara, 1976 and After." In *The Organization of American Historical Writing and Teaching of American History*, edited by Richard S. Kerkendall, 317–22. New York: Oxford University Press, 2011.

Graves, J. A. *My Seventy Years in California, 1857–1927.* Los Angeles: Times-Mirror, 1929.

Greenberg, Erik. "Peter 'Pete' Kahn: Los Angeles Jewish Leader, 1878–1952." *Western States Jewish History* 38, no. 1 (2005): 17–43.

Greene, Harlan, and Dale Rosengarten. "In Distinguished Company: A Profile of Solomon Breibart." *Southern Jewish History* 7 (2004): 3–4.

Greenspan, Sophie. *Westward with Fremont: The Story of Solomon Carvalho.* Philadelphia: Jewish Publication Society, 2018.

"Greetings by Jacob R. Marcus." *Michigan Jewish History* 1, no. 1 (March 1960): 3.

Gross, Rachel Beth. "Objects of Affection: The Material Religion of American Jewish Nostalgia." PhD diss., Princeton University, 2014.

Grossman, Grace Cohen. "Jewish Museums in America." *Encyclopedia Judaica*, 2nd ed., 631–34. New York: Macmillan Reference, 2007.

———. "Project Americana: Collecting Memories and Exploring the American Jewish Experience." In *New Beginnings: The Skirball Museum Collection and Inaugural Exhibit*, edited by Grace Cohen Grossman, 89–109. Los Angeles: Skirball Cultural Center, 1996.

Gurock, Jeffrey. "Cyrus Adler's Vision of American Jewish Historical Writing." *American Jewish History* 101, no. 4 (2017): 489–99.

———. "From *Publications* to *American Jewish History*: The Journal of the American Jewish Historical Society and the Writing of American Jewish History." *American Jewish History* 81, no. 2 (1993–94): 155–270.

———. "Jacob Rader Marcus, Salo W. Baron, and the Public's Need to Know American Jewish History." *American Jewish Archives Journal* 56 (1998): 23–27.

Gutstein, Morris. *The Story of the Jews of Newport: Two and a Half Centuries of Judaism, 1658–1908.* New York: Bloch, 1936.

Hall, Martin. "The Jews of Los Angeles." *Chicago Jewish Forum* 16, no. 4 (1958): 223–27.

Handlin, Oscar. "New Paths in American Jewish History." *Commentary*,

January 8, 1949, 388–94.

———. "Our Unknown American Jewish Ancestors: Fact and Myth in History." *Commentary*, January 1, 1948, 104–10.

Harmon, Wendell E. "The Bootlegger Era in Southern California." *Southern California Quarterly* 37, no. 4 (1955): 335–46.

Harrison, Rodney. "Forgetting to Remember, Remembering to Forget: Late Modern Heritage Practices, Sustainability and the 'Crisis' of Accumulation of the Past." *International Journal of Heritage Studies* 19, no. 6 (2013): 579–95.

Henle, Alea. "Preserving the Past, Making Histories: Historical Societies in the Early U.S." PhD diss., University of Connecticut, 2012.

Herberg, Will. *Protestant—Catholic—Jew: An Essay in American Religious Sociology*. New York: Doubleday, 1955.

Herman, Alice, and Steven Bayme. "Celebrating the 350th." *American Jewish Yearbook* 106 (2006): 115–32.

Higham, John. "The Ethnic Historical Society in Changing Times." *Journal of American Ethnic History* 13, no. 2 (1994): 30–44.

Hirsh, Pauline. "Two Pair Pants Come with This Coat, a Perfect Fit: History of the Jews in the Southern California Apparel Business." *Legacy: Journal of the Southern California Jewish Historical Society* 1, no. 2 (1988).

"Historian to Give Talk." *Los Angeles Times*, November 15, 1973.

"Historian to Speak." *Los Angeles Times*, April 8, 1974.

Hoffman, Abraham. "Dr. Norton B. Stern: A San Francisco Treat in Jewish History." *Western States Jewish History* 41, no. 1 (2008): ix–xi.

Hollinger, David. "Communalist and Dispersionist Approaches to American Jewish History in an Increasingly Post-Jewish Era." *American Jewish History* 95, no. 1 (March 2009): 1–32.

Howe, Barbara J. "Reflection on an Idea: NCPH's First Decade." *The Public Historian* 11, no. 3 (1989): 69–85.

Isaacson, Michael. *Jewish Music As Midrash: What Makes Music Jewish*. Woodland Hills, CA: Isaac Nathan, 2007.

Jackson, Andrew. "Local and Regional History As Heritage: The Heritage Process and Conceptualising the Purpose and Practice of Local Historians." *International Journal of Heritage Studies* 14, no. 4

(2008): 362–79.

Jaroszynska-Kirchman, Anna, and Suzanne M. Sinke. "Ethnic Historical Associations at the Crossroads: An Introduction." *Polish American Studies* 65, no. 1 (2008): 7–10.

"Jewish Federation Council to Honor Pauline Hirsh." *Los Angeles Times*, November 23, 1981.

"Jewish Role in American Civil War Depicted in Los Angeles Exhibit." *Jewish Telegraph Agency*, January 2, 1963.

"Jews of Wild and Wooly West." *Los Angeles Times*, October 23, 1977.

Johnson, Grove L. "A Gentile Reproves an Anti-Semite: Fresno, 1893." *Western States Jewish Historical Quarterly* 9, no. 4 (1977): 299–300.

Joselit, Jenna Weissman. "Best-in-Show: American Jewish Museums Exhibitions, and the Search for Community." In *Imagining the American Jewish Community*, edited by Jack Wertheimer, 141–53. Hanover, MA: Brandeis University Press, 2007.

"Justin George Turner Papers: Finding Aid." Huntington Library (Online Archive of California), http://pdf.oac.cdlib.org/pdf/huntington/mss/turnerj.pdf.

Kaganoff, Nathan M., and Melvin I. Urofsky, eds. *Turn to the South: Essays on Southern Jewry*. Waltham, MA: American Jewish Historical Society and Charlottesville: University of Virginia Press, 1979.

Kahn, Ava F., ed. *Jewish Voices of the California Gold Rush: A Documentary History, 1849–1880*. Detroit: Wayne State University Press, 2002.

———. "Review of *Jews on the Frontier*." *Journal of Jewish Identities* 12, no. 2 (2019): 230–31.

Kahn, Ava F., and Marc Dollinger. "Introduction: The Other Side." In *California Jews*, edited by Ava F. Kahn and Marc Dollinger, 1–16. Hanover, NH: University Press of New England, 2003.

Kahn, Ellie. *Meet Me at Brooklyn & Soto: Celebrating the Jewish Community of East Los Angeles*. Teaneck, NJ: Ergo Media, 1998, DVD.

Kammen, Carol. *On Doing Local History*, 3rd. ed. Lanham, MD: Rowman and Littlefield, 2014.

———. "On Doing Local History: The Future Survival of Historical Societies." *History News* 59, no. 1 (2004): 3–4.

Kammen, Michael. "The Mississippi Valley Historical Association, 1907–52." In *The Organization of American Historians and the Writing and Teaching of American History*, edited by Richard S. Kerkendall, 17–32. New York: Oxford University Press, 2011.

Kaplan, Elisabeth. "We Are What We Collect, We Collect What We Are: Archives and the Construction of Identity." *The American Archivist* 63 (2000): 126–51.

Kapstein, Jonathan. "Captain John J. Kapstein, U.S. Army Air Force: In War and Peace." *Rhode Island Jewish Historical Notes* 17, no. 4 (2018): 664–80.

Karp, Abraham. "From Tercentenary to Bicentennial." *American Jewish History* 64, no. 1 (1974): 3–13.

Kassof, Anita. "Maryland's Treasure House: The Jewish Museum and Its Collections." *Generations* (2000): 35–42.

Kerstetter, Todd M. *God's Country, Uncle Sam's Land: Faith and Conflict in the American West.* Urbana and Chicago: University of Illinois Press, 2006.

Kessler, Barry. "Chronology: Jewish Museum of Maryland." *Generations* (2000): 46–51.

Kirshenblatt-Gimblett, Barbara. "From Ethnology to Heritage: The Role of the Museum." In *Museum Studies: An Anthology of Contexts*, edited by Bettina Messias Carbonell, 199–205. Malden, MA: Blackwell, 2012.

Klyberg, Albert T. "A Rhode Island Historian Looks at the *Rhode Island Jewish Historical Notes*." *Rhode Island Jewish Historical Notes* 13, no. 1 (1999): 9–16.

Korn, Bertram W. *American Jewry and the Civil War.* Philadelphia: Jewish Publication Society, 1951.

———. "Jews and Negro Slavery in the Old South, 1789–1865." *Publications of the American Jewish Historical Society* 50, no. 3 (1961): 151–201.

Kramer, William M. "Chinese-Jewish Moh-ist." *Western States Jewish History* 42, nos. 2–3 (2010): 30–31.

———. "The Life of Edgar Magnin, Part I." *Western States Jewish History* 42, nos. 2–3 (2010): 141–42.

———. "The *Los Angeles Times* Noted Rabbi Magnin's Arrival." *Western States Jewish History* 42, nos. 2–3 (2010): 15–16.

———. "Magnin Regarding Colleges." *Western States Jewish History* 42, nos.

2–3 (2010): 46.

———. "My Life of Careers." *Western States Jewish History* 30, no. 3 (1998): 202–11.

———. "Rabbi Magnin Answers." *Western States Jewish History* 42, nos. 2–3 (2010): 40.

———. "Review of *History of the Jews of Los Angeles*." *Journal of the American Academy of Religion* 40, no. 1 (1972): 133–34.

———. "'They Have Killed Our Man But Not Our Cause': The California Jewish Mourners of Abraham Lincoln." *Western States Jewish Historical Quarterly* 2, no. 4 (1970): 187–216.

———. "Tree Art in Western Jewish Cemeteries." *Western States Jewish Historical Quarterly* 2, no. 2 (1970): 91–100.

———. "Young Magnin, Part III." *Western States Jewish History* 42, nos. 2–3 (2010): 145–46.

———. "The Youth of Edgar Magnin, Part II." *Western States Jewish History* 42, nos. 2–3 (2010): 143–44.

Kramer, William M., and Reva Clar. "Los Angeles Rabbi Edgar Magnin's 1906 San Francisco Earthquake-Fire Memories." *Western States Jewish History* 27, no. 3 (1995): 143–45.

———. "Rabbi Edgar F. Magnin and the Modernization of Los Angeles Jewry, Part I." *Western States Jewish History* 19, no. 3 (1987): 233–51.

———. "Rabbi Edgar F. Magnin and the Modernization of Los Angeles Jewry, Part II." *Western States Jewish History* 19, no. 4 (1987): 246–62.

———. "Rabbi Edgar F. Magnin in Stockton (1914–1915): Rehearsal for Los Angeles." *Western States Jewish History* 17, no. 2 (1985): 99–121.

Kramer, William M., and Norton B. Stern. "Archival Sources for the History of Religion in California, Part II: Jewish Religious Archives and Ethnic Histories." *Southern California Quarterly* 72, no. 3 (1990): 275–89.

———. "A Guide to California Jewish History, Part I." *Western States Jewish History* 24, no. 4 (1992): 378–83.

———. "A Guide to California Jewish History, Part II." *Western States Jewish History* 25, no. 4 (1993): 325–58.

———. "A Jewish History of Oakland: A Review Essay." *Western States Jewish Historical Quarterly* 9, no. 4 (1977): 371–77.

———. "Some 'Warts' on the Face of Early Western Jewry." *Western States Jewish Historical Quarterly* 14, no. 1 (1981): 82–87.

———. "The Study of Los Angeles History: An Analytical Consideration of a Major Work." *Western States Jewish Historical Quarterly* 3, no. 1 (1970): 38–58.

Kraut, Alan M., and David A. Gerber, eds. *Ethnic Historians and the Mainstream: Shaping America's Immigration Story.* New York: Routledge, 2013.

Kronzek, Lynn C. "Fairfax: A Home, a Community, a Way of Life." *Legacy: Journal of the Southern California Jewish Historical Society* 1, no. 4 (1990).

Kun, Josh, ed. *Songs in the Key of Los Angeles: Sheet Music from the Collection of the Los Angeles Public Library.* Santa Monica: Angel City, 2013.

Kunin, Samuel A. *Circumcision: Its Place in Judaism, Past and Present.* Woodland Hills, CA: Isaac Nathan, 1998.

Kyvig, David E., Myron A. Marty, and Larry Cebula. *Nearby History: Exploring the Past Around You*, 4th ed. Lanham, MD: Rowman and Littlefield, 2019.

LaFantasie, Glenn W., ed. *The Correspondence of Roger Williams*, 2 vols. Providence, RI: Brown University Press, 1988.

Lampard, Eric E. "American Historians and the Study of Urbanism." *American Historical Review* 67, no. 1 (1961): 49–61.

Langston, Scott M., and Bryan Edward Stone. "Teaching Southern Jewish History: A Dialogue." *Southern Jewish History* 15 (2012): 1–40.

"Lecture on Jews." *Los Angeles Times*, May 12, 1974.

"A Letter and a Jewish Article in Chinese." *Western States Jewish History* 26, no. 2 (1994): 112.

Levine, Peter. *Ellis Island to Ebbets Field: Sport and the American Jewish Experience.* New York: Oxford University Press, 1993.

Levy, William. "A Jew Views Black Education: Texas, 1890." *Western States Jewish History* 8, no. 4 (1976): 351–60.

Lincolniana: A Catalogue of Historic Autograph Letters and Documents from the Justin G. Turner Collection of Americana. Los Angeles: Occidental College, 1957.

Lippman, Joan. "From the Editor." *Generations* 1, no. 1 (1978): 1.

Livingston, John. "Introduction." In *Jews of the American West*, edited by Moses Rischin and John Livingston, 15–25. Detroit: Wayne State University Press, 1991.

"Local Jewish Historical Societies in the United States and Canada." *American Jewish Historical Quarterly* 59 (1969): 118–20.

"Local Jewish Historical Societies in the United States and Canada." *American Jewish Historical Quarterly* 66, no. 4 (1977): 538–40.

"The Los Angeles Jewish Community Council." In *Southwest Jewry*, vol. 3, edited by Joseph L. Malamut, 18–24. Los Angeles: Los Angeles Jewish Institutions and Their Leaders, 1957.

Luce, Caroline. "Western States Jewish History Special Collections: Reflections." *Western States Jewish History* 41, no. 3 (2009): xv–xxii.

Lustig, Jason. "Building a Home for the Past: Archives and the Geography of American Jewish History." *American Jewish History* 102, no. 3 (2018): 375–400.

Lutzki, Morris. *Catalogue of Geniza Fragments (now British Library ms. Or. 13,153): From the Collection of Justin G. Turner*. London: Hebrew Section, Oriental and India Office Collections, The British Library, 1994.

MacLeod, Celeste L. "The Western Jewish History Center." *American Jewish Historical Quarterly* 58, no. 2 (1968): 271–77.

Marcus, Jacob R. "Address of the President." *Publications of the American Jewish Historical Society* 46, no. 4 (June 1957): 465–66.

———. "After Twenty-Five Volumes." *American Jewish Archives Journal* 26, no. 1 (1974): 3–4.

———. "Congratulatory Message." *Michigan Jewish History* 10, no. 2 (1970): 4.

———. "Greetings, Jewish Historical Society and Similar Societies." *Michigan Jewish History* 1, no. 1 (1960): 3.

———. "Foreword." *The Journal of the Southern Jewish Historical Society* 1, no. 1 (1958): 3.

———. *How to Write the History of an American Jewish Community*. Cincinnati: American Jewish Archives, 1953.

———. "The Periodization of American Jewish History." *American Jewish Historical Society* 47, no. 3 (1958): 1–9.

———. "The Theme in American Jewish History." *Publications of the American Jewish Historical Society* 48, no. 3 (1959): 141–48.

Maze, Jacob M. "Jewish Farmers in California." *Jewish Farmer* 51, no. 5 (1958): 83–84, and 52, no. 5 (1959): 71–80.

McKelvey, Blake. "American Urban History Today." *American Historical Review* 57, no. 4 (1952): 919–29.

McLeod, Celeste L. "Historical News and Comments: Western Jewish History Center." *American Jewish Historical Quarterly* 58, no. 2 (1968): 271–77.

McLoughlin, William G. *Rhode Island: A Bicentennial History*. New York: W.W. Norton, 1978.

———. *Rhode Island: A History*. New York: W.W. Norton, 1986.

Mendelsohn, Adam. "An Interview with Bernard Wax." *Southern Jewish History* 17 (2014): 131–44.

Moghadam, Yaara Shteinhart. "Practitioners and Practices in Museum Jewish Education." PhD diss., Jewish Theological Seminary, 2011.

"Names in the News." *Jewish Post*, January 16, 1970.

"New School for Jewish Adults Opens." *Los Angeles Times*, January 29, 1966.

Newmark, Harris. *Sixty Years in Southern California, 1853–1913*. Edited by Maurice H. Newmark and Marco R. Newmark. New York: Knickerbocker, 1916.

Newmark, Marco R. "Dr. Philip Seman." *The Historical Society of Southern California Quarterly* 41, no. 1 (1959): 79.

———. *Jottings* in Southern California History. Los Angeles: Ward Ritchie, 1955.

———. "Wilshire Boulevard Temple: Congregation B'nai B'rith, 1862–1947." *Southern California Quarterly* 38, no. 2 (1956): 167–84.

Norman, Amanda, and Amie Oliver. "Cultivating Class Projects in the Archives." *Archival Outlook* (May/June 2014): 10–11.

Novick, Peter. *That Noble Dream: The "Objectivity Question" and the American Historical Profession*. Cambridge: Cambridge University Press, 1988.

Oates, Marylouise. "Driving Force Behind Jewish Exhibit." *Los Angeles Times*, April 20, 1981.

Olitzky, Kerry M. "A Memorial Tribute to Malcolm H. Stern." *American Jewish History* 82, no. 1 (1994): 329–30.

Ordeal of the Union: Civil War Manuscripts and Documents. Los Angeles: University of Southern California, 1963.

"Periodical Reflections." *Western States Jewish Historical Quarterly* 13, no. 4 (1981): 377–78.

Proctor, Samuel, Louis Schmier, and Malcolm Stern, eds. *Jews of the South: Selected Essays from the Southern Jewish Historical Society*. Macon, GA: Mercer University Press, 1984.

Proffitt, Kevin. "Jacob Rader Marcus and the Archive He Built." In *New Essays in American Jewish History Commemorating the Sixtieth Anniversary of the Founding of the American Jewish Archives*, edited by Pamela Nadell, Lance Sussman, and Jonathan Sarna, 5–18. Cincinnati: American Jewish Archives, 2010.

Raab, Earl. "There's No City Like San Francisco: Profile of a Jewish Community." *Commentary* 10, no. 4 (1950): 369–78.

"Rabbi Max Vorspan, 86; Scholar and Historian." *Los Angeles Times*, June 16, 2002.

Rabin, Shari. *Jews on the Frontier: Religion and Mobility in Nineteenth-Century America*. New York: New York University Press, 2017.

Rafael, Ruth. "Selected Acquisitions, Western Jewish History Center, Judah L. Magnes Memorial Museum." *Western States Historical Quarterly* 6, no. 2 (1974): 234.

———. "Selected Acquisitions, Western Jewish History Center, Judah L. Magnes Memorial Museum." *Western States Historical Quarterly* 8, no. 1 (1975): 92.

Rain, Leo J. "Dr. Jacob Rosenfeld: A Jewish Commander in a Chinese Army, 1903–1952." Edited by Malgert Cohen. *Western States Jewish History* 33, no. 4 (2001): 291–302.

Raphael, Marc Lee. "Beyond New York: The Challenge to Local History." In *Jews of the American West*, edited by Moses Rischin and John Livingston, 48–65. Detroit: Wayne State University Press, 1991.

Resnick, Edie. "The Jewish Historical Society of Michigan is Celebrating." *Michigan Jewish History* 49 (2009): 4–15.

Riche, Aaron. "Zionism in Los Angeles on Its Twenty-Fifth Anniversary." *Western States Jewish History Journal* 23, no. 1 (1991): 31–3.

Rischin, Moses. *Inventory of American Jewry*. Cambridge, MA: Harvard University Press, 1954.

———. "Jewish Studies in Northern California: A Symposium." *Judaism* 44, no. 4 (1995): 417–19.

———. "Review Essay: Jacob Rader Marcus: Historian-Archivist of Jewish Middle America." *American Jewish History* 85, no. 2 (1997): 175–81.

———. "Review of *The Colonial Jew, 1492–1776*, Jacob R. Marcus." *William and Mary Quarterly* 30, no. 2 (1973): 353–55.

Rischin, Moses, and John Livingston, eds. *Jews of the American West*. Detroit: Wayne State University Press, 1991.

Rochlin, Harriet. "Norton B. Stern: Pioneer Western Jewish Historian and Founding Editor of the First *Western Jewish Historical Quarterly*." *Western States Jewish History* (1998): 218–19.

Rochlin, Harriet, and Fred Rochlin. *Pioneer Jews: A New Life in the Far West*. Boston: Houghton Mifflin, 1984.

"Romance of the Jews." *Los Angeles Times*, January 16, 1976.

Romer, Margaret. "Pioneer Builders of Los Angeles: Part II." *Southern California Quarterly* 43, no. 3 (1961): 342–49.

Rosen, Judith Friedman. "In Search of . . . Early American Jewish Anniversary Celebrations: 1905–54." *American Jewish History* 92 (2004): 481–97.

Rosenbaum, Fred. *Visions of Reform: Congregation Emanu-El and the Jews of San Francisco, 1849–1999*. Berkeley: Judah L. Magnes Museum, 2000.

Rothstein, Edward. "The Problem with Jewish Museums." *Mosaic* (February 2016). https://mosaicmagazine.com/essay/history-ideas/2016/02/the-problem-with-jewish-museums/.

Rubin, Saul J. "The Pioneer Period of the SJHS (1976–1983)." *Southern Jewish History* 10 (2007): 5–11.

Russo, David. *Keepers of Our Past: Local Historical Writing in the United States 1820s–1930s*. New York: Greenwood, 1988.

Sarna, Jonathan. "The Cult of Synthesis in American Jewish Culture." *Jewish Social Studies* 5, nos. 1–2 (1998): 52–79.

———. "Jacob Rader Marcus (1896–1995)." In *The Dynamics of American Jewish History: Jacob Rader Marcus's Essay on American Jewry*, edited by Gary P. Zola, 3–12. Hanover, MA: Brandeis University Press, 2004.

———. "What's the Use of Local Jewish History?" *Rhode Island Jewish Historical Notes* 12, no. 1B (1995): 77–83.

Scarpino, Philip, and Daniel Vivian. "What Do Public History Employers Want?" *Report of the Joint AASLH-AHA-NCPH-OAH Task Force on Public History Education and Employment*, https://ncph.org/wp-content/uploads/2019/02/What-do-Public-History-Employers-Want-A-Report-of-the-Joint-Task-Force-on-Public-History-Education-and-Employment.pdf.

Schappes, Morris U. *A Documentary History of the Jews in the United States, 1654–1875*. New York: Schocken, 1950.

Segal, Beryl. "Introduction." *Rhode Island Jewish Historical Notes* 1, no. 1 (1954): 5–7.

Seligman, Ben B. "They Came to Hollywood: How Jews Built the Movie Industry." *Jewish Frontier* (July 1953): 19–29.

Seman, Philip L. "The Jewish Community in Mexico City, 1924–1935." *Western States Jewish History* 43, no. 1 (2011): 176–90.

"Series on Los Angeles Jews to Begin with Pioneers." *Los Angeles Times*, February 2, 1981.

Showman, Richard K., Margaret Cobb, Robert E. McCarthy, and Dennis M. Conrad, eds. *The Papers of General Nathanael Greene*, 13 vols. Chapel Hill: University of North Carolina Press for the Rhode Island Historical Society, 1971–2005.

"Shul v. Shul: Judge McConnell's Decision." *Rhode Island Jewish Historical Notes* 17, no. 2 (2016): 316–61.

The Signers of the Declaration of Independence: A Loan Exhibition of Manuscripts by the Signers, from the Justin G. Turner Collection. Los Angeles: Los Angeles County Museum, 1955.

Simonoff, Harry. *Jewish Participants in the Civil War*. New York: Arco, 1963.

"The Society's New President, Justin George Turner." *Newsletter: The Historical Society of Southern California* 1, nos. 1–2 (1962): 6–7.

Solis-Cohen, J., Jr. "A California Pioneer: The Letters of Bernard Marks to Jacob Solis-Cohen (1853–1857)." *Publications of the American Jewish*

Historical Society 44, no. 1 (1954): 12–57.

Soref, Irwin. "The Jewish Community of Los Angles in Retrospect." *Reconstructionist* 18, no. 15 (1952): 8–12.

Souvenir Program: First Annual Meeting and Installation, Thursday, February 4, 1954. Los Angeles: Southern California Jewish Historical Society, 1954.

Starr, Kevin. *California: A History.* New York: Modern Library, 2005.

———. *Material Dreams: Southern California through the 1920s.* New York: Oxford University Press, 1990.

Stein, E. P. "General Two-Gun Cohen: Morris Abraham Cohen, the Chinese Connection, 1887–1970, Part I." *Western States Jewish History* 32, no. 1 (1999): 4–21.

———. "General Two-Gun Cohen: Morris Abraham Cohen, the Chinese Connection, 1887–1970, Part II." *Western States Jewish History* 32, nos. 2–3 (2000): 162–83.

Stern, Norton B. *Baja California: Jewish Refuge and Homeland.* Los Angeles: Dawson, 1973.

———. *The Birth of Modern Los Angeles Jewry.* Santa Monica, CA: Stern, 1977.

———. *California Jewish History: A Descriptive Bibliography.* Glendale, CA: Arthur H. Clark, 1967.

———. "The Editor's Corner." *Western States Jewish Historical Quarterly* 3, no. 2 (1970): 124–25.

———. "The Editor's Page." *Western States Jewish Historical Quarterly* 2, no. 1 (1969): 62–64.

———. "The Editor's Page." *Western States Jewish Historical Quarterly* 12, no. 2 (1980): 191–92.

———. *Jews in Early Santa Monica: A Centennial Review.* Los Angeles: Jewish Federation Council of Greater Los Angeles, 1975.

———. *The Jews of Los Angeles: Urban Pioneers.* Los Angeles: Southern California Jewish Historical Society, 1981.

———. "Judah L. Magnes of Oakland: Errors and Omissions in His Life Story." *Western States Jewish History* 17, no. 4 (1985): 352–57.

———. *Mannie's Crowd: Emmanuel Lowenstein, Colorful Character of Old Los Angeles.* Glendale, CA: Arthur H. Clark, 1970.

———. "A Murder to be Forgotten." *Western States Jewish Historical Quarterly* 9, no. 2 (1977): 176–85.

———. "A San Francisco Synagogue Scandal of 1893." *Western States Jewish Historical Quarterly* 6, no. 3 (1974): 196–203.

Stern, Norton B., and Benjamin Efron. "Rabbi Edgar F. Magnin: Summary of an Interview at Wilshire Boulevard Temple, Los Angeles, California, February 18, 1966." *Western States Jewish History* 41, no. 3 (2009): 547–50.

Stern, Norton B., and William M. Kramer. "Anti-Semitism and the Jewish Image in the Early West." *Western States Jewish Historical Quarterly* 6, no. 2 (1974): 129–40.

———. "Emil Harris: Los Angeles Jewish Police Chief." *Southern California Quarterly* 55, no. 2 (1973): 163–92.

———. "The Major Role of Polish Jews in the Pioneer West." *Western States Jewish Historical Quarterly* 8, no. 4 (1976): 326–44.

———. *Morris L. Goodman: The First American Councilman of the City of Los Angeles*. Santa Monica, CA: Lipton, 1981.

———. *San Francisco's Artist: Toby E. Rosenthal*. Northridge: California State University, Northridge, 1978.

Straus, Oscar. *Roger Williams: The Pioneer of Religious Liberty*. New York: Century, 1894.

Sturman, Gladys. "History Takes Many Forms." *Western States Jewish History* 37, no. 2 (2005): 98.

———. "A Letter from the New Editor." *Western States Jewish History* 30, no. 3 (1998): 197.

Sturman, Gladys, and David W. Epstein. "Dedication of WSJH Archives, UCLA, March 3, 2009." *Western States Jewish History* 41, no. 4 (2009): ix–xviii.

Sturman, Gladys, and David W. Epstein. "Postscript: The Western States Jewish History Archives." In *A Cultural History of Jews in California*, edited by Bruce Zuckerman, William Deverell, and Lisa Ansell, 47–54. West Lafayette, IN: Purdue University Press, 2009.

Sussman, Lance. "'Historian of the Jewish People': A Historiographical Reevaluation of the Writings of Jacob R. Marcus." *American Jewish*

Archives Journal 50 (1998): 11–21.

Szasz, Ferenc Morton. *Religion in the Modern American West.* Tucson: University of Arizona Press, 2001.

"Talk on 'Early Santa Monica.'" *Los Angeles Times*, November 11, 1976.

Toll, William. "Review of Jews in America: Four Centuries of an Uneasy Encounter." *American Jewish Archives Journal* 45, no. 2 (1993): 252–58.

Topf, Mel A. "Introduction to the First Circuit Opinion," and "Decision in Congregation Jeshuat Israel v. Congregation Shearith Israel." *Rhode Island Jewish Historical Notes* 17, no. 3 (2017): 515–52.

Townsend, Robert. *History's Babel: Scholarship, Professionalization and the Historical Enterprise in the United States, 1889–1940.* Chicago: University of Chicago Press, 2013.

Tugend, Tom. "Western Jewish History Collection Gets Broken Up among Local Academic Institutions." *Jewish Journal of Greater Los Angeles*, February 16, 2007.

Turner, Justin G. "The First Decade of Los Angeles Jewry: A Pioneer History, 1850–1860." *American Jewish Historical Quarterly* 54 (1964): 123–64.

———. *The First Decade of Los Angeles Jewry: A Pioneer History, 1850–1860.* Philadelphia: Press of Maurice Jacobs, 1964.

———. "In Memoriam: Marco Newmark." *California History* 39, no. 2 (1960): 175–76.

———. "Manuscripts and History." Paper presented at the American Association for State and Local History at Houston, Texas, October 24, 1952.

———. *A Note on Solomon Nuñes Carvalho and his Portrait of Abraham Lincoln*. Los Angeles: Plantin, 1960.

———. "Southern California Jewish Historical Society." In *Southwest Jewry*, vol. 3, edited by Joseph L. Malamut, 194–95. Los Angeles: Los Angeles Jewish Institutions and Their Leaders, 1957.

Turner, Justin G., and Norton B. Stern. "Marco Ross Newmark, 1878–1959: First Jewish Historian of the Southland." *Western States Jewish Historical Quarterly* 1, no. 1 (1968): 3–8.

Turner, Justin G., and Linda Levitt Turner. *Mary Todd Lincoln: Her Life and Letters.* New York: Alfred Knopf, 1972.

Tyrrell, Ian. *Historians in Public: The Practice of American History 1890–1970.* Chicago: University of Chicago Press, 2005.

Urofsky, Melvin I. *Community and Commonwealth: The Jewish Experience in Virginia*. Charlottesville: Virginia Historical Society, 1997.

———. *The Levy Family and Monticello, 1834–1923.* Chapel Hill: University of North Carolina Press, 2002.

Viener, Saul. "Roots of the Southern Jewish Historical Society: The Recollections of Saul Viener." *Southern Jewish Historical Society Newsletter* (July 1982): 2–3.

Vorspan, Max. "How the 'Vest was Von': An Irreverent Account of the Conservative Jewish Occupation of Los Angeles." *Western States Jewish History* (1997): 219–30.

———. "Los Angeles 1970 to the Present: An Encyclopedic Essay." *Western States Jewish History* 26, no. 2 (1994): 127–44.

Vorspan, Max, and Lloyd P. Gartner. *History of the Jews of Los Angeles*. San Marino, CA: Huntington Library, 1970.

Vorspan, Max, and Sheldon Teitelbaum. "Los Angeles." *Encyclopedia Judaica*, vol. 13, 2nd ed., 195–211. New York: Macmillan Reference, 2007.

Warner, J. J., Benjamin I. Hayes, and Joseph Pomeroy Widney. *An Historical Sketch of Los Angeles County, California*. Los Angeles: Louis Lewin and Co., 1876.

Warsen, Allen A. *Autobiographical Episodes.* Oak Park, MI: n.p., 1971.

———. "Founding Our Society." *Michigan Jewish History* 1, no. 1 (1960): 1–2.

Watts, Steven. *The People's Tycoon: Henry Ford and the American Century.* New York: Vintage, 2005.

Wax, Bernard. "Comment: Solutions to Contemporary Problems of National Ethnic Historical Societies." *Journal of American Ethnic History* 13, no. 2 (Winter 1994): 59–62.

———. "Local Jewish Historical Societies in the United States and Canada." In *The Jacob Dolnitzky Memorial Volume Studies in Jewish Law, Philosophy, Literature and Language*, edited by Morris Casriel Katz, 228–46. Skokie, IL: Hebrew Theological College, 1982.

———. "Postscript: Reminiscences and Observations." *Southern Jewish History* 17 (2014): 145–47.

———. "Ruminations about the SJHS." *Southern Jewish History* 10 (2007): 1–11.

Waxman, Deborah. "Review of the National Museum of American Jewish History, Philadelphia." *Pennsylvania History* 79, no. 1 (2012): 65–75.

Weber, Francis J. "Review of California Jewish History: A Descriptive Bibliography." *Southern California Quarterly* 49, no. 4 (1967): 463–64.

Weiner, Deborah R. "A Sense of Connection to Others: A Profile of Stephen J. Whitfield." *Southern Jewish History* 7 (2004): 58.

Weinfeld, David. "Two Commemorations: Richmond's Jews and the Lost Cause During the Civil Rights Era." *Southern Jewish History* 23 (2020): 77–123.

Weissbach, Lee Shai. *Jewish Life in Small-Town America*. New Haven, CT: Yale University Press, 2005.

Wenger, Beth S. *History Lessons: The Creation of American Jewish Heritage.* Princeton: Princeton University Press, 2010.

Whitfield, Stephen J. "The Achievement of Mark K. Bauman." *Southern Jewish History* 20 (2017): 1–32.

Wolfson, Ron. *A Time to Mourn, A Time to Comfort: A Guide to Jewish Bereavement and Comfort.* Woodstock, VT: Jewish Lights, 1996.

Wurl, Joel. "Ethnicity as Provenance: In Search of Values and Principles for Documenting the Immigrant Experience." *Archival Issues* 29, no. 1 (2005): 65–76.

Yaco, Sonia, Caroline Brown, and Lee Konrad. "Linking Special Collections to Classrooms: A Curriculum-to-Collection Crosswalk." *The American Archivist* 79, no. 2 (2014): 417–77.

Zadora, Anna. "Review of *History's Babel* Robert Townsend." *Alberta Journal of Educational Research* 62, no. 1 (2016): 117–20.

Zesch, Scott. *The Chinatown War: Chinese Los Angeles and the Massacre of 1871.* New York: Oxford, 2012.

Zola, Gary P. "Jacob Rader Marcus and the Dynamics of American Jewish History." In *The Dynamics of American Jewish History: Jacob Rader Marcus's Essays on American Jewry*, edited by Gary P. Zola, xiii–xxxi. Hanover, MA: Brandeis University Press, 2004.

———. "To Our Readers." *The American Jewish Archives Journal* 42, no. 2

(2010): vii–xi.

———. "Why Study Southern Jewish History?" *Southern Jewish History* 1 (1998): 1–21.

Contributors

Jeanne E. Abrams holds a PhD in American history from the University of Colorado. She is a professor in the University of Denver Libraries and Center for Judaic Studies, where she has also served as the longtime director of the Rocky Mountain Jewish Historical Society and Beck Archives. Abrams is the author of many books and articles in the fields of American and American Jewish history that have appeared in academic presses and journals and in popular media, including *Jewish Women Pioneering the Frontier Trail: A History in the American West* and her latest book, *A View from Abroad: The Story of John and Abigail Adams in Europe.*

Mark K. Bauman, professor of history at Atlanta Metropolitan College (retired), has written or edited eleven books, including most recently a volume of his collected essays, *A New Vision of Southern Jewish History* (2019), as well as over fifty scholarly articles. He serves as founding and current editor of *Southern Jewish History* and co-edits the series "Jews and Judaism: History and Culture" for the University of Alabama Press. Holder of master's degrees from Lehigh and Chicago Universities and a doctorate from Emory, he taught at the College of William and Mary as a Mason Fellow and received Starkoff and Director's Fellowships to conduct research at the American Jewish Archives, as well as the first Samuel Proctor Outstanding Career Scholarship Award in Southern Jewish History from the Southern Jewish Historical Society.

Lawrence Bell received his bachelor's degree in history from Arizona State University and his master's and PhD degrees in history from The Ohio State University. For the past fifteen years, Dr. Bell has served as the executive director of the Arizona Jewish Historical Society, where he has been involved in restoring Phoenix's first synagogue as the Cutler-Plotkin Jewish Heritage Center, a museum and cultural center open to people of all backgrounds. The center now hosts a variety of programs, including regular exhibitions of Jewish history and art, a monthly documentary film series, book discussion group, Holocaust speaker seminar, genealogy society, and community archive. Dr. Bell is also very passionate about promoting good interfaith relations and serves on the board of the Arizona Interfaith Movement.

Catherine Cangany has been executive director of the Jewish Historical Society of Michigan since 2018. Previously, she was a tenured associate professor of history at the University of Notre Dame. She received her PhD in history from the University of Michigan in 2009.

Jonathan L. Friedmann, PhD, is professor of Jewish music history and academic dean of the Master of Jewish Studies Program and Rabbinical School at the Academy for Jewish Religion California, president of the Western States Jewish History Association, director of the Jewish Museum of the American West, editor of the journal *Western States Jewish History*, and the author or editor of thirty books on Judaism, music, and religion. He also leads Adat Chaverim–Congregation for Humanistic Judaism in Los Angeles.

Joel Gereboff, PhD, is associate professor of religious studies at Arizona State University and professor of Bible and Jewish history at the Academy for Jewish Religion California. His research and publications focus on early rabbinic Judaism, American Judaism, Jewish ethics, and Judaism and the emotions.

George M. Goodwin, a native of Los Angeles, has broad interests in art, architecture, and cultural history. He has taught at many levels, conducted extensive oral history interviews, designed exhibitions, collected folk art, and traveled widely. Having lived in Providence for thirty-five years, Goodwin co-edited *The Jews of Rhode Island* (Brandeis University Press, 2004) and has edited *Rhode Island Jewish Historical Notes* for nineteen years. He and his wife, Betsey, live in an Arts & Crafts bungalow and belong to Temple Beth-El in Providence.

Index

www.ingramcontent.com/pod-product-compliance
Lightning Source LLC
Chambersburg PA
CBHW020444100426
42812CB00036B/3447/J
* 9 7 8 1 6 8 2 8 3 1 8 1 6 *